Shannon T. Bischoff, Carmen Jany (Eds.)
Functional Approaches to Language

Trends in Linguistics
Studies and Monographs

Volume 248

Functional Approaches to Language

Edited by
Shannon T. Bischoff, Carmen Jany

DE GRUYTER
MOUTON

ISBN 978-3-11-048476-2
e-ISBN 978-3-11-028532-1
ISSN 1861-430

Library of Congress Cataloging-in-Publication Data
A CIP catalog record for this book has been applied for at the Library of Congress.

Bibliographic information published by the Deutsche Nationalbibliothek
The Deutsche Nationalbibliothek lists this publication in the Deutsche Nationalbibliografie;
detailed bibliographic data are available in the Internet at http://dnb.dnb.de.

© 2013 Walter de Gruyter GmbH & Co. KG, Berlin/Boston
Typesetting: PTP-Berlin Protago-T$_E$X-Production GmbH, Berlin
Printing: Hubert & Co. GmbH & Co. KG, Göttingen
♾ Printed on acid-free paper
Printed in Germany

www.degruyter.com

Contents

Shannon T. Bischoff and Carmen Jany
Introduction

1 Introduction

Functional approaches to language are mainly concerned with examining the question of why language structure is the way it is and with finding explanations in language use. Functionalism views language as a dynamic, adaptive, and emergent system representing crystallizations of recurrent patterns and frequent use and outcomes of internal and external competing motivations. This point of view has implications for three levels of linguistic inquiry: description, explanation, and methodology. At a descriptive level, functionalism is concerned with spontaneous, naturally-occurring language use in real time in different social situations, as most notably reflected in topics such as preferred argument structure (Du Bois 1987), conversation analysis (Schegloff 2007), and common ground management (Krifka 2008), in addition to, as Haspelmath (2008: 92–93) notes, "describing languages in an ecumenical, widely understood descriptive framework". Unlike in generative linguistics, functionalist descriptions do not serve the purpose of being restrictive and therefore explanatory. Rather, they deal with cross-linguistic differences and linguistic idiosyncracies, alongside regular patterns. Description, then is separated from explanation in functionalism (Haspelmath 2008: 93). At the explanatory level, functionalism aims at finding explanations for linguistic structures on the basis of language use and the evolutionary and adaptive processes leading to current language usage. Functional explanations rest upon cognitive and communicative aspects of human behaviour, the changing nature of language (i.e. diachrony) and the origins of structural patterns (i.e. grammaticalization), regularities and patterns arising from frequent language use (i.e. ritualization, automatization, and exemplar-based models), and generalizations based on a wide range of languages (i.e. functional-typological approach). Grammar is not viewed as an autonomous system, because explanation can be sought in system-internal interaction (i.e. semantics explains syntax or phonology explains pragmatics, etc). Functionalism, then is data-driven and more empirically oriented than formal approaches to language, and it depends on studying real language use rather than abstract representations of language. As a result, functional approaches to language demand specific methodological choices. At the methodological level, functionalism has been linked to a wide variety of methods ranging from corpus-based linguistics (Gries 2011), psychological experimentation as in cognitive linguistics and language acquisition (Bates and MacWhinney 1982), conversation analysis (Fox et al. 2012), descriptive grammar writing (Dryer 2006), to computer-generated exemplars (Wedel 2006), among others.

Given this broad range of phenomena related to the notion of functionalism, functional approaches have penetrated various linguistic subfields over the past four decades. Since the 1970s, inspired by the work of those such as Jespersen, Bolinger, Givón, Dik, Halliday, and Chafe, functionalism has been attached to a variety of movements and models making major contributions to linguistic theory and its subfields, such as syntax, discourse, language acquisition, cognitive linguistics, neurolinguistics, typology, and documentary linguistics. Further, functional approaches have had a major impact outside linguistics in fields such as psychology and education, both in terms of theory and application. The main goal of functionalist approaches is to clarify the dynamic relationship between form and function (Thompson 2003: 53). While in so-called formal approaches performance does not motivate competence, explanations generalizing in nature are sought on the basis of abstract linguistic representations, and crosslinguistic generalizations are due to the innate Universal Grammar, functionalists find explanation in the ways performance affects competence assuming that "language structure can be influenced by regularities of language use through language change" (Haspelmath 2008: 75).

Functional research into grammar offers new explanations for linguistic structure whereby grammar is "conceived in terms of the discourse functions from which it can be said to have emerged" (Thompson 2003: 54). This somewhat narrow view of functionalism has led to important work on discourse and grammar by Sandra A. Thompson, Paul Hopper, T. Givón, Joan Bybee, and others. Another major contribution of the functional perspective is found in linguistic typology. Building on the insights of Greenberg, Comrie's seminal work on language universals (Comrie 1981) and his linking of typology and functional accounts of linguistic phenomena has had a profound impact on the field with the *World Atlas of Language Structures* (Dryer and Haspelmath 2011) as an exceptional resource for linguists across subfields, including researchers in documentary linguistics. Documentary linguistics, informed by and contributing to linguistic typology, has defined itself as a new subfield within linguistics, and data from previously unstudied languages are constantly re-shaping current linguistic theory. Work in language documentation is based on how actual language use is reflected in linguistic structure, a key issue in functionalism.

In the last decade there has been a sea change in linguistic inquiry as a direct result of technological advancement that has allowed for increased experimentation, corpus building and analysis, and greater communication among linguists. Moreover, during this same decade there has been a shift in the previously dominant Transformation Generative approach which has many 'formal' linguists looking for answers and direction in functionalism, which in previous years was looked at as a *competing* approach, but today even to 'formalists' looks to hold promising alternatives to investigating language.

This volume thus reflects the widespread and in-depth impact of functionalism on the present-day linguistic scene. We now have a substantial body of literature from various perspectives on functionalism, making a positive impact on the field of linguistics in general and the various subfields, and pointing researchers in new and interesting directions. In an effort to bring leading scholars in this area together and to provide recognition to the impact of functionalist approaches on current linguistic theory, this volume highlights the nature of functionalism as an important force within linguistics defining its current and future directions. Due to the ecletic nature of functionalism, the seven papers in this volume deal with a broad range of topics from a historical overview of functionalist thinking to the examination of explanatory and methodolgical issues.

2 The Volume Papers

The papers in this volume remind us that language, and thus linguistics, cannot be reduced to one subfield or another. Additionally, these papers illustrate that language and linguistic inquiry can not be reduced to structure alone if we wish to understand language in its totality. Throughout this volume authors argue that the study of structure and function play crucial roles in expanding our understanding of language, but that functional approaches offer the most compelling explanation for linguistic phenomena.

In the first of seven papers in this volume **T. Givón** provides an overview of the history of functionalism in linguistic, intellectual thought and inquiry since antiquity. Starting with Platonic rationalism and Aristotelian empiricism and touching briefly upon Medieval logicians, Givón traces the direct antecedence of late-20th Century functionalism through von Humboldt, Paul and Jespersen, and subsequent work by Bolinger and Halliday. The impact of the two giants of structuralism – Saussure, Bloomfield – and of Chomsky is viewed by Givón as an important catalyst, which he traces from the late-1960s advent of functionalist thinking to the Generative Semantics rebellion of Ross, Lakoff, and others. Following what he refers to as a "despair of Chomskian structuralism", Givón asserts that one may interpret the expanding agenda of the 1970s "as an attempt to integrate the multiple strands of the adaptive correlates of language structure: discourse/ communication, cognition, language diversity and universals, diachrony, acquisition, and evolution".

Unlike others (e.g. Allen 2007) who make similar claims regarding the historical antecedents of functionalism in linguistics, Givón uses parallel historical antecedents in biology to make the claim that an approach to linguistic inquiry modelled on biology is preferable to that of physics which has dominated the Transformation Generative approach of Chomsky. Givón concludes with a call to look outside linguistics to allied fields such as evolutionary psychology and ethology for insights into linguistic phenomena and explanation. This call is echoed by a number of the contributing authors in this volume, a reflection of the often inter- and intra-disciplinary nature of contemporary functionalist approaches in linguistics.

In a similar vein, looking to other sciences and functionalism, **Esa Itkonen** examines the notion of function as it applies in the human sciences and the uses of functional explanation in linguistics. He argues that the methods actually used by linguists ought to be the focus of concentration in regards to explanation rather than model disciplines such as physics or biology, a seemingly opposing view to Givón's position. His argument is grounded in a set of examples (e.g. zero morphology, number systems) that are meant to illustrate the methods actually employed by linguists, in this case typologists. Itkonen concludes that typological-functional explanation, when analyzed more narrowly, is ultimately based on the notion of empathy, which according to him is by definition functional in nature, and on pattern explanation. Accordingly, Itkonen argues that this approach renders deterministic explanation unnecessary, statistical explanation valuable, but not capable of explanations in and of themselves, and Darwinist explanation simply not applicable. This final claim, regarding Darwinist explanation, is also taken up by both Givón and Harder in this volume who arrive at somewhat contrary perspectives to Itkonen – demonstrating that as with formal approaches, within functionalism there is still room for debate regarding the role and nature of evolutionary approaches to linguistic explanation.

Before moving to evolutionary arguments, **Peter Harder** claims that the division between formalist and functionalist approaches depends in part on a difference of focal research interests. Formalists, Harder explains, are interested in language structure and believe one has to start out with structure in order to understand how language functions, while functionalists believe that structure can only be understood as embedded in function – and therefore the two groups focus on different sets of problems. This seems to echo the sentiments of Chafe, who also addresses this issue from the perspective of function and structure but takes the discussion in a different direction. Harder notes that although this difference is not likely to go away, the familiar polarization is not the only possible form of the argument, and in fact there have been developments towards discussions targeted at finding common ground.

Harder then turns to recent developments in evolutionary theory, specifically in recent claims regarding niche construction and cultural evolution. Following Harder, from this position, both groups are right in their main claim: functions of units in human language as we know it presuppose structure, just as structural units presuppose function. Harder argues that from a panchronic perspective, this form of circularity can be reanalysed as reflecting a co-evolutionary spiral which reflects a series of niche-constructional bootstrapping relations between structure and function. To capture this, it is necessary for linguists to see the structure of a specific language as constituting a socioculturally entrenched system in the speakers' environment, to which learners have to adapt – until they crack the structural code, they are functionally incapacitated.

The position Harder defends belongs on the functionalist side of the divide: it sees structural categories as reflecting a partial order imposed on communicative resources, ultimately sustained by functional relations (analogous to functional relations that shape the biological evolution of organs). However, Harder argues that this view differs from some functionalist claims in seeing structural properties as distinct from the properties of online usage events. Among the issues considered in the light of this hypothesis are variability, grammaticalization, and recursion.

Wallace Chafe, like Harder, addresses the division between formalism and functionalism. Chafe begins with the question of how one goes about interpreting how something functions. Chafe argues that there are two ways to interpret how something functions. Using the notion of the automobile to illustrate, Chafe says you can study how the automobile is used to go from place to place or how it is constructed for such use. He focuses on the second approach and argues that language functions by "associating thoughts with sounds" and by "organizing thoughts in ways that make the association possible". Chafe proceeds to explore the concept of "thought" and two contrasting perspectives of "language design": syntax-dominated (formal) versus thought-based (functional). The remainder of the paper is dedicated to explaining and exemplifying his proposed thought-based language design tackling the relationship between thoughts and semantics, semantics and syntax, syntax and phonology, and more generally between language and thoughts. Chafe concludes that syntax is the greatest source of diversity (rather than universality) and states that language universals "may be maximally present in thoughts, a bit less in semantics, and much less in syntax".

Finally, Chafe argues that linguists need to develop a better understanding of thought, and that this understanding can and should be reached, in part, by looking to other disciplines. This call to look outside of linguistics for answers to linguistic questions emerges elsewhere in the volume. Similarly Menn, Duffield, and Narasimhan argue that questions of linguistic structure can be further addressed by looking beyond functional explanation. This openness to other disciplines and subfields within linguistics is perhaps a hallmark of functionalism.

Chafe suggests that what unites functionalists is an agreement that language, and thus linguistic inquiry, cannot be simply reduced to formal syntax. This argument is made throughout this volume in nearly every chapter whether directly or indirectly and demonstrates what Chafe refers to as the comprehensiveness of functionalism. For Chafe this comprehensiveness reveals a different kind of unity in functionalism among scholars, as compared to formal approaches, "one that embraces cognitive linguistics, ethnolinguistics, sociolinguistics, psycholinguistics, pragmatics, discourse studies, corpus linguistics, language documentation, and more".

Perhaps another hallmark of functionalism is the belief that, in general, language learning or acquisition involves the same set of cognitive mechanisms responsible for other types of learning, as opposed to views that see language learning or acquisition as unique and thus necessitating some type of language specific organ. This is the view pursed by **Michael P. Kaschak and Morton Ann Gernsbacher**. Kaschak and Gernsbacher explore linguistic change over short spans of time, i.e. minutes, days, and weeks. They look to a series of empirical studies of syntactic and phonological learning and adapation effects from psycholinguistics to argue that the language system is quite malleable over short stretches of time, which reflects procedural learning common in other types of learning. For example, they find the following similarities between syntactic adaptation and perceptual learning: adaptations a) occur quickly, b) are long-lasting, c) are somewhat context-specific, and d) seem to follow general principles of learning and memory. Kaschak and Gernsbacher argue that this type of implicit learning, found in syntactic adaptation, follows the same general principles of implicit and procedural learning found in other domains of knowledge.

The next paper returns to issues of structure, specifically discourse structure. **Bernd Heine, Gunther Kaltenböck, Tania Kuteva, and Haiping Long** argue that attempts to reduce discourse structure to canonical principles of sentence grammar have not been successful. They further argue that most frameworks of linguistic analysis highlight phenomena of language use and/or language knowledge such as sentence and word structure, while backgrounding or ignoring other phenomena that are interpreted as being of more marginal interest for the linguist. In particular, they identify certain forms of discourse structures, such as formulae of social exchange, vocatives, interjections, and what are traditionally known as parenthetical constructions, which have turned out to pose problems to grammatical analysis. The authors argue that such units do not conform to canonical principles of sentence grammar, and rather than being located at the periphery of language use, they play an important role in discourse organization. Heine et al. find a place for such elements in structure by appealing to Sentence Grammar (SG) which concerns itself primarily with propositional content and clauses and Thetical Grammar (TG) which in contrast subsumes elements that are seen outside SG: parenthetical constructions. They argue that SG and TG are the major components of Discourse Grammar which they outline in the paper by elaborationg on the role of TG, its relationship to SG, and its role in accounting for parentheticals in grammatical structure. Heine et al. conclude, like many of the papers in the volume, by offering suggestions on how to further research in linguistic inquiry by appealing to allied fields and subfields.

Lise Menn, Cecily Jill Duffield, and Bhuvana Narasimhan further the call to look to other fields and methodologies to pursue linguistic inquiry by highlighting the benefits of combining functional approaches with greater experimental research. The authors discuss experimental methods which test functionalist explanations for formal choices, such as information flow and word order. First, they outline three problem areas for functional explanations: competing factors, constraints imposed by how the brain works, and circularity of purely text-based functional explanations. Then, they discuss how these can be addressed by experimental methods focusing on the motivations of speakers in their formal choices (rather than on the listeners). They argue that such choices are influenced by "automatic consequences of the way the brain works", such as lexical and structural priming. Thus, the consequence is that functional explanations do not account for all instances in which particular structures are preferred over others as they may result from processing demands of the brain. However, Menn et al. argue that functional ideas can help tease apart interactions of cognitive factors that influence a particular choice. They conclude that experimental methods to test functionalist explanations are possible and necessary, but need to go through various stages of re-design as they turn out to be very tricky due to too many unanticipated variables.

Overall, the seven papers in this volume demonstrate that as a theory functionalism is answering age-old questions and raising exiciting new ones. The authors remind us that there is much work to be done and that linguists may not always agree, but they do agree more than we might expect.

Acknowledgments

The editors wish to thank the members of the 2011 LSA Symposium *Functions, Functionalism, and Linguistics* which was the genesis of this volume: Suzanne Kemmer, Brian MacWhinney, William Greaves, Craig Hancock, Wallace Chafe, and T. Givón.

References

Allen, Keith. 2007. *The Western Classical Tradition in Linguistics*. Equinox: London.
Bates, Elizabeth and Brian MacWhinney. 1982. Functionalist approaches to grammar. In *Language Acquisition: The State of the Art*. E. Wanner and L. Gleitman eds. Cambridge: Cambridge University Press. 173–218.
Comrie, Bernard. 1981. *Language Universals and Linguistic Typology: Syntax and Morphology*. Oxford: Blackwell.
Dryer, Matthew S. 2006. Descriptive Theories, Explanatory Theories, and Basic Linguistic Theory. In *Catching Language: The Standing Challenge of Grammar Writing*. Felix K. Ameka, Alan Dench, and Nicolas Evans eds. Berlin: Mouton de Gruyter. 207–234.
Dryer, Matthew S. and Martin Haspelmath (eds.). 2011. *The World Atlas of Language Structures Online*. Munich: Max Planck Digital Library.
Du Bois, John W. 1987. The discourse basis of ergativity. *Language 64*. 805–855.
Fox, Barbara A., Sandra A. Thompson, Cecilia A. Ford, and E. Couper-Kuhlen. 2012. Conversation Analysis and Linguistics. In *The Handbook of Conversation Analysis*. Jack Sidnell and Tanya Stivers eds. Wiley-Blackwell. 726–740.
Gries, Stefan Th. 2011. Corpus data in usage-based linguistics: What's the right degree of granularity for the analysis of argument structure constructions? In *Cognitive linguistics: convergence and expansion*. Mario Brdar, Stefan Th. Gries, and Milena Žic Fuchs eds. Amsterdam and Philadelphia: John Benjamins. 237–256.
Haspelmath, Martin. 2008. Parametric versus functional explanations of syntactic universals. In Theresa Biberauer ed. *The limits of syntactic variation*. Amsterdam: John Benjamins. 75–107.
Krifka, M. 2008. Basic notions of information structure. *Acta Linguistica Hungarica 55*. 243–276.
Schegloff, Emanuel A. 2007. *Sequence Organization in Interaction: A Primer in Conversation Analysis, Volume 1*, Cambridge: Cambridge University Press.
Thompson, Sandra A. 2003. Functional Grammar. In William Frawley, ed., *Oxford International Encyclopedia of Linguistics*, 2nd edition. Oxford: Oxford University Press.
Wedel, Andrew. 2006. Exemplar Models, Evolution and Language Change. *The Linguistic Review 23*. 247–274.

T. Givón
On the Intellectual Roots of Functionalism in Linguistics

1 Antiquity

In Biology, the mother of all functionalist disciplines, one can trace two traditional lines of adaptive-functional thought. The first, global or macro functionalism, is the Darwinian discussion of **adaptive selection**, whereby organisms or populations adapt to their external environmental (Darwin 1859), or to their self-created niche (Waddington 1942, 1953; Odling-Smee *et al.* 2003). In this sense, one may consider language an adaptation selected for a particular niche in which communication enhanced sociality and conferred various adaptive-reproductive advantages (Darwin 1871; Washburn and Lancaster 1968; Lieberman 1984 Greenfield 1991; Dunbar 1992, 1998; Knight 1998; Számadó and Sathmáry 2006; Tomasello *et al.* 2005; Bickerton 2005, Givón 2009; *inter alia*).

The second line, concerning the **functional motivation** for the structure of individual bodily organs, harkens back to Aristotle, the founder of empirical biology. Two structuralist schools dominated Greek biological thought prior to Aristotle, both seeking to understand bio-organisms like inorganic matter. Empedocles proposed to explain organisms by their **component elements**, while Democritus opted for understanding them through their **component parts** – their structure.

In *De Partibus Animalium*, Aristotle first argued against Empedocles' elemental approach, pointing out the relevance of histological and anatomical macro-structure:

(1) "...But if men and animals are natural phenomena, then natural philosophers must take into consideration not merely the ultimate substances of which they are made, but also flesh, bone, blood and all the other homogeneous parts; not only these but also the heterogenous parts, such as face, hand, foot..." (McKeon ed. 1941, p. 647)

Aristotle next noted the inadequacy of Democritus' structuralism:

(2) "...Does, then, configuration and color constitute the essence of the various animals and their several parts?... No hand of bronze or wood or stone constituted in any but the appropriate way can possibly be a hand in more than a name. For like a physician in a painting, or like a flute in a sculpture, it will be unable to do the *office* [= function] which that name implies..." (*ibid.*, p. 647; italics & bracketed translations added)

Next, Aristotle offered his functionalist touchstone – the teleological interpretation of living organisms, using the analogy of usable artifacts:

> (3) "...What, however, I would ask, are the forces by which the hand or the body was fashioned into its shape? The woodcarver will perhaps say, by the axe and auger; the physiologist, by air and earth. Of these two answers, the artificer's is the better, but it is nevertheless insufficient. For it is not enough for him to say that by the stroke of his tool this part was formed into a concavity, that into a flat surface; but he must state the *reasons* why he struck his blow in such a way as to affect this, and what his final *object* [= purpose] was..." (*ibid.*, pp. 647–648; italics added)

Finally, Aristotle outlined the governing principle of functionalism, the isomorphic mapping between form and function:

> (4) "...if a piece of wood is to be split with an axe, the axe must of necessity be hard; and, if hard, it must of necessity be made of bronze or iron. Now exactly in the same way the body, which like the axe is an *instrument* – for both the body as a whole and its several parts individually have definite operations for which they are made; just in the same way, I say, the body if it is to do its *work* [= function], must of necessity be of such and such character..." (*ibid.*, p. 650; italics and brackets added)

Ever since Aristotle, **structuralism** – the idea that structure is autonomous, arbitrary and requires no 'external' explanation; or worse, that structure somehow explains itself – has been a dead issue in biology, a discipline where common-sense functionalism is taken for granted like mother's milk. Thus, from a contemporary introductory anatomy text:

> (5) "...anatomy is the science that deals with the structure of the body... physiology is defined as the science of function. Anatomy and physiology have more meaning when studied together..." (Crouch 1978, pp. 9–10)

Paradoxically, Aristotle, following Epicure, is also the father of structuralism in linguistics, as may be seen in the opening paragraph of *De Interpretatione*:

> (6) "Now spoken sounds [=words] are symbols of affections of the soul [=thoughts], and written marks are symbols of spoken sounds. And just as written marks are not the same for all men [=are language specific], neither are spoken sounds. But what these are in the first place signs of – affections of the soul – are the same for all [=are universal]; and what are these affections are likenesses of – actual things – are also the same for all men..." (J.L. Ackrill ed. 1963; bracketed translation added)

From Aristotle's **empiricist** perspective, thoughts ('affections of the soul') reflect external reality ('actual things') faithfully, iconically ('are likenesses of'). What is more, this reflecting relation is universal ('the same for all men'). In contrast, linguistic expressions ('words') bear an arbitrary relation to ('are symbols of') thoughts. And this relation is not universal ('not the same for all men').

Paradoxically again, Aristotle wound up hedging his bets about language. In his treatment of grammar in *The Categorie,* and in various other works on logic (*Prior Analytic, Posterior Analytic*), an **isomorphism** – functionally motivated relation – is postulated between grammatical categories and sentences, on the one hand, and logical meaning.

A similar hedging of bets is found in Plato's *Cratylus* dialog (Hamilton and Cairns eds 1961), where Cratylus argues for the Aristotle/Epicure arbitrariness position (*nomos*), while Socrates argues for a motivated, natural, isomorphic relation (*physis*); and further, that language is an *organ* dedicated to the expression of meaning.

Socrates' (i.e. Plato's) naturalness position was extended to grammatical analysis in the works of the Alexandrine philosopher Marcus Terrenius Varro (116–26 BC) and the Roman philosopher Apollonius Dyscolus (80–160 AD). This extension merged Plato's 'naturalness' position concerning the compositionality of lexical words with Aristotle's functionalist analysis of grammatical categories (Itkonen 2010).

2 Middle Ages to the 19th Century

Most later Platonists opted for Socrates' naturalism and universality. And indeed, from early on there tended to be a less-than-perfect clustering of approaches to language along the philosophical dichotomy of Aristotelian **empiricism** vs. Platonic **rationalism**.

(7) | domain | functionalism | structuralism |
|---|---|---|
| epistemology: | rationalism | empiricism |
| motivation: | naturalness | arbitrariness |
| universals: | universality | diversity |
| mind: | mentalism | externalism |
| ontogeny: | innateness | input-dependence |
| diachrony: | emergence | ??? |
| **evolution**: | evolution | ??? |

That the clustering in (7) was imperfect was obvious from two glaring exceptions. The first goes back to Aristotle: Medieval Latin grammarians/logicians, the

Modistae, subscribed to St. Thomas Aquinas' Aristotelian empiricism, but also to the logical functionalism and universalism of *The Categories* (e.g. St. Anselm's *De Grammatico*; also Boethius of Dacia, Sigerus de Cortraco; William Ockham; see discussion in Itkonen 2010).

Subsequently, the *Port Royal* French grammarians (Arnauld 1662; Lancelot & Arnauld 1660) reverted, via Descartes, to Platonic rationalism, thus conforming better to the clustering in (7). The second exception is Chomsky (see below).

3 The 19th Century

In philosophy, there was a subtle sea change at the end of the 18th Century, with Kant and the emergence of the **pragmatic middle-ground** between the two extreme schools of epistemology. Its impact was not immediate, and the birth of linguistics proper in the early 19th Century took place in a context of a continuing Platonic/rationalist perspective and an implicit functionalism. However, the 19th Century contributed three important ingredients to the mix in (7). The first came with linguistics itself – **diachrony**. The other two emerged through contact with other disciplines: First, the expansion of Platonic mentalism from logic and meaning to a broader concept of **cognition** under the impact of nascent psychology. And second, the addition of **evolution** under the impact of Darwinian biology. The most conspicuous exponents of this enriched mix were Franz Boop (1816), W. von Humboldt (1836), and Hermann Paul (1890). Their perspective carried over into the 20th Century with illustrious exponents such as Otto Jespersen (1921, 1924) and Edward Sapir (1921), as well as the oft-forgotten functionalism of George Zipf (1935), who seems to have retained a great reservoir of common sense about language:

> (8) "...language is primarily a representation of experience. It may represent [it] as a report of direct perceptual experience... Or it may represent tendencies to act...[thus] potential activity, such as oration to persuade others to modify their behavior in accord with the wishes of the speaker... A function of the linguistic representation is to restore equilibrium. The equilibrium may be of two types: (a) inter-personal and (b) intra-personal..." (Zipf 1935, pp. 294–295)

4 Structuralism

The rise of structuralism in the social sciences in the early 20th Century is sometimes seen as a reaction to so-called naive functionalism of the late 19th Century Romantics. The real impetus, however, was again external, coming from a radical brand of empiricism – **Logical Positivism** in philosophy. To the infant disciplines of psychology, anthropology and linguistics, two towering exponents of Logical Positivism, Bertrand Russell (Russell 1956) and Rudolph Carnap (Carnap 1963), offered the deceptive analogy of physics, inadvertently reaching back to pre-Aristotelian biology.

In tracing the roots of 20th Century structuralism to Positivist philosophy, one must recall that the descent of Positivism in the philosophy of science goes back to Aristotle's objectivist epistemology. This is fairly transparent in, e.g., Rudolph Carnap's later reflection upon the physicalism of the Vienna Circle:

(9) "...The thesis of physicalism, as originally accepted in the Vienna Circle, says roughly: Every concept of the language of science can be explicitly defined in terms of observables; therefore every sentence of the language of science is translatable into a sentence concerning observable properties..." (Carnap 1963, p. 59)

Bertrand Russell's objectivism, couched in somewhat forbidding terms, is evident in his discussion of the relation between particular entities and the universal concept to which they give rise:

(10) "...We may then define a *particular* in our fourth sense as an entity that cannot be in or belong to more than one place at any particular time, and a *universal* as an entity that either cannot be in or belong to any place, or can be in or belong to many places at once... Owing to the admission of universals in our fourth sense, we can make an absolute division between percepts and concepts. The universal whiteness is a *concept*, whereas a particular white patch is a *percept*...Such *general qualities* as whiteness never exist in time, whereas the things that do exist in time are all particular [percepts]..." (*Relations of universals & particulars*; in Russell 1956, p. 122)

The core notions of functionalism, *purpose* or *function*, are invisible teleological constructs that defy translation into Carnap's 'language of science'; as are psychological concepts such as *meaning, intent, mind, knowledge* or *belief*. The critical element that makes something a biological code, or in C.S. Peirce's (1934, 1940) words "something by knowing of which one knows something more", is the signal's association with some purpose or function. This is where the world of living organisms stands in stark contrast to the pre-biological universe of physics and chemistry, where teleological notions are senseless, except perhaps in reference to the Divine. To quote the physicist I. Rabi:

(11) "...My view of physics is that you make discoveries but, in a certain sense, you never really understand them. You learn how to manipulate them, but you never really understand them. "Understanding" would mean relating them to something else – to something more profound..." (Rabi 1975, p. 96)

Aristotle's doctrine of the arbitrariness of the linguistic sign – thus the arbitrariness of cross-language diversity – pertained explicitly only to the semiotic relation between concepts and sounds or letters, i.e. the lexicon. But latter-day structuralists unreflectively extended the doctrine to grammar. In the intellectual climate fostered by Logical Positivism, F. de Saussure (1915) elaborated the three central dogmas of structuralism:

- **arbitrariness**: The detachment of the visible signal from invisible mental – purposive – correlates,
- **idealization**: The reification of the underlying system – *langue* – as against the manifest behavior – *parole*,[1]
- **segregation**: The detachment of synchrony (product) from diachrony (process).

Leonard Bloomfield, the father of American structuralism, owed his conception of meaning to the empiricism of behaviorist psychology:[2]

> (12) "...We must study people's habits of language – the way they talk – without bothering about mental processes that we may conceive to underlie or accompany habits. We must dodge the issue by a fundamental assumption, leaving it to a separate investigation, in which our results will figure as data along the results of other social sciences..." (Bloomfield 1922, p. 142)

> (13) "...In order to give a scientifically accurate definition of meaning for every form of the language, one should have to have a scientifically accurate knowledge of everything in the speaker's world... In practice, we define the meaning of a linguistic form, whenever we can, in terms of some other science..." (Bloomfield 1933, pp. 139–140)

In the same vein, Bloomfield's rejection of universals and theory harkens back to Aristotle's and Saussure's arbitrariness:

> (14) "...North of Mexico alone there are dozens of totally unrelated groups of languages, presenting the most varied types of structures. In the stress of recording utterly strange forms of speech, one soon learns that philosophical presuppositions were only a hindrance... The only useful generalizations about language are inductive generalizations..." (1933, pp. 19–20).

---

1 Saussure's idealized *langue* harkens back to Plato's *eidon* ('essence'; see Bostock 1994; Williams 1994).

2 Bloomfield got his behaviorism from his Chicago colleague Weiss, thus indirectly from Watson. He and his structuralist followers never adopted the Platonic/Saussurean idealization, an anathema to empiricists.

5 Chomsky

Noam Chomsky's theoretical perspective displays a baffling melange of functionalist and structuralist features. On the one hand, Chomsky's structuralist provenance is clearly evident in his subscription to Saussure's **arbitrariness** ('autonomous syntax'), **idealization** ('competence') and **segregation** (irrelevance of diachrony). In ch. 1 of *Aspects* (1965), idealization is introduced as follows:

> (15) "...Linguistic theory is concerned primarily with an idealized speaker-listener, in a completely homogeneous speech-community, who knows its language perfectly and is unaffected by such grammatically irrelevant conditions as memory limitation, distractions, shifts of attention and interest, and errors (random or characteristic) in applying his knowledge of the language to actual performance...This seems to me to have been the position of the founders of modern general linguistics, and no cogent reason for modifying it has been offered. In the study of actual linguistic performance, we must consider the interaction of a variety of factors, of which the underlying competence of the speaker-hearer is only one. In this respect, the study of language is no different from empirical investigation of other complex phenomena..." (Chomsky 1965, pp. 3–4; italics added)

There is nothing *in principle* inimical to functionalism in idealization – provided it is strictly **methodological**. Data is always simplified during analysis. Theory is always more abstract than the data it purports to organize and explain. However, once cognition was relegated to the realm of 'performance', and with disinterest in change and variation, 'competence' became a theoretical prime, the endgame of both description and theory.

Underscoring the connection between idealization and structuralism is Chomsky's (1961) description of grammar as a formal algorithmic machine:

> (16) "...By "grammar of the language L" I will mean a device of some sort (that is, a set of rules) that provides, at least, a complete specification of an infinite set of grammatical sentences of L and their structural description. In addition to making precise the notion "structural description", the theory of grammar should meet requirements of the following kind. It should make available:

(1) (a)   a class of possible grammars $G1$, $G2$...

(b)   a class of possible sentences $S1$, $S2$...

(c)   a function f such that $f(i,j)$ is a set of structural descriptions of the sentence Si that are provided by the grammar Gj,

(d)   a function $m(i)$ which evaluates Gi,

(e)   a function *g* such that *g(i,n)* is the description of a finite automaton that takes sentences of (b) as input and gives structural descriptions assigned to these sentences by *Gi*..." (*On the notion 'rule of grammar'*, 1961, p. 6)

This **formalism** has remained a foundational leitmotif, running through multiple reincarnations of Generative Grammar. Over the years, it has grown ever more extreme, as Chomsky eventually (1992) dispensed with the last vestiges of concrete syntactic structures altogether:[3]

(17) "...[Early generative grammar proposed that] each language is a rich and intricate system of rules that are, typically, construction-particular and language-particular... The principles-and-parameters approach that has developed in recent years, and that I assume here, breaks radically with this tradition... The notion of grammatical construction is eliminated, and with it, construction-particular rules. Constructions such as verb phrase, relative clause, passive, etc., are taken to be *taxonomic artifacts*, collection of phenomena explained through the interaction of the principles of UG, with the values of parameters fixed..." (Chomsky 1992, p. 3; bracketed material and italics added)

By the time *Aspects* (1965) came along, the feature mix of Generative Grammar has become rather heterogenous. First, the transformational relation between 'deep' and 'surface' structures has always hinged on **meaning** (propositional semantics). This was obscured by Harris' (1965) terminology ('co-occurrence'), but was explicitly embraced in ch. 2 of *Aspects*, and is only marginally compatible with structuralism (or empiricism).

Next came the assumption of Cartesian **mentalism** (1965, ch. 1, 1966, 1968). But this clashed head on with 'competence', which ruled psychology out of bounds. The mentalism Chomsky envisioned thus turned out to be so abstract and formal so as to have relatively little to do with empirically-studied mental representation and mental processing.

Next Chomsky (1959, 1965 ch. 1, 1966, 1968) came up with an extreme **innatist** account of language acquisition, again a move toward Cartesian Platonism. This was confounded, however, by Chomsky's puzzling resistance to a biologically-plausible account of language **evolution**, coupled with a life-long insistence on Cartesian **exceptionalism** (1968; see also Hauser *et al.* 2002).[4]

———

3 In the same vein, the rules of grammar were boiled down to a single abstract one, 'merge' (Rizzi 2009; Bickerton 2009)

4 The logical contradiction here is quite glaring, since innateness implies genetic coding, which is itself the cumulative product of adaptive-selected evolution. Many functionalists accept language evolution but reject innateness, the converse of Chomsky's contradiction.

Lastly, there is the puzzling contradiction between the implicit functionalism of ch. 2 of *Aspects*, where 'deep structure' is said to be isomorphic to propositional semantics ('logical structure'), and ch. 3, where the communicative correlates of transformations are ignored ('transformations don't change meaning'), or dismissed as 'stylistic options'. Chapter 2 was the real launching pad of the **Generative Semantics** rebellion (Ross and Lakoff 1967). And the frustration of chapter 3's mid-stream retreat to structuralism forced many of us to undertake the empirical study of the communicative underpinnings of syntax (Hooper and Thompson 1973; Givón 1979, ed. 1979; Hopper ed. 1982; *inter alia*).

The schizophrenic legacy of *Aspects* has haunted subsequent functionalist work for years to come, with persistent focus on the relation between grammar and propositional meaning, to the exclusion of communicative pragmatics (Chafe 1970; Lakoff 1970; Dik 1978; Foley and van Valin 1984; Langacker 1987, 1991; *inter alia*).

6 The 1970's pragmatic synthesis

Many could claim credit for the functionalist rebellion of the 1970s. My own take may sound a bit perverse, but I think the rebellion started with Chomsky himself, in *Aspects* (1965) and even before. Chomsky had managed, rather explicitly, to build so many apparent contradictions into his position, it was almost impossible to ignore them:

- Universality without the study of language diversity
- Mentalism without psychology ('performance')
- Logic/semantics without communication/discourse
- Innateness without evolution
- The centrality of acquisition without real child language data
- Native speaker's intuition without spontaneous speech data
- Ordered rules that mimicked diachrony, but Saussurean segregation

In 1965–1967, each one of us focused on one – or at best a few – of these contradictions. But sooner or later it became clear that the emperor was stark naked.

The functionalism that emerged out of the anti-Generative rebellion of the late 1960s assembled its intellectual baggage gradually, piecemeal and often retroactively. The philosophical background, whether acknowledged or not, was the re-emergence of the Kantian-Peircean **pragmatic middle ground** between the two reductionist schools of epistemology, empiricism and rationalism. This went with a corresponding middle ground between extreme inductivism and extreme deductivism in the philosophy of science (Hanson 1958). As Chomsky (1959, 1966) had it, there was no middle ground. But a closer examination reveals a persistent pragmatic middle in both epistemology and methodology. Consequently, many of the stark dichotomies in (7) turned out to be empirically untenable. A more fine-grained approach to language, incorporating elements of both extremes, could now emerge. The main strands of this approach may be given as follows.[5]

6.1 Communicative (discourse) function

Ch. 3 of *Aspects* was a clear challenge to functionalists – they had to demonstrate that transformations *were* communicatively motivated. That is, that surface-structure variation among clause types was not a mere matter of 'stylistics' (Hooper and Thompson 1973). What was needed, above all, were structure-independent criteria – or empirical tests – for hypotheses about the communicative function of syntactic structures. The initial step here was to study the **text-distribution** of morpho-syntactic structures (Chafe ed. 1980, 1994; Givón 1979, ed. 1983). But this was only a first step toward a more direct experimental validation of the notion 'communicative function'.

6.2 Iconicity

A relatively short-lived boom in iconicity studies, inspired by Peirce (1934, 1940), took place in the 1980s, purporting to demonstrate the non-arbitrariness of grammar (Haiman 1985, ed. 1985). Unfortunately the notion of 'iconicity' involved in the discussion never transcended the relatively concrete pictorial level. Underlying cognitive, neurological and bio-evolutionary mechanism were seldom invoked, in spite of the near-certainty that pictorial iconicity was the surface product of complex emergence (Givón 1995).

6.3 Universality cum variation

Here, under the clear influence of Joseph Greenberg, a convergence took place between the extreme Bloomfieldian/Aristotelian approach of unconstrained diversity and the extreme Chomskian approach of abstract universality. Both were

---

5 Few of the participants in the functionalist renaissance of the 1970s explicitly acknowledge all these strands. They nonetheless hang together coherently as a broad *research programme*.

recognized as necessary ingredient in a mature empirical perspective, whereby universals did not contrast with diversity but rather predicted and constrained it. And further, the emphasis now shifted from formal to substantive universals, thus to the interplay between purely-structural (linguistic) and substantive (cognitive, neurological, biological) universals. And finally, universals were increasingly ascribe to the process of emergence (Heine and Kuteva 2007; Givón 2009).

6.4 Cognition and neurology

The relation between language and cognition ought to have become, at least in principle, a crucial ingredient of the pragmatic synthesis of the 1970s; first in relation to lexical-semantic memory (Atkinson and Shiffrin 1968; Swinney 1979; Spitzer 1999, *inter alia*); then in relation to working memory and attention (Carpenter and Just 1988; Just and Carpenter 1992; Garthercole and Baddeley 1993; *inter alia*); but perhaps most crucially in relation to episodic memory and discourse processing (Kintsch & van Dijk 1978; Loftus 1980; Anderson *et al.* 1983; Gernsbacher 1990, ed. 1994; Kintsch 1992, 1994; Ericsson and Kintsch 1995; *inter alia*).[6]

In the same vein, understanding the neurology of visual information processing (Ungerleider and Mishkin 1982; Squire 1987; Squire and Zola-Morgan 1991), and of the attentional and working-memory systems (Schneider and Chein 2005; Posner and Fan 2008), is crucial to an eventual account of language processing and language evolution (Givón 1995, ch. 9). Of most immediate relevance are the neurology of lexical semantics (Petersen et al. 1988; Raichle et al. 1993; Snyder et al. 1995; Posner and Pavese 1997; Abdulaev and Posner 1997; Caramazza 2000; Martin and Chao 2001; Bookheimer 2002; Pulvermüller 2003; Badre and Wagner 2007; *inter alia*) and the processing of simple and complex clauses (Friederici 2009; Friederichi and Frisch 2000; Fridederici et al. 2006a, 2006b; Grodzinmsky and Friederici 2006; Pulvermüller 2003; *inter alia*).[7]

---

6 Unfortunately, the vast majority of self-designated functionalists, of whatever sect, tend to expostulate about cognition without studying the cognitive literature.

7 While of great relevance in principle, current experimental work in neuro-linguistics suffers from two related, self-imposed methodological strictures: (a) Single-word or single-clause language stimuli, which remain largely out of the functional range of grammar; and (b) excessive focus on grammaticality judgements, ignoring the adaptive role of grammar in communication.

6.5 Emergence-I: Diachrony & grammaticalization

The resurgent interest in diachronic syntax and grammaticalization in the 1970's and beyond (Givón 1971, 1979; Li ed. 1977; Heine *et al.* 1991; Heine and Traugott eds 1991; Heine and Kuteva 2007; Hopper and Traugott 1993; Bybee *et al.* 1994; *inter alia*) represented an integral strand in the functionalist tapestry and a return to F. Bopp and H. Paul. The resurgence of diachrony dovetailed with the interest in typological diversity and universals, and in the diachronic underpinnings of synchronic typology (Givón 2002, 2009). It also dovetailed – Labov (1994) notwithstanding – with the functional motivation for change and emergence, an issue that is central to bio-evolution (see below).

6.6 Emergence-II: Child language acquisition

The rise of the middle-ground pragmatic approach to child language acquisition was another important strand in the functionalist tapestry. Rather than an automatic consequence of innate, abstract universal parameters, the ontogeny of language was now seen as an **interaction** between multiple innate factors – neuro-cognition, communication, learning strategies, maturational sequences – and the care-giver's socio-affective, communicative and linguistic input (Ervin-Tripp 1970; Scollon 1976; Bates 1976; *Bates et al.* 1979; Bates and MacWhinney 1979; Ochs and Schieffelin eds. 1979; MacWhinney ed. 1999). Rather than an instantaneous single process, language acquisition turned out to be a gradual multi-stage emergence (Carter 1974; Bloom 1970/1973; Bowerman 1973; Bates *et al.* 1975).

6.7 Emergence-III: Evolution

The third process of emergence, adaptive-selected evolution, is just as compatible with functionalism in linguistics, meshing well with core preoccupation such as variation-and-change and functional-adaptive motivation (Heine and Kuteva 2007; Givón 2002, 2009). While seemingly unprecedented in biology (as against ontogeny and phylogeny), language diachrony nonetheless recapitulates many of the general features of biological evolution. This may be summed up in the following observations:
– Today's micro-variation within the species/language engenders, at least potentially, tomorrow's macro-variation across species/languages.
– Conversely, today's starkly diverse extant species, genera, families, and phyla in biology, or starkly diverse languages, dialects and families, can be

traced back to earlier variation at lower taxonomic levels (sub-species, sub-dialects).

– Consequently, gradual step-by-step *micro-variation* can yield, over time, stark and seemingly unbridgeable gaps of *macro-variation* among extant species or languages.

– The process of change itself, the invisible teleological hand that guides the ever-shifting but still roughly-isomorphic matching of structures and functions, is driven by adaptive selection, i.e. by functional-adaptive pressures.

– The overlaying of adaptively-driven changes in temporal order can lead, over time, to considerable restructuring and arbitrariness of structure-function mapping, thus to seemingly non-adaptive *relic features* ('excess structure', 'spandrels').

– Universal principles do not control observed surface features directly, but rather control the developmental processes that, in turn, give rise to observed surface features.

In addition, six general principles seem to characterize both language diachrony and biological evolution:
– Graduality of change
– Adaptive-selectional motivation
– Functional change and ambiguity before structural change and specialization
– Terminal addition of new structures to older ones
– Local causation (but global consequences).
– Uni-directionality of change

To drive these points home, here are a few salient quotes from the evolutionary biologists E. Mayr and D. Futuyma. First, concerning Platonic idealization:

> (17) "...Plato's concept of the *eidos* is the philosophical codification of this form of thinking. According to this concept the vast observed variability of the world has no more reality that the shadows of an object on a cave wall...Fixed, unchangeable "ideas" underlying the observed variability are the only things that are permanent and real. Owing to its belief in essences this philosophy is also referred to as *essentialism*...[which] dominated the natural sciences until well into the nineteenth century. The concepts of unchanging essences and of complete discontinuity between every *eidos* (type) and all others make genuine evolutionary thinking well-nigh impossible..." (Mayr 1969, p. 4)

> (18) "...variation is at the heart of the scientific study of the living world. As long as *essentialism*, the outlook that ignores variation in its focus on fixed essences, held sway, the possibility of evolutionary change could hardly be conceived, for variation is both the product and the foundation of evolution. Few other sciences take variation as a primary focus of study as does evolutionary biology..." (Futuyma 1986, p. 82)

The profound difference between biological and pre-biological science, what Aristotle insisted on in the 4th Century BC, indeed hinges on variation. That is:

(19) "...Until a few years ago, when an evolutionist or a systematist opened the book on the philosophy of science, and read about the basic concepts, methods and objectives of science, he was bound to be distressed to discover how little all this had to do with his own particular endeavor. The reason for this incongruity is that these books were written either by logicians or physicists. These authors did not realize that the physical sciences are a very specialized branch of science. Its ideal is to explain everything under a few general laws and to subordinate all diversity under a limited number of broadly-based generalizations[...] Perhaps the outstanding aspect of the physical sciences is the identity of the entities with which it deals. A sodium atom is a sodium atom no matter where you encounter it and what its chemical history might have been. It always has exactly the same properties. The same is true for the elementary particles, the protons, electrons, mesons, etc., or for the aggregates of atoms, the molecules. It is the sameness of these entities that permits the determination of extremely precise constants for all the properties of these constituents as well as their inclusion in general laws. How different is the material of the systematist and evolutionist! Its outstanding characteristic is uniqueness. No two individuals in a sexually reproducing population are the same (not even identical twins), no two populations of the same species, no two species, no two higher taxa[...]..." (Mayr 1976, pp. 408–409).

Both variation and its limits are adaptively motivated, exhibiting a fluid trade-off relation. Excessively-constrained variation deprives a population of evolutionary dynamism, as innovative adaptive solutions to potential novel conditions are diluted and re-absorbed into the common gene pool. Unconstrained variation leads to reproductive isolation and speciation, whereby the creative adaptive innovations of dynamic outlier populations cease to contribute to the common gene-pool (Bonner 1988).

The source of variation in biological populations is both genetic (genotypic) and non-genetic (phenotypic, behavioral). While both can be adaptive, it is only genetic variation that has direct evolutionary consequences. However, the adaptive interaction of genes with the environment – natural selection – is mediated by the individual's phenotypic structural and behavioral traits. As a result, non-genetic variation does partake in the actual mechanism of adaptive selection. In this way, synchronic variation in the phenotypic behavior, thus the adaptive experimentation of individuals, contributes, in a fashion reminiscent of the Lamarckian program, to the eventual direction of adaptive evolution. Or, as Ernst Mays puts it:

(23) "...Many if not most acquisitions of new structures in the course of evolution can be ascribed to selection forces exerted by newly-acquired behaviors (Mayr 1960). Behavior, thus, plays an important role as the pacemaker of evolutionary change. Most adaptive radiations were apparently caused by behavioral shifts..." (Mayr 1982, p. 612)

Synchronic variation *within* a biological population is at the very heart of the mechanism of evolutionary change, whereby such micro-variation can become, in time, macro-variation *across* distinct populations. In linguistics, this is akin to saying that today's synchronic variants are but the potential reservoir of tomorrow's diachronic changes, the *Labov Principle* (Givón 2009, ch. 3).

Lastly, a line of research that is highly relevant to the evolution of language may be found in the works of primatologists and animal ethologists (de Wall 1982, 2001; Cheney and Seyfarth 1990, 2007; Hrdy 2009; Tomasello and Call 1997, Tomasello *et al*. 2005; Boesch and Boesch-Achermann 2000; Crockford and Boesch 2002, 2005; *inter alia*); and likewise in the works of evolutionary psychologists (Barkow *et al*. eds 1992; Geary 2005; *inter alia*) and cognitive anthropologists (Richerson and Boyd 2005, *inter alia*). Even when not directly pointing to language, this magnificent body of work lays out the parameters of gradual socio-cultural evolution in primates, hominids and *homo sapiens*, which is in turn the real context for the evolution of human communication.

References

Abdulaev, Yalchin G. and Michael I. Posner. 1997. "Time-course of activating brain areas in generating verbal associations", *Psychological Science*, 8.1.

Anderson, A., S. C. Garrod and A. J. Sanford. 1983. "The accessibility of pronominal antecedents as a function of episodic shift in narrative text", *Quarterly J. of Experimental Psych.*, 35A.

Anselm, St. 1964. *De Grammatico*, in D.P. Henry, *The De Grammatico of St. Anselm*, Notre Dame, IN: University of Notre Dame Press.

Aristotle. 1941a. *De Partibus Animalium*, in McKeon (ed.).

Aristotle. 1941b. *The Categories*, in McKeon (ed.).

Arnauld, A. 1662. *La Logique, ou l'Art de Panser*, tr. in J. Dixon and P. James (1964) *The Art of Thinking*, Indianapolis: Bobbs-Merrill.

Atkinson, R.C. and R.M. Shiffrin. 1968. "Human memory: A proposed system and its control processes", in K.W. Spence and T. Spence (eds) *The Psychology of Learning and Motivation,* vol. 2, NY: Academic Press.

Badre, D. and A.D. Wagner. 2007. "The left ventrolateral prefrontal cortex and the cognitive control of memory", *Neuropsychologia*, 45.

Barkow, Jerome H., Leda Cosmides, and John Tooby (eds). 1992. *The Adapted Mind: Evolutionary Psychology and the Generation of Culture*, Oxford: Oxford University Press.

Bates, Elizabeth. 1976. *Language in Context: The Acquisition of Pragmatics*, NY: Academic Press.

Bates, Elizabeth, L. Benigni, I. Bretherton, L. Camioni, and V. Voltera. 1979. *The Emergence of Symbols: Cognition and Communication in Infancy*, NY: Academic Press.

Bates, Elizabeth, L. Camioni and V. Voltera. 1975. "The acquisition of performatives prior to speech", *Bobbs-Merrill Quarterly*, 21.

Bates, Elizabeth and Brian MacWhinney. 1979. "A functional approach to the acquisition of grammar", in E. Ochs and BV. Schieffelin (eds 1979).

Bickerton, Derek. 2005. "The origin of language in niche construction", University of Hawaii, Honolulu (ms).

Bickerton, Derek. 2009. "Recursion: Core of complexity or artifact of analysis?", in T. Givón and M. Shibatani (eds 2009).

Bloom, Lois. 1970/73. *One Word at a Time: The Use of Single-Word Utterances Before Syntax*, The Hague: Mouton.

Bloomfield, Leonard. 1922. "Review of Sapir's Language", *The Classical Weekly*, 18.

Bloomfield, Leonard. 1933. *Language*, NY: Holt, Rinehart and Winston.

Boesch, Cristophe and Hedwige Boesch-Achermann. 2000. *The Chimpanzees of Tai Forest: Behavioral Ecology and Evolution*, Oxford: Oxford University Press.

Bonner, John Tyler. 1988. *The Evolution of Complexity in Animals*, Princeton: Princeton University Press

Bookheimer, Susan. 2002. "Functional MRI of language: New approaches to understanding the cortical organization of semantic processing", *Ann. Rev. of Neuroscience*, 25.

Bopp, Franz. 1816. *Über das Konjugationssystem der Sanskritsprache in Vergleichung mit jenem der griechischen, lateinischen, persischen und germanischen Sprache.*

Bostock, D. 1994. "Plato on understanding language", in S. Everson (ed. 1994).

Bowerman, Melissa. 1973. *Early Syntactic Development*, Cambridge: Cambridge University Press.

Bybee, Joan, Wiliam Pagliuca and Revere Perkins. 1994. *The Evolution of Grammar: Tense, Aspect and Modality in the Languages of the World*, Chicago: University of Chicago Press.

Caramazza, Alfonso. 2000. "The organization of conceptual knowledge in the brain", in M. Gazzaniga (ed.) *The New Cognitive Science*, 2nd edition, Cambridge, MAL: MIT Press.

Carnap, Rudolph. 1963. *The Philosophy of Rudolph Carnap*, ed. by P.A. Schillp, LaSalle, IL: Open Court.

Carpenter, P. and M. Just. 1988. "The role of working memory in language comprehension", in D, Klahr and D. Kotovsky (eds) *Complex Information Processing: The Impact of Herbert Simon*, Hillsdale, NJ: Erlbaum.

Carter, Anne. 1974. *Communication in the Sensory-Motor Period*, PhD dissertation, UC at Berkeley (ms).

Chafe, Wallace. 1970. *Meaning and the Structure of Language*, Chicago: University of Chicago Press.

Chafe, Wallace. 1980 (ed). *The Pear Stories*, Norwood, NJ: Ablex.

Chafe, Wallace. 1994. *Discourse, Consciousness and Time: The Displacement of Conscious Experience in Speaking and Writing*, Chicago: University of Chicago Press.

Cheney, Dorothy, and Robert Seyfarth. 1990. *How Monkeys See the World*, Chicago: University of Chicago Press.

Cheney, Dorothy, and Robert Seyfarth. 2007. *Baboon Metaphysics*, Chicago: University of Chicago Press.

Chomsky, Noam. 1959. "Review of B.F. Skinner's *Verbal Behavior*", *Language*, 35.

Chomsky, Noam. 1961. "On the notion 'rule of grammar'", in *The Structure of Language and its Mathematical Aspects,* Providence RI: American Mathematical Society.

Chomsky, Noam. 1965. *Aspects of the Theory of Syntax*, Cambridge, MAL: MIT Press.

Chomsky, Noam. 1966. *Cartesian Linguistics*, NY: Harper and Row.

Chomsky, Noam. 1968/72. *Language and Mind*, NY: Harcourt, Brace, Jovanovich.

Chomsky, Noam. 1992. "A minimalist program for linguistic theory", *MIT Occasional Papers in Linguistics*, Cambridge, MA: MIT.

Crockford, Catherine and Christoph Boesch. 2003. "Context specific calls in wild chimpanzees, *pan troglodytus verus*: Analysis of barks", *Animal Behavior*, 66.

Crockford, Catherine and Christoph Boesch. 2005. "Call combinations in wild chimpanzees", *Behaviour*, 142.

Crouch, James Esign. 1978. *Functional Human Anatomy*, 3rd edition, Philadelphia: Lea and Fabiger.

Darwin, Charles. 1859. *On the Origin of Species by Means of Natural Selection*, London: John Murray.

Darwin, Charles. 1871. *The Descent of Man and Selection in Relation to Sex*, London: John Murray.

de Wall, Frans. 1982. *Chimpanzee Politics: Power and Sex among the Apes*, London: Unwin/ Counterpoint.

de Wall, Frans. 2001. *The Ape and the Sushi Master*, NY: Basic Books.

Dik, Simon. 1978. *Functional Grammar*, Amsterdam: North Holland.

Dunbar, R. 1992. "Co-evolution of cortex size, group size and language", *Brain and Behavior Science*, 16.4.

Dunbar, R. 1998. "Theory of mind and the evolution of language", in J. R. Hurford *et al.* (eds 1998).

Ericsson, Karl Anders, and Walter Kintsch. 1995. "Long term working memory", *Psych. Review*, 102.2.

Ervin-Tripp, Susan. 1970. "Discourse agreement: How children answer question", in J.R. Hays (ed.) *Cognition and the Development of Language*, NY: Wiley.

Everson, Stephen (ed.). 1994. *Language, Companion to Ancient Thought*, 3, Cambridge: Cambridge University Press.

Foley, William, and Robert van Valin. 1984. *Functional Syntax and Universal Grammar*, Cambridge: Cambridge University Press.

Friederici, A. 2009. "Brain circuits of syntax", in D. Bickerton and E. Szathmáry (eds) *Biological Foundations and Origin of Syntax*, Cambridge, MA: MIT Press.

Friederichi, A. and S. Frisch. 2000. "Verb-argument structure processing: The role of verb-specific and argument-specific information", *J. of Memory and Language*, 43.

Fridederici, A., J. Bahlmann, S. Heim, R.I. Schubotz, and A. Anwander. 2006a. „The brain differentiates human and non-human grammar: Functional localization and structural connectivity", *Proc. Nat. Acad. of Sci.*, USA, 103.

Friederici, A., C.J. Fiebach, M. Schlesewsky, I. Bornkessel and D.Y. von Cramon. 2006b. "Processing linguistic complexity and grammaticality in the left frontal cortex", *Cerebral Cortex*, 16.

Futuyma, Douglas. 1986. *Evolutionary Biology*, 2nd edition, Sunderland, MA: Sinauer.

Gathercole, Susan E., and Alan D. Baddeley. 1993. *Working Memory and Language*, Hillsdale, NJ: Erlbaum.

Geary, David C. 2005. *The Origin of Mind: The Evolution of Brain, Cognition and General Intelligence*, Washington, DC: American Psychological Association.

Gernsbacher. Morton A. 1990. *Language Comprehension as Structure Building*, Hillsdale, NJ: Erlbaum.

Gernsbacher, Morton A. (ed.). 1994. *Handbook of Psycholinguistics*, NY: Academic Press.

Givón, T. 1971. "Historical syntax and synchronic morphology: An archaeologist's field trip", *CLS #7*, Chicago: University of Chicago, Chicago Linguistics Society.

Givón, T. 1979. *On Understanding Grammar*, NY: Academic Press.

Givón, T. (ed) 1979. *Discourse and Syntax, Syntax and Semantics 12*, NY: Academic Press.

Givón, T. (ed) 1983. *Topic Continuity in Discourse*, TSL #3, Amsterdam: J. Benjamins.

Givón, T. 1995. *Functionalism and Grammar*, Amsterdam: J. Benjamins.

Givón, T. 2002. *Bio-Linguistics: The Santa Barbara Lectures*, Amsterdam: J. Benjamins.

Givón, T. 2009. *The Genesis of Syntactic Complexity: Diachrony, Ontogeny, Neuro-Cognition, Evolution*, Amsterdam: J. Benjamins.

Givón, T., and Masayoshi Shibatani (eds). 2009. *Syntactic Complexity*, TSL #85, Amsterdam: J. Benjamins.

Greenfield, P.M. 1991. "Language, tools and brain: The ontogeny and phylogeny of hierarchically organized sequential behavior", *Brain and Behavior Sciences*, 14.4.

Grodzinsky, Yosef and Angela Friederici. 2006. "Neuroimaging of syntax and syntactic processing", *Current Opinion in Neurobiology*, 16.

Haiman, John. 1985. *Natural Syntax*, Cambridge: Cambridge University Press.

Haiman, John. (ed) 1985. *Iconicity in Syntax*, TSL #6, Amsterdam: J. Benjamins.

Hamilton, Edith, and Huntington Cairns (eds). 1961. *Plato: The Collected Dialogues*, Princeton: Princeton University Press.

Hanson, Russell Norwood. 1958. *Patterns of Discovery*, Cambridge: Cambridge University Press.

Harris, Zelig. 2002. "Co-occurrence and transformations in linguistic structure", *Language*, 33.3.

Hauser, M., N. Chomsky and W.T. Fitch. 2002. "The faculty of language: What it is, who has it, how did it evolve", *Science*, 298, Nov. 2002.

Heine, Bernd, Ulrike Claudi, and Friederike Hünnemeyer. 1991. *Grammaticalization: A Conceptual Framework*, Chicago: University of Chicago Press.

Heine, Bernd and Tania Kuteva. 2007. *The Genesis of Grammar*, Oxford: Oxford University Press.

Heine, Bernd and Elizabeth Traugott (eds). 1991. *Approaches to Grammaticalization*, TSL #19 (2 vols), Amsterdam: J. Benjamins.

Hooper, Joan, and Sandra A. Thompson. 1973. "On the application of root transformations", *Linguistic Inquiry*, 4.

Hopper, Paul (ed.). 1982. *Tense and Aspect: Between Semantics and Pragmatics*, TSL #1, Amsterdam: J. Benjamins.

Hopper, Paul and Elizabeth Traugott. 1993. *Grammaticalization*, Cambridge: Cambridge University Press.

Hrdy, Sarah Blaffer. 2009. *Mothers and Others*, Cambridge, MA: Harvard University Press.

Humboldt, Wilhelm von. 1836. *Linguistic Variation and Intellectual Development*, tr. by G.C. Buck, Coral Gables, FL: University of Florida press [1961].

Hurford, James R., Michale Studdard-Kennedy, and Chris Knight (eds). 1998. *Approaches to the Evolution of Language*, Cambridge: Cambridge University Press.

Itkonen, Esa. 2010. "Philosophy of Linguistics", *Oxford Encyclopedia of Philosophy of Science*, Oxford: Oxford University Press (in press).

Jespersen, Otto. 1921. *Language: Its Nature, Development and Origin*, NY: Modern Library

Jespersen, Otto. 1924. *The Philosophy of Grammar*, NY/London: W.W. Norton & Co. [1965].

Just, Marcel and Patricia Carpenter. 1992. "A capacity theory of comprehension: Individual differences in working memory", *Psych. Review*, 99.1.

Kintsch. Walter. 1992. "How readers construct situation models of stories: The role of syntactic cues and causal inference", in A.F. Healy, S. Kosslyn and R.M. Shiffrin (eds) *Essays in Honor of William K. Estes*, Hillsdale, NJ: Erlbaum.

Kintsch. Walter. 1994. "The psychology of discourse processing", in M.A. Gernbacher (ed. 1994).

Kintsch, Walter and Teun van Dijk. 1978. „Toward a model of text comprehension and production", *Psych. Review*, 85.

Knight, Chris. 1998. "Ritual/speech co-evolution: A solution to the problem of deception", in J.R. Hurford *et al.* (eds 1998).

Labov, William. 1975. "Empirical foundations of linguistic theory", in R. Austerlitz (ed.) *The Scope of American Linguistics*, Lisse: Peter de Ridder.

Labov, William. 1994. *Principles of Linguistic Change*, vol. 1: Internal Factors, Oxford: Basil Blackwell.

Lakoff, George. 1970. "Linguistics and natural logic", *Studies in Generative Semantics*, 2, Ann Arbor, MI: University of Michigan.

Langacker, Ronald. 1987. *Foundations of Cognitive Grammar*, vol. I, Stanford: Stanford University Press.

Langacker, Ronald. 1991. *Foundations of Cognitive Grammar*, vol. II, Stanford: Stanford University Press.

Li, Charles N. (ed). 1977. *Mechanism of Syntactic Change*, Austin: University of Texas Press.

Lieberman, Philip. 1984. *The Biology and Evolution of Language*, Cambridge, MA: Harvard University Press.

Loftus, Elizabeth F. 1980. *Eyewitness Testimony*, Cambridge: Harvard University Press.

MacWhinney, Brian (ed.). 1999. *The Emergence of Language*, Mahwah, NJ: Erlbaum.

Martin, A. and L.L. Chao. 2001. "Semantic memory and the brain: Structure and processes", *Current Opinion in Neurobiology*, 11.

Mayr, Ernst. 1969. *Populations, Species and Evolution*, Cambridge, MA: Harvard University Press.

Mayr, Ernst. 1976. *Evolution and the Diversity of Life*, Cambridge, MA: Harvard University Press.

Mayr, Ernst. 1982. *The Growth of Biological Thought*, Cambridge, MA: Harvard University Press.

McKeon, Richard (ed.). 1941. *The Basic Works of Aristotle*, NY: Random House [22nd edition]

Lancelot, Claude and Antoine Arnauld *et al.* 1660. *Grammaire Générale et Raisonée*.

Ochs, Elinor and Bambi Schieffelin (eds.). 1979. *Developmental Pragmatics*, NY: Academic Press.

Odling-Smee, F. John, Kevin N. Laland and Marcus D. Feldman. 2003. *Niche Construction: The Neglected Process in Evolution*, Monographs in Population Biology #37, Princeton: Princeton University Press.

Peirce, Charles S. 1934. *Collected Writings*, vol. V, Cambridge, MA: Harvard University Press.

Peirce, Charles S. 1940. *The Philosophy of Peirce*, d. by J. Buchler, NY: Harcourt, Brace.

Paul, Hermann. 1890. *Principles of the History of Language*, Tr. by H.A. Strong, London: Swann, Sonnenschein & Co.

Petersen, S.A., P.T. Fox, M.I. Posner, M. Mintun, and M.E. Raichle. 1988. „Positron emission tomographic studies of the cortical anatomy of single words", *J. of Cognitive Neuroscience*, 1.2.

Plato. *Cratylus*, in E. Hamilton and H. Cairns (eds 1961).

Posner, M.I., and J. Fan. 2008. "Attention as an organ system", in J. Pomerantz (ed.) *Neurobiology of Perception and Communication: From Synapses to Society*, 4th De Lange Symposium, Cambridge: Cambridge University Press.

Posner, M.I., and A. Pavese. 1997. "Anatomy of word and sentence meaning", in M. Posner and M. Raichle (orgs) *Colloquium on Neuroimaging of Human Brain Functions*, UC Irvine (ms).

Pulvermüller, Friedemann. 2003. *The Neuroscience of Language*, Cambridge: Cambridge University Press.

Rabi, I. I. 1975. interview in *The New Yorker*, Oct. 20, 1975.

Raichle, M.E. et al. 1993. «Practice-related changes in the human brain functional anatomy during non-motor learning», *Cerebral Cortex*, (ms).

Richerson, Peter J., and Robert Boyd. 2005. Not by Genes Alone: How Culture Transformed Human Evolution, Chicago: University of Chicago Press.

Rizzi, L. 2009. "Recent advances in syntactic theory", in D. Bickerton and E. Szathmáry (eds) *Biological Foundation and Origin of Syntax*, Cambridge, MA: MIT Press.

Ross, John Robert, and George Lakoff. 1967. "Is deep structure necessary?", First La Jolla Conference on Linguistics Theory (ms).

Russell, Bertrand. 1956. *Logic and Knowledge*, selected essays, 1901–1950, ed. E.C. Marsh, London: Routledge.

Sapir, Edward. 1921. *Language*, NY: Harcourt, Brace & World [1929].

Saussure, Ferdinand de. 1915. *Course in General Linguistics*, ed. by C. Bally and S. Sechehaye, tr. by W. Baskin, NY: Philosophical Library [1959].

Schneider, W. and J.M. Chein. 2003. „Controlled and automated processing: Behavior, theory and biological mechanisms", *Cognitive Science*, 27.

Scollon, Ronald. 1976. *Conversations with a One-Year-Old Child*, Honolulu: University of Hawaii Press.

Snyder, A., Y Abdulaev, M.I. Posner, and M.E. Raichle. 1995. "Scalp electric potentials reflect regional cerebral blood flow responses during processing of written words", *Proc. Nat. Acad. of Science*, USA, 92.

Spitzer, Manfred. 1999. *The Mind within the Net: A Model of Learning, Speaking and Acting*, Cambridge, MA: MIT Press.

Squire, Larry. 1987. *Memory and Brain*, Oxford: Oxford University Press.

Squire, Larry, and S. Zola-Morgan. 1998. "Episodic memory, semantic memory and amnesia", *Hippocampus*, 8.

Swinney, D. 1979. "Lexical access during language comprehension: (Re)consideration of context effects", *J.V.L.V.B.*, 18.

Számadó, S. and E. Szathmáry. 2006. "Competing selective scenarios for the emergence of natural language", *Trends in Ecology and Evolution*, 2.

Tomasello, Michael, and Joseph Call. 1997. *Primate Cognition*, Oxford: Oxford University Press.

Tomasello, Michael, J. Carpenter, J. Call, T. Behne, and H. Moll. 2005. "Understanding and sharing intentions: The origins of cultural cognition", *Brain and Behavior Sciences*, 28.

Ungerleider, L.A. and M. Mishkin. 1982. „Two cortical visual systems", in D.J. Ingle, M.A. Goodale and R.J.K. Mansfield (eds) *Analysis of Visual Behavior*, Cambridge, MA: MIT Press.

Waddington, Conrad Hal. 1942. "Canalization of development and the inheritance of acquired characters", *Nature*, 150.

Waddington, Conrad Hal. 1953. "Genetic assimilation of an acquired character", *Evolution*, 7.

Washburn, Sherwood L., and C. Lancaster. 1968. "The evolution of hunting", in R.B. Lee and I. deVore (eds) *Man the Hunter*, Chicago: Aldine.

Williams, Bernard. 1994. "Cratylus theory of names and its refutation", in S. Everson (ed. 1994).
Zipf, George. 1935. *The Psycho-biology of Language: An introduction to Dynamic Philology*, Cambridge, MA: MIT Press.

Esa Itkonen
Functional Explanation and its Uses

1 Preliminary Remarks

It is the purpose of this paper to analyze the notion of explanation as it is used in the typological literature. First, it is argued that, instead of involving either a set of zeros or one multiply ambiguous zero, the 'minimal' structures of verb morphology should be interpreted as exemplifying a 'basic use', justified by considerations of economy. Next, the notion of (binary) implicational universal is unfolded in successive steps. The seemingly equivalent formulations 'if A, then B' and 'if not-B, then not-A' are directly confirmed by opposite linguistic types, whereas neither of them is directly confirmed by the third (= prevalent) type. Therefore a more adequate format is suggested, in terms of 'expressive needs' (directly satisfied only by the third type). This analysis is then extended to implicational hierarchies in general and ultimately to non-binary types. In the following two sections more examples are adduced in confirmation of the preceding account. An examination of the grammaticalization process highlights the explanatory roles of empathy and analogy (already implicit in what precedes). In the next section linguistic behavior is conceptualized as partaking in problem-solving: the problem is to achieve a goal and the solution is the behavioral means chosen by the agent. This type of explanation-by-goal is defined more narrowly as 'rational explanation'. Because it relies on the use of empathy, this notion needs in turn to be explicated. It proves to be a half-way house between introspection and intuition: empathy is vicarious introspection while intuition is conventionalized empathy. The key term 'function' is divided into social-psychological goal and biological function, producing two distinct notions of 'functional explanation'. Finally, a third type of explanation is introduced, namely 'pattern explanation', intended to explain particular languages by showing how their grammars fit in with the general typological framework (designated as 'universal grammar').

2 Explaining the Zero in Verb Morphology

In classical structuralism the morpheme was the basic form–meaning unit. This notion was divided into several subtypes, including zero morpheme. On reflection, however, it turns out that zero morpheme is not just one type of morpheme on a par with others. Let us consider the following Yoruba example:

(1) ó   rà   á
     3SG.AG   buy   3SG.PAT
     '[S]he bought it'

It is immediately evident that vital information is lacking in the morpheme- by-morpheme gloss. Example (1) differs e.g. from the sentence *yó rà á* ('[s]he will buy it'), where *yó* = FUT and 3SG.AG = zero. Therefore – as shown by the English translation – the tense of (1) is preterite (= PRET), even if it remains unexpressed (or – as it seems – is expressed by zero). Clearly we have to correct our example as follows:

(2) ó   rà-Ø   á
     3SG.AG   buy-PRET   3SG.PAT
     '[S]he bought it'

Moreover, the translation of (1) shows the aspect of *rà* to be completive (= CMP), as becomes evident if (1) is compared e.g. with the sentence *ó ńrà á (nígbánáà)* ('[s]he used to buy it [at the time]'), where the prefix *ń-* expresses habituality. We again correct our example:

(3) ó   rà-Ø-Ø   á
     3SG.AG   buy-PRET-CMP   3SG.PAT
     '[S]he bought it'

The translation further shows the modality of (1) to be factive (= FCT). In Yoruba non-factive modalities are expressed (in subordinate clauses) e.g. by the conjunction *kí* or by the (pre-verbal) auxiliary *bá*; for instance, *mo ní **kí** ó rà á* ('I told him/her to buy it') or *mo bi í léèrè bí ó **bá** fé. rà á* ('I asked him/her if [s]he wanted to buy it'), where *bi ...léèrè* = 'to ask', *bí* = 'if', and *fé.* = 'to want'. Rowlands (1969) calls the *kí* construction and the *bá* construction dependent verb (Chapter 13) and indefinite clause (Chapter 18), respectively. The factive modality of (1) is evident from the fact that *kí* and *bá* are lacking, which means (or seems to mean) that it is expressed by zero. As a consequence, we again need to correct our example:

(4) ó   rà-Ø-Ø-Ø   á
     3SG.AG   buy-PRET-CMP-FCT   3SG.PAT
     '[S]he bought it'

The translation of (1) also shows the voice of the *rà* verb-form to be active (=ACT) (and not e.g. passive). The presence of this grammatical meaning may be somewhat less obvious than that of the three previous meanings (=PRET, CMP, FCT). It makes sense to speak of ACT only in a language with at least one other type of voice, in particular PASS. Unlike e.g. English, Yoruba has no passive with optional agents à la *It was bought by him/her*, but it does have an agentless passive, for instance *ó di rírà* ('it was bought'), where *di* ='become'. To be sure, this construction may not be very frequent (cf. Rowlands 1969: 189–190). With this qualification, we revise our example as follows:

(5) ó   rà-Ø-Ø-Ø-Ø   á
     3SG.AG buy-PRET-CMP-FCT-ACT   3SG.PAT
     '[S]he bought it'

Our analysis of (1) cannot stop here. This is obvious as soon as we compare (1) with a question like *ó rà á bí?* ('did [s]he buy it?'). Thus, (1) also expresses an assertion (= ASS). The same grammatical meaning is elicited by comparing an assertion like *o rà á* ('you.2SG bought it') with a command like *rà á!* ('buy it!'). Notice that a command is even more economical than the corresponding assertion because now 2SG.AG = zero. In any event, ASS has no dedicated exponent, which is why the following addition has to be made:

(6) ó   rà-Ø-Ø-Ø-Ø-Ø   á
     3SG.AG buy-PRET-CMP-FCT-ACT-ASS 3SG.PAT
     '[S]he bought it'

Finally it needs to be noted that the meaning of (1) is affirmative (= AFF), as shown by comparing it with a negated sentence like *kò rà á* ('[s]he did not buy it'), with 3SG.AG – zero. In sum, the total meaning of (1) contains six grammatical meanings none of which is overtly expressed:

(7) ó   rà-Ø-Ø-Ø-Ø-Ø-Ø   á
     3SG.AG buy-PRET-CMP-FCT-ACT-ASS-AFF 3SG.PAT
     '[S]he bought it'

The gloss of (7) is so formulated as to claim that (7) contains six (dedicated) zeros each of which expresses one grammatical meaning. On an alternative interpretation, (7) contains only one zero and six meanings that have accumulated behind it. Both of these interpretations are quite artificial.

The foregoing should not be taken to mean that the notion of zero morpheme simply has to be abandoned. It certainly has a meaningful use e.g. in distinguishing between SG and PL, as in *boy-Ø* vs. *boy-s*. But its use becomes more and more implausible when the number of zero-expressed grammatical meanings increases, as shown by (1–7). But what is, then, the alternative interpretation?

Although we may instinctively think that every meaning should have an overt expression (and, moreover, only one such expression), a moment's reflection is enough to show that it would be unreasonable – and uneconomical – to accept this as a generally valid principle. In linguistics and elsewhere, some meanings are basic in the sense that they are understood to be there even when they are not overtly expressed, or rather, just because they are not expressed at all. Alternatively, it may be said that the linguistic form-category (e.g. verb) with which these meanings are correlated occurs here in its basic use. It needs to be understood that this is not just a reformulation of the zero morpheme interpretation (= either one multiply ambiguous zero or several dedicated zeros). Rather, one needs to adopt a different way of thinking.

This different way is certainly no novelty. The underlying principle is only too well known: "what is **familiar** is given reduced expression" (Haiman 1985: 18). Jespersen (1924: 264), for his part, anticipated the notion of basic use as follows: "it cannot be called illogical to omit the designation of what goes without saying: situation and context make many things clear which a strict logician in a pedantic analysis would prefer to see stated." Jespersen had in turn been preceded by Hermann Paul: "Such expressions must develop everywhere as contain no more material than is required for the hearer to understand the meaning" (1975 [1880]: 313). And when we dig deeper, we discover that Apollonius Dyscolus already inaugurated this view, focussing on the expressive power of the verb form, just as we are doing right now: "in finite verbs there are very many meanings implicit"; and he is quite explicit in counting both ASS and AFF, i.e. cases (6) and (7), among these "implicit meanings" (cf. Itkonen 1991: 208).

Thus, the notion of basic use is not new in itself. What is perhaps new, is the realization that it is incompatible with unrestricted use of zero morphemes. In general, people do not care to distinguish between these two options. But they should be understood to exclude each other. Moreover, it should be realized that there have never been generally accepted criteria for what counts or not as a zero morpheme. This has devastating consequences for any approach that tries to classify languages on some kind of category-per-word basis, in addition to the fact that, most of the time, the term 'category' is allowed to stand both for units of form and for units of meaning (cf. Itkonen & Pajunen 2011: 107–108).

It is certainly more economical to express meaning 'X' by zero than by some overt form Y. Therefore the basic use is more economical than non-basic uses. Now, the fact that the basic use of a given sentence-form is economical illustrates the very essence of linguistic **functionalism**. The form in its basic use is likely to be the most frequent one among possible alternatives, and it is rational (in the sense of 'energy-saving') that this type of form should be as short as possible. Even better than by means of (1)–(7), the rationality implicit in basic use is exemplified by the command that was cited above, i.e. *rà á!* ('buy it!'). Unlike in assertions in general, there is no need to express the agent of the action expressed by the command because it is the person who the command is addressed to.

Since the notion of basic use is based on the absence of (dedicated) formatives, it is grasped most easily in connection with analytic languages (like Yoruba). But once it has been grasped, it is seen to apply everywhere. The structure of (1) consists of a (transitive) verb root plus (pronominal) markers for AG and PAT. But exactly the same basic structure occurs in synthetic languages like Finnish and in polysynthetic languages like West Greenlandic.

In Yoruba, the meaning 'I bought it' is expressed by *mo rà á* while in Finnish an equally simple sentence structure expresses the meaning 'I buy it':[1]

(8) osta-n   se-n
    buy-1SG   3SG.N-ACC

Thus, just as with (1), there are no dedicated exponents for grammatical meanings other than AG = 1SG and PAT = 3SG(N). To be sure, the Finnish example is slightly complicated by the fact that the ACC case ending of the PAT word indicates the CMP aspect.

While the structure of the polysynthetic (here: West Greenlandic) verb is potentially very complex, it is only the more significant that in its basic use it is just as simple, or close-to-zero, as its analytical counterpart (cf. Fortescue 1984: 289):

(9) pisi-vaa
    buy-3SG→3SG
    '(S)he bought it'

The AG vs. PAT relation is expressed here by the cumulative (or portmanteau) morpheme *-vaa*.

Thus, languages of all major types (i.e. analytic, synthetic, polysynthetic) converge on this point. What is, then, the (tentative) generalization to be made on the basis of examples (1), (8), and (9)? Which are – cross-linguistically – the verb-related grammatical meanings that need no overt expression (or are the least in need of such expression)? ASS, AFF, FCT, and ACT are shared by all the examples.

---

1 The subject person of (8) is 1SG, and not 3SG, due to facts of Finnish verb morphology that are irrelevant to the present discussion.

On the other hand, there is some variation as to whether the tense is PRE or PRET, and whether the aspect is CMP or INCMP. Here the basic use of a sentence depends on the lexical meaning of the finite verb. For instance, the tense/aspect meaning of (1), i.e. *ó rà á*, is PRET&CMP, whereas the tense/aspect meaning of an equally minimalist sentence *ó le* ('[s]he/it is hard') is PRE&INCMP (cf. Rowlands 1969: 11, 18–19). The default assumption seems to be that in its basic use a verb expresses "past actions or present states" (Haiman 1980: 136). Abondolo (1998: 27) postulates the same principle for the Uralic proto-language: "the lexical, i.e. intrinsic, aspect of verb roots determines the semantic force of their finite forms: an inherently stative verb had a present meaning while an inherently punctual verb had a past meaning".

But **why** should it be the case that precisely these, and not some other, grammatical meanings are left unexpressed or, alternatively, are expressed just by zero?[2] Givón (2001: 105) provides the answer: "the simple – main, declarative, affirmative, active – clause serves as the reference point for grammatical description. ... simple clauses exhibit the strongest isomorphism between semantics and syntax, as compared to all other clause types." This justification becomes more cogent when isomorphism and semantics are replaced by iconicity and ontology, respectively. Once this is done, we become aware of the mutual interdependence – via basic use – between **functionalism** and **iconicity**. Hence iconicity is an integral part of functionalism, and not something that can freely be either added to or subtracted from it.

In the present context, functionalism unites the notions of economy and iconicity. This is not always the case: "I believe that the tendencies to maximize economy and to maximize iconicity are two of the most important **competing** motivations for linguistic forms in general" (Haiman 1985: 18; emphasis added).

Up to now, the notion of basic use has been assumed to be a rather uncontroversial one. But it is in stark conflict with the following kind of statement made in *The World Atlas of Language Structures* (= *WALS*) (Haspelmath et al. 2005):

> Exponence refers to the number of categories that cumulate into a single formative. The universal default is to express each category by a dedicated formative. These are monoexponential (or separative) formatives. Polyexponential (or cumulative) formatives, i.e. formatives which simultaneously code more than one category, **are much rarer** (Bickel & Nichols 2005: 90; emphasis added, original emphasis deleted).[3]

---

2 Notice that speaking of zero does not yet commit us to positing zero morphemes.
3 Notice the following inconsistency: category is here a meaning unit but in measuring category-per-word values it is a formal unit (cf. Itkonen & Pajunen 2011: 107–108).

It is (or should be) self-evident that this view is mistaken. The "default" on which it is based applies to **no** language, and every analytical language is a clear counter-example to it. According to Bickel & Nichols (2005), **every** category normally has its dedicated formative. But in the prototypical analytical structure, represented by (1)–(7), no category (= grammatical meaning) has its dedicated formative. Significantly, the same is true of the verb forms in their basic use both in synthetic and in polysynthetic languages as well, as shown by (8) and (9). What we have here is a complete (but perhaps not unusual) misunderstanding that goes to the very foundations of typological linguistics (cf. Itkonen & Pajunen 2011: 109–111).

To avert any objections, it is good to add that all of the meanings (or categories) elicited in connection with (1)–(7) are among those that, according to Bickel & Nichols (2005: 94), are typically "coded on the verb".

Thus, the monoexponential view proves to be blatantly contrary to facts. How is it possible for such a view to have emerged, in the first place? Here I mention only one possible source. The monoexponential view is identical with the so-called principle of one meaning – one form (= 1M1F principle), if this is taken literally. But the 1M1F principle should not be taken literally. Its use e.g. in explaining linguistic change has been recommended, among others, by Anttila (1989 [1972]: Ch. V) and Itkonen (1983: 208–211, 2005b: 106–108). But closer examination of the data reveals that the principle is always meant to apply only to a couple of focal meanings, never to all possible meanings (= e.g. those elicited in connection with (1)–(7), including the AG/PAT meanings).

For instance, in the Latin copula, *es* and *est* had the meanings '(2SG) are' and '(3SG) is', thus exemplifying 2M2F (= two meanings – two forms). In Proto-Romance, these forms coalesced as *es* (or threatened to do so), exemplifying 2M1F. In Spanish, the 'normal' 2M2F situation was restored by means of the forms *eres* (borrowed from the future paradigm) and *es*; and analogous developments took place in Italian and French as well. Notice that this (explanatory) account concentrates on the two (focal) meanings 2SG and 3SG, and takes everything else for granted.

For the sake of completeness, let us consider the category of person qua exemplification of the AG/PAT/RES roles. Which person, if any, is coded on the verb by zero? This question is answered by Mithun (1999: 69): "Many languages have no third person pronouns. Third persons are referred to either by a full noun phrase, by a demonstrative ('that one') or ... by no form at all." Here the term pronoun subsumes word, clitic, and affix. The examples given by Mithun show that what is meant is, more particularly, third person singular. This is confirmed by Dixon (2002: 363): "most commonly, zero is used just for 3SG".

The 3SG = Ø principle is explained in terms of (paradigmatic) iconicity: "Benveniste [1946] argued that in such cases, the formal contrast between non-null and null forms reflected a conceptual contrast which the traditional terminology of the Western linguistic tradition has obscured. For the Arab grammarians, ... the third person, who did not participate in the speech act, was characterized as *al-ya'ibu* 'the absent one'. The non-person was iconically represented by a non-desinence" (Haiman 1985: 5; cf. also Foley 1986: 66). Once again, instead of competing with each other, iconicity and economy coincide.

Above, the 3SG = Ø principle was exemplified by the FUT and NEG constructions of Yoruba, i.e. *yó rà á* and *kò rà á*, where 3SG = AG (cf. 1, 6). Another example, even more economical than (1), comes from Italian: *lo compra-Ø* ('[s]he buys it', with *[s]he* = Ø). Just as often 3SG = Ø, when 3G = PAT/REC. This is the case e.g. in Hua: Ø-*ko-e* = 3SG-see-1SG[4] = 'I saw it' (as opposed to e.g. *p-koe* = 'I saw you.PL/them').

As was noted above, forms in basic use are likely to be the most frequent ones. But their nature is not explained by their frequency. Rather, frequency itself needs to be explained: "text frequency reflects characteristics of human cognition and communicative choices" (Croft 2003: 111). According to Comrie (1986: 104), for instance, "those constructions that involve less formal markedness [i.e. are closest to zero] linguistically correspond to those extralinguistic situations which – in fact or in our conceptualizations – are more **expected**" (emphasis added).

Finally, it might be suggested that the notion of verb-form in its basic use is identical with, or should even be replaced by, some such notion as maximally **unmarked** verb-form. The reason why I personally reject this suggestion is that reference to unmarkedness seems to me clearly less explanatory than joint reference to economy and iconicity. It goes without saying that there are, of necessity, all kinds of differences between linguistic forms *X, Y, Z*, etc. Some of these differences are symmetrical or equipollent while others are asymmetrical. It is differences of the latter type that can be summarized in terms of (un)markedness. But they are just data in need of explanation. (Un)markedness is a label, not an explanation.

The preceding account takes grammatical paradigms to be networks where the identity of any unit is determined by its relations to all other units. This could be called Word-and-Paradigm model; but it just repeats the basic insight of structuralism.

---

4 1SG.AG is actually expressed by a suffix-cum-ablaut combination.

3 Explaining Grammatical Asymmetries and Hierarchies

Implicational universals are customarily invoked to account for asymmetric relations exhibited by typological data. Although useful, this notion does not seem to be as differentiating as one would like to think. This is the classic example of a universal ('material') implication:

X = For all x, if x is a raven, then x is black', or $\forall x(Rx \rightarrow Bx)$.

When the antecedent of X is true, propositional logic and common sense agree: X is confirmed by the occurrence of a black raven, i.e. by the truth of (e.g.) *Ra & Ba*, and X is falsified by the occurrence of a non-black raven, i.e. by the truth of (e.g.) *Ra & ~Ba*. But when the antecedent of X is false, propositional logic and common sense part ways. For propositional logic, X is also confirmed by the occurrence of a black piece of paper (= *~Ra & Ba*) or of a white piece of paper (= *~Ra & ~Ba*), which gives rise to the paradoxes of confirmation (cf. Hempel 1965b [1945]: 14–20). To put it differently, $\forall x(Rx \rightarrow Bx)$, or X, is logically equivalent to its contraposition:

X* = For all x, if x is not black, then x is not a raven, or $\forall x(\sim Bx \rightarrow \sim Rx)$

It follows that, in propositional logic, not only X* but also X is (counter- intuitively) confirmed by the truth of (e.g.) *~Ra & ~Ba*, i.e. by the occurrence of (e.g.) a white piece of paper. For common sense, by contrast, occurrences truthfully described by *~Ra & Ba* or *~Ra & ~Ba* are equally irrelevant to the truth of X.

Next, let us consider the following implicational universal, or Y, concerning the structure of nouns:

Y = For all languages x, if x has a non-zero morpheme for the singular (= SG), then x has a non-zero morpheme for the plural (= PL)

Let us summarize Y as 'If A, then B'. The first thing to notice is that, in contradistinction to such predicates as 'raven' and 'black', a predicate like 'having a non-zero morpheme (either in SG or in PL)' is a **binary** one. Both non-A and non-B have here substantive meanings, instead of just denoting all those innumerable things that are not either A or B. These facts are evident from the following tetrachoric table (where 'no morpheme' means 'no **overt** morpheme'):

Table 1: The cross-linguistic distribution of zero vs. non-zero marking in singular vs. plural

	A SG morpheme	~A no SG morpheme
B PL morpheme	Swahili	English
~B no PL morpheme	–	Chinese

We are right now examining the implication Y = 'If A, then B'. It goes without saying that Y is explicitly confirmed by A & B (exemplified here by Swahili) and would be falsified by A & ~B (not exemplified, systematically, by any language). Moreover, as shown by Table 1, Y is implicitly confirmed both by ~A & B and by ~A & ~B, i.e. the two cases where the antecedent is false. Why? because, thanks to the binary character of the predicates A and B, both ~A & B and ~A & ~B stand here for positive or well-defined options (exemplified by English and Chinese, respectively). In this respect Y crucially differs from X, which, to repeat, is not confirmed at all by (the counterparts of) ~A & B and ~A & ~B.

On closer reflection, however, things turn out to be somewhat more complicated. Consider Y*, i.e. the contraposition of Y:

Y* = For all languages x, if x has a zero morpheme for the plural,
x has a zero morpheme for the singular (If not-B, then not-A)

Now, Y* is explicitly confirmed by a language like Chinese, because it makes the antecedent (as well as the consequent) of Y* true. Y, by contrast, was just seen to be explicitly confirmed by a language like Swahili. It is significant that Y and Y* are explicitly confirmed by opposite types of language, i.e. a strongly synthetic language like Swahili (= A & B) and an analytical language like Chinese (= ~A & ~B). This should be taken to mean that although Y (= if A, then B) and Y* (= if not-B, then not-A) are logically equivalent, they are not synonymous. To be sure, both Y and Y* are falsified by the same type of language, i.e. A & ~B.

The status of ~A & B (exemplified by English) still remains to be examined. It seems to involve a paradox. On the one hand, a language like English explicitly confirms neither Y nor Y*. On the other hand, it is the very purpose of these two implications to express the fact that it is precisely English, and not Swahili or Chinese, which represents the most frequent, and thus normal, type of language: it has no morpheme in the singular and has a morpheme in the plural. Therefore one can only conclude that the implicational format is a somehow inadequate way to express those cross-linguistic regularities which it is meant to express.

But what would then be a more adequate and, hopefully, a more explanatory format? To find an answer, let us spell out the contents of the four options:

Table 2: The iconic, non-iconic, and anti-iconic markings in singular vs. plural

		A		~A
B	(1)	SG ≠ PL	(3)	SG < PL
~B	(2)	SG > PL	(4)	SG = PL

where X < Y means 'X is shorter than Y' while X ≠ Y means 'X and Y are non-identical but of equal length'

The options (3) and (2) are of central importance insofar as (3) represents the normal case while (2) represents the abnormal (= non-existent) case. Their mutual relation is most clearly brought out by the ubiquitous presence of (noun) reduplication: wherever it occurs, it is always the case that the reduplicated and non-reduplicated forms express PL and SG, respectively, never the other way around. What is, then, the explanation of (3) and (2)? The answer is obvious at once: it is (quantitative) iconicity, formulated as the principle "what is ontologically less vs. more is expressed by what is linguistically less vs. more".

The primary cases (3) and (2) may be called iconic and anti-iconic, respectively. The secondary cases (1) and (4), in turn, qualify as non-iconic.[5]

This format of accounting for the SG vs. PL relation is adequate insofar as the important or primary cases (3) and (2) are described in non-implicational, i.e. iconic, terms. It is the secondary cases (1) and (4) that are described implicationally, i.e. by Y and by Y*, respectively.

According to Croft (2003: 89), "languages such as Swahili and Chinese conform to the [implicational] universal Y just as much as English and Tatar do".[6] But this is exactly what is wrong with the implicational format. It conceals the crucial distinctions between English, on the one hand, and Swahili and Chinese, on the other, distinctions that the present account, summarized in Table 2, puts in relief.

Assuming that Y and Y* are adequate ways of expressing (1) and (4), how are they justified, exactly? Their non-iconic status provides the key. On closer reflec-

---

5 Croft (2003: 102) calls (1) and (4) "iconic", thus mistaking the 1M1F principle for iconicity (cf. Itkonen 2004).

6 To make this quotation consonant with what precedes, 'Zulu', 'Minor Mlabri', and 'in 4' have been replaced by 'Swahili', 'Chinese', and 'Y', respectively.

tion, what Y and Y* are saying is that even if iconicity is not achieved, as in (3), at least **anti-iconicity is avoided** in (1) and (4).

The SG < PL relation, exemplified by (3), iconically describes the corresponding ontological relation. The asymmetry between SG and PL can be expressed by saying that there is a primary need for overt marking of PL, but only a secondary need for overt marking of SG. Accordingly, the situation could be conceptualized in terms of expressive needs.[7] Y and Y* may now be reformulated in terms of primary and secondary needs:

Y = if secondary needs (for formal distinction) are satisfied, primary needs are too (= Swahili)

Y* = if primary needs are not satisfied, neither are secondary needs (= Chinese)

The notion of expressive need may seem *ad hoc*. Therefore it will be clarified with the aid of an additional example. Consider the following implicational universal Z and its contraposition Z*:

Z = if the intransitive subjects have overt case-marking, then the transitive subjects have it too

Z* = if the transitive subjects have no overt case-marking, neither have the intransitive subjects

30 years ago I suggested the following explanation for this universal: "People have a universal need to make distinctions between things that are important to them. Communication is important, and therefore linguistic units used in communication are important too. ... It is immediately evident that there is a greater **need for differentiation** in the latter [transitive] case, i.e. {N, N, V}, than in the former [intransitive] one, i.e. {N, V}. Now, if the required differentiation is to be achieved by overt case-marking, and not (only) by word order, then it goes without saying that there is a greater need to have {N-S, N-O, V} than to have {N-S, V}. And because greater needs are by definition satisfied before smaller ones, it follows that if a language has {N-S, V}, we can 'predict' that it also has {N-S, N-O, V}, but not vice versa" (Itkonen 1983: 216–217; emphasis added).

Y/Y* and Z/Z* exemplify the same logic. First, there is the primary or non-implicational case. Second, there are two secondary or implicational cases, seem-

---

7 Coseriu (1974 [1958]) repeatedly uses such terms as Ausdruckserfordernis and Ausdrucksbedürfnis (cf. Itkonen 2011a).

ingly opposite but logically equivalent. These three options can be illustrated with the following everyday example:
(i)   It is more important to have food than to have a cell phone
(ii) If one has money for a cell phone, then one has money for food
(iii) If one does not have money for food, then one does not have money for a cell phone

For clarification, let us add one more example:
(i)   C happens before D
(ii) If D happens, C has happened
(iii) If C has not happened, D does not happen

It is obvious that in all these cases we have to do with a relation of presupposition:
(i)   C is presupposed by D
(ii) If D is there, C is there
(iii) If C is not there, D is not there

In linguistics, relations of presupposition are often expressed in terms of (un)markedness. Tables 1–2 illustrate the notion of **typological** (un)markedness. As shown by cross-linguistic evidence (and explained by iconicity), English represents the unmarked case: it has zero in SG and non-zero in PL. It follows that Swahili and Chinese represent marked cases, but in opposite ways. The former has non-zero in SG whereas the latter has zero in PL:
If marked, then unmarked
Swahili = if non-zero in SG, then non-zero in PL
Chinese = if zero in PL, then zero in SG

This is the standard way to express markedness relations, but it is clearly somewhat counter-intuitive. To find a better way, consider the following. The standard translation of a logical equivalence $(p \equiv q)$ is 'if, and only if, p then q', which is more fully expressed as a conjunction of two implications: 'if p then q, and only if p then q'. On the other hand, the equivalence $p \equiv q$ is itself equivalent to a conjunction of two inverse implications, i.e. $(p \to q)\,\&\,(q \to p)$, translated as 'if p then q, and if q then p'. Hence, there is an equivalence between 'only if p then q' and 'if q then p', which makes it possible to express markedness relations in a more natural way. Thus, Y and Y* will be reformulated as follows:

Y = **only if** there is non-zero in PL, there is non-zero in SG (= Swahili)

Y* = **only if** there is zero in SG, there is zero in PL (= Chinese)

And more generally:

Only if unmarked, then marked
Only if primary needs are satisfied, then secondary needs are too

Up two now, we have been considering an asymmetric relation between two binary predicates. The same relation may be extended to three or more such predicates by means of a chain of implications. For instance, the relations between singular, plural, and dual inflections are such that there is PL inflection, only if there is (at least equally complex) SG inflection, and there is DL inflection only if there is PL inflection (cf. Corbett 2000: 38, Croft 2003: 126). This produces a (typological) grammatical hierarchy W, summarized as follows:

W = SG < PL < DL

How should W be explained? It is immediately evident that, unlike in the case of Y (= zero vs. non-zero marking of SG vs. PL), iconicity is ruled out here because, in terms of (quantitative) iconicity, DL should be placed between, not after, SG and PL. Still, it is not too difficult to imagine such expressive needs as would explain the SG < PL < DL ranking. It is easy to understand that there are more occasions to speak about individual persons/things than about persons/things as collectivities; and DL, being a special case of PL, can well dispense with an expression of its own.

Plausible as such speculations may seem, they certainly court the danger of committing a *virtus dormitiva* type fallacy. Observing a distinction between A and B, we postulate the existence of some unobservable entities α and β such as to explain the A vs. B distinction. Clearly, some additional support is needed for postulating α and β. In the present context such support is provided by the **analogy** with how the universals Y and Z are explained. This 'argument from analogy' may be spelled out as follows: Explanations of Y and Z in terms of expressive needs are acceptable; Y, Z, and W are structurally similar; therefore explanations of W in terms of expressive needs are acceptable too.

How do we identify expressive needs, or how are they accessible to us? This is how I justified my own explanation of Z: "Although this term may once again seem out of place, one cannot help realizing that such explanations are contrived on the basis of a certain type of **empathy**, or of imagining what **we** would do, if the unconscious goals that we hypothetically assume to exist were our conscious goals" (Itkonen 1983: 217). We were implicitly relying on the notion of empathy already in what precedes. Let us recall that Comrie (1986: 104) notes the correlation between zero expression and those extralinguistic situations that are expected; and it takes at least some minimal amount of empathy to grasp what in a given culture is or is not expected. Notice also that empathy may equally well be said to apply either to needs or to goals, because satisfying a need constitutes a goal.

The most familiar example of a grammatical hierarchy is the animacy hierarchy (also known as empathy hierarchy). It is established on the basis of a set of converging criteria. If we single out plural inflection vs. the lack of it, we get the following hierarchy (cf. Corbett 2000: 56, 90; Croft 2003: 128–129, 134):

first/second PRO < third PRO < human N < animate N < inanimate N

This hierarchy is explained by the fact that "similarity in form ... reflects in turn similarity in **function**. ... other humans are the most similar to the speaker and addressee, other animates are the next most similar, and inanimates are the least similar" (Croft 2003: 137; emphasis added). Thus, the hierarchy is defined by decreasing similarity to the speech act participants (= first and second person). But the form vs. function terminology is not differentiating enough. The human vs. animate vs. inanimate distinctions are ontological, and insofar as there is a corresponding three-way categorization in language, we have to do with qualitative iconicity in just the same sense as in the (paradigmatic) case of the thing/action vs. noun/verb correlation. On the other hand, pronouns are distinguished from nouns on functional rather than ontological grounds. But how do we explain this hierarchy? It is not for nothing that it is called empathy hierarchy. It borders on a tautology to state that speakers and hearers identify more strongly with, or feel greater empathy for, the points on this continuum when moving toward its left end. This direction coincides with increasing importance and, once again, it is uncontroversial to state that greater expressive needs attach to important things rather than to less important ones. Finally, how is this hierarchy accessible to us qua linguists? – on the basis of a sort of meta-empathy, of course.

A few qualifications need to be added to conclude this section. First, all grammatical predicates that have been considered so far are binary, as shown by the fact that the contrapositions are just as lawlike as the original implications. To illustrate, let us concentrate on the human < animate section of the animacy/empathy hierarchy:

only if PL in humans, then PL in animates =
if PL in animates, then PL in humans =
if no PL in humans, then no PL in animates

Let us, however, consider two such non-binary predicates as (basic) word order and accessibility to relativization; and let us, for the sake of argument, assume the validity of a universal like if the word order is VOS, then only subjects are relativized. We then realize that its contraposition, i.e. if not subject-only, then not VOS, has no definite meaning. Not subject-only stands for 4 distinct options, combining subject with direct object, plus indirect object, plus oblique (and including the option of **no** relativization), while not VOS stands for 6 distinct options (including **no** basic word order). There can be no lawlike connection between two sets constituted by such heterogeneous materials (cf. Itkonen 1998). The result is analogous to the implication X*, i.e. If non-black, then non-raven.

Second, implications are made use of to express many other things in addition to relations of presupposition, for instance, cause-to-effect (= "if it has been raining during the night, the streets are wet in the morning") or effect-to-cause (= "if the streets are wet in the morning, it has been raining during the night"). Applied to linguistics, this means that not all if A, then B statements express markedness relations to be explained by a hierarchy of expressive needs.

4 Explaining Grammaticalization

The general nature of grammaticalization is well understood. Still, it could be argued that the standard accounts are not differentiating enough. We need to distinguish between (at least) **four** stages in this process. While doing this, we shall also clarify the transition from parataxis to hypotaxis (cf. Heine & Kuteva 2007: 241):

(10) [Ich sehe **das**] [Er ist zufrieden]
    [I see **that**] [He is satisfied]

(11) [Ich sehe [**dass** er zufrieden ist]
    [I see [**that** he is satisfied]]

(12) [Ich bin **überzeugt** [**dass** er zufrieden ist]]
[I am **convinced** [**that** he is satisfied]]

(13) [[**Dass** er zufrieden ist] **verwundert** mich sehr]
[[**That** he is satisfied] **puzzles** me a lot]

Paul (1975 [1880]: 229) describes the development from (10) to (13) as follows:
"After *das* had been incorporated into the subordinare clause and reanalyzed by
the same token as a conjunction, it was possible to extend this construction also
to cases where *das* was inapplicable". Thus, to begin with, Paul distinguishes
between reanalysis (*Verwandlung*) and extension (*Übertragung*). But it is important to realize that the latter subprocess is **repeated** in the sequel. For clarity, the
entire process will now be depicted with the aid of examples (10–13), distinguishing between these three "moments": input, change, output:

Parataxis   (10)
Reanalysis   (10) > (11)
Hypotaxis-1   (11)
Extension-1   (11) > (12)
Hypotaxis-2   (12)
Extension-2   (12) > (13)
Hypotaxis-3   (13)

In reanalysis one clause of a paratactic structure is interpreted as part of another
clause, i.e. as a subordinate clause. More precisely, reanalysis applies to the word
das. This word, like any other word, is a form–meaning unit. Therefore reanalysis
necessarily applies both to its form and to its meaning. The form of *das* ceases to
be a demonstrative pronoun and becomes the conjunction *dass*, and its meaning
changes accordingly. These two processes are called decategorialization and
desemantization by Heine & Kuteva (2007: 34). According to de Saussure's metaphor, form and meaning are like the two sides of a sheet of paper, and so are
decategorialization and desemantization too.

(11) is the hypotactic output of reanalysis, but the structure of the paratactic
input (10) is still visible in (11). By contrast, extension (i.e. extension-1) is defined
by the fact that its output (12) no longer has any recognizable connection with
parataxis. There is no such construction as *[Ich bin **das** überzeugt] [Er ist zufrie-
den]*. Rather, the input to extension-1 is an (abstract) model provided by any verb
that takes a *dass* clause as an object, for instance, the verb *sehen*, as in (11). This is
exactly why the output of extension is said to be based on analogy, as confirmed
by Matisoff (1991: 385): "all grammatization involves analogy". And this is indeed

the term that Hopper & Traugott (1993) use instead of extension. An attempt at disentangling these complicated relations is made in Itkonen (2005a: 110–113).

Extension need not stop at (12). In (11–12) the *dass* clause functions as an object. In (13), which is the output of extension-2, the *dass* clause functions as a subject. The (analogical) model for (13) is simply any SVO structure, for instance *Peter verwundert mich sehr*. In other words, the use of the *dass* clause in (13) is based on the following analogical principle: "The subordinate clause behaves in reality just like a grammatical unit (*Satzglied*)" (Paul 1975 [1880]:123). "The subordinate clause has the same function as a grammatical unit (*Satzglied*)" (p. 296). Because (13) presupposes the analogy used in constructing (12), (13) itself does not just result from an analogy, but from a chain of analogies.

The post-paratactic developments illustrated by (12–13) justify the following résumé by Paul: "It is wrong to think – as is generally done – that each and every case of hypotaxis has emerged out of parataxis" (p. 145).

What right do we have to postulate such cognitive processes as reanalysis and extension? How are they accessible to us? Such questions are seldom asked and even less often answered. And yet the answer is self-evident: all this is made possible by empathy, and nothing else. To give a random example, Mithun (1988: 341) notes that "it is not too difficult to imagine how a particle of this type [i.e. *hni'* in Cayuga] could develop from an adverbial into a syntactic conjunction". This is precisely the point. I, as a linguist, am in a position first to postulate and then to analyze processes of grammaticalization only because I can **imagine** performing them **myself**. This is the only reason why, when faced with the explanatory problem of filling the gaps between (10) and (11), on the one hand, and between (11) and (12), on the other, I assume that, first, *das* has been reanalyzed as *dass* and, second, the *dass* construction has been extended to a new context. And what is true of me is true of you as well. If we cannot imagine ourselves performing a putative process of grammaticalization, we just reject it.

This last claim may be confirmed in the following way. In grammaticalization studies it is a standard procedure to show that what at first glance looks like one inexplicable change is in reality a chain of several changes each of which is explicable in itself. This is how, for instance, Heine (2002: 88–89) explains the change from the reflexive to the agent-passive construction in !Xun, namely by postulating two intermediate constructions between these extremes. In explaining how the form that originally expresses the completive preterite meaning has acquired the general subjunctive meaning, Givón (2001: 362–366) follows the same logic, namely by postulating "three main steps in this analogical extension" (p. 365).

Let us make this a little more precise. We observe that one and the same form expresses the quite dissimilar (grammatical) meanings A and D. This constitutes a prima facie problem. Why? – because we cannot imagine a change like A > D (or vice versa); and this we cannot do because we cannot imagine performing such a change ourselves. Now, either we try to explain the variation A ~ D or we give up. If we choose the former option, we typically proceed as follows. We postulate (e.g.) the changes A > B, B > C, and C > D, each of which is such that we can imagine performing it. (Our acts of imagination are conscious but the changes that we imagine are supposed to have occurred unconsciously.) Our task is easier if the meanings B and C happen to be attested, but this is strictly speaking not necessary. As a result of our efforts, we now understand the change A > D, even if indirectly, whereas each of the particular changes A > B etc is understood directly.

In this context, explanation of X equals (empathy-based) understanding of X, and what is understood is, more exactly, the history of X: "Once the histories of these [lexical] affixes are determined, their special characteristics are easily understood" (Mithun 1997: 358). This echoes what August Schleicher asserted in 1863: "If we do not know how something has come into being, we do not understand it" (quoted in Arens 1969: 260).

Once again, the section will be rounded off with a few additional remarks. As I see it, reanalysis is the first, and essential, component of grammaticalization. Heine & Kuteva (2007: 35, n. 25) seem to contest this, claiming that "we will not use the term 'reanalysis' in this work". But this disclaimer does not amount to much because they just substitute reinterpretation for reanalysis, for instance: "S2 is reinterpreted as a complement clause. The demonstrative object argument (DEM) is reinterpreted as a complementizer (CPL)" (p. 241). And occasionally the offending term actually intrudes into the text: "the subordinator [= *dass*] starts out as a constituent of the matrix clause [= *das*] but is later reanalyzed as introducing the complement clause" (p. 257).

The role of analogy cannot be stressed too much in this context. First, reanalysis is always based on some analogical model while extension is an explicitly analogical process. Second, there is a high-level analogy between the process of grammaticalization, divided into reanalysis and extension, and the hypothetico-deductive method, divided into abduction and prediction (cf. Itkonen 2002, 2005a: 110–113).[8]

But why should there be such a process as grammaticalization at all? The answer has to do, ultimately, with economy. In reanalysis, analogy establishes a one meaning – one form uniformity between the model and the modelled (e.g. between grammatical units and clauses); and in making the data conform to the result of reanalysis, extension too is economical. But then there are deeper ques-

---

8 It could also be argued that integration and expansion, as defined by Heine & Kuteva (2007), exemplify one and the same process, based on the analogy between grammatical unit (*Satzglied*) and subordinate clause (*Nebensatz*), as noted by Paul (1975 [1880]: 123, 296); cf. Itkonen (2011c).

tions that are likely to remain unanswered: Why this model and not some other? Ultimately, one just has to accept the brute fact of free will and/or chance.

5 Additional Examples of Typological Explanation

In Sections 2–4 I have proposed explanations for such central and well- known phenomena as zero, hierarchy, and grammaticalization. The present section contains four examples of how typological explanation has been applied in the literature.

First, Mithun (1988) notes that, cross-linguistically, there are relatively few instances of the conjoined-nominals construction. Rather than simply accepting this fact, she wants to explain it:

> This rarity [of N-and-N constructions] is not altogether inexplicable: several factors con-verge to minimize the **need** for conjoined nominals in connected speech. Most important, speakers typically introduce only one major piece of information into discourse at a time. Conceptually distinct entities [referred to by nominals] are introduced by distinct intona-tion units, often separate clauses. [...] Once they have been introduced individually, sets of entities can be referred to by plural pronouns, so the **need** for conjoined noun phrases is bypassed (p. 337; emphasis added; notice the connection with the "expressive needs" postulated in what precedes).

Let us next give an analysis of the preceding quotation, and more precisely an analysis formulated in terms of problem-solving:

Problem: Why are there, cross-linguistically, so few cases of *N1-and-N2*?

Solution: In general, referents of *N*'s are introduced in separate clauses: *X&V1&N1*, *Y&V2&N2* (where *X* and *Y* represent arbitrary material, and *V1* and *V2* are verbs connected with *N1* and *N2*, respectively); and later, if needed, the referents of *N1* and *N2* are re-identified by the pronouns *PRO-1* and *PRO-2*, respectively. Now, if the referents of *N1* and *N2* have to be re-identified **together**, this is done by *PRO-1&2* (meaning, roughly, 'they'). Thus, at no stage is there any need for an expression like *N1-and-N2*.

Comment: This explanation is achieved by means of empathy, or by adopting the speaker's perspective. The goal of the speaker is to re-identify two entities in a situ-ation where they have already been introduced by *N1* and *N2*. Now he is confronted with the following problem: Which means should he choose to achieve his goal? His solution is to choose *PRO-1&2* (assuming that a corresponding pronominal system is available). There is no need for him to choose *N1-and-N2*. Why is there no need for *N1-and-N2* when *PRO-1&2* is available? Because the latter is a more economical means for achieving the goal than the former. Thus, what we have here is a rational (= means-to-end) explanation (since it is inherent to rationality to choose – ceteris paribus – the more economical alternative). The preceding account (rationally) explains the rarity of *N1-and-N2* (when a pronominal system is available). Of course, the rationality involved is of unconscious nature; it is the same type of rationality that governs not only human but also animal behavior. Our example shows that empathy culminates in rational explanation (cf. below).

Notice also that the proposed explanation is *eo ipso* a generalization: it is meant to apply to all languages that lack the conjoined-nominals construction.

In conceptualizing typological explanations as solutions to problems that speakers are confronted with, I follow a well-established practice: "It is possible to view the various types of coding of the same functional domain as alternative **solutions** to the same communicative task" (Givón 1984: 145; original emphasis). "Grammaticalization can be interpreted as a process that has problem solving as its main goal, whereby one object is expressed in terms of another" (Heine et al. 1991: 29).

We have already seen that the solution to the problem is reached by means of empathy. But how does this work in practice? What kind of inference yields the (tentative) solution? We have to do here with a very general figure of thought that applies equally well to the exegesis of philosophical texts and to the explanation of historical events:

> One and the same passage states [Leibniz's] solution and serves as evidence of what the problem was. The fact that we can identify his problem is proof that he has solved it; for we only know what the problem was by arguing back from the solution. If anybody chooses to deny this, I will not try to convince him. Everybody who has learnt to think historically knows it already; and no amount of argument could teach it to a person who has not learnt to think historically. How can we discover what the tactical problem was that Nelson set himself at Trafalgar? Only by studying the tactics he pursued in the battle. We argue back from the solution to the problem. What else could we do? (Collingwood 1983 [1939]: 147).

As our second example, let us consider converb constructions. Implicit- subject converbs and same-subject converbs tend to coincide, and so do explicit-subject converbs and different-subject converbs. This form – meaning correlation is explained by Haspelmath (1995) as follows:

> The functional motivation [i.e. explanation] for these connections should be apparent: when the subject is mainly implicit, only the same subject reference **ensures** that its subject can be identified. When the subject is necessarily different from superordinate clause con-

stituents, only explicit expression **ensures** that its reference can be identified (p. 11; emphasis added).[9]

On the one hand, suppose you hear a sentence containing an implicit- subject converb like *Listening to the conversation, John felt embarrassed*. Who did the listening? It requires little imagination to for you realize that it must be John (i.e. that what was to be expressed is a same-subject meaning), and the speaker too knew that you would realize it; and now I, as a linguist, know these facts about you and the speaker by means of empathy. It does not make sense to assume that it was e.g. Mary who did the listening (i.e. that what was to be expressed is a different-subject meaning), because it would be impossible to recover this information from the sentence-form. On the other hand, suppose the speaker intends to say that John felt embarrassed while, or because, Mary was listening (i.e. the speaker intends to convey a different-subject meaning). Then, for reasons just explained, he must use an explicit-subject converb, like *With Mary listening to the conversation, John felt embarrassed*. Notice, in particular, that here the proposed explanation assumes that the speaker can solve his/her problem of shaping the linguistic form only by considering what is needed for the listener to solve his/her own problem of understanding the linguistic form-as- shaped, i.e. identifying the (semantic) subject of the converb construction. This reveals the inherently social (i.e. minimally dialogical) nature of language.

Let us reformulate this explanation in terms of rationality. It is possible, of course, to express same-subject meanings by means of explicit-subject converbs, as in *With John listening to the conversation, John felt embarrassed*. But this would be less economical, and therefore less rational, than to use the implicit-subject converb. By contrast, it is not possible to express different-subject meanings by means of implicit-subject converbs; and therefore it would be downright irrational to do so. Therefore, explicit-subject converbs are the only solution to this communicative task.

Again, this explanation is meant to be cross-linguistically valid. It applies to all converb constructions in all languages.

Let us consider our third example. In Hua, a Papuan language of the Eastern Highlands of New Guinea, the aorist (or declarative) paradigm of the verb *do-* ('to eat') looks like this, with the dual omitted (cf. Haiman 1980: 51; also Itkonen 2005b:59–60):

---

9 It is somewhat confusing that the same term, i.e. subject, stands here both for a semantic unit (same/different subject) and for a syntactic one (implicit/explicit subject). Still, I have retained the original terminology in what follows.

Table 3: The aorist paradigm in Hua

	SINGULAR	PLURAL
1.	do-e	do-**ne**
2.	da-**ne**	da-e
3.	de-e (> de)	da-e

From our Western point of view, two facts cry out for explanation. First, why is the 2PL form identical with the 3PL form? Second, why is the 2SG suffix identical with the 1PL suffix? It needs to be emphasized that these features are not just idiosyncrasies of Hua but recur in many Papuan languages.

The first fact is explained by Foley (1986: 69) as follows: "It is the **diffuseness** and passivity of the second plural that associates it with the absent non-participants of the third person" (emphasis added).

As for the second fact, Foley (1986: 73) appeals to the empathy hierarchy (cf. Section 3):

> This conflation is only attested in languages without an exclusive/inclusive distinction in first nonsingular categories. This suggests that the motivation for this conflation may be the presence of the addressee, corresponding to the second singular, in a statistically large number of uses of the undifferentiated first nonsingular, those corresponding semantically to the inclusive. A conflation motivated by the inclusive grouping [= *I-and-you*] can be **explained** by its higher **salience** than the exclusive [= *I-and-(s)he*] (see Silverstein 1976); presumably a grouping of the primary speech-act participants, speaker and addressee, would be regarded as more **important** by the speaker than a grouping of himself and some non-participants" (emphasis added).

This agrees with everything that has been said in what precedes. In trying to figure out what speakers of Hua and of similar languages (unconsciously) find "diffuse" or "salient" or "important", Foley is just practicing empathy. He is making the same hermeneutic effort as any historian who, in Collingwood's (1946) words, is "rethinking people's thoughts".

Fourth, and finally, let us mention the 'Early Immediate Constituents' hypothesis that Hawkins (1994) proposes in order to explain the cross-linguistic facts of word order. This hypothesis is explicitly couched in the terminology of rational goal-directed behavior:

> I believe that words and constituents occur in the orders they do **so that** syntactic groupings and their immediate constituents can be recognized (and produced) as rapidly and **efficiently** as possible in language performance (p. 57; emphasis added).

6 Explanations: From Typological via Teleological to Rational

The argument of the preceding sections may be summed up as follows: "People use language to achieve purposes and goals" (Heine 1997: 4). This is certainly true. But what does it mean? In particular, what is the role of "purposes and goals" in the causation of linguistic behavior? This question will be answered in the present section.

I propose the following as a general schema (= rational explanation, or RE) for explaining human actions:

RE: $\{[G{:}X \ \& \ B{:}(A \rightarrow X)] \vdash G{:}A\} \Rightarrow A$; and if all goes as planned, $A \rightarrow X$

The prefixes G and B stand for the propositional attitudes of wanting and believing, respectively. X and A stand for states of affairs and actions, respectively. The simple arrow and the double arrow stand for ordinary causation and mental causation, respectively, while the sign ⊢, as usual, stands for entailment (= 'it is necessarily the case that if p, then q'). RE says that if someone wants to achieve the goal X and believes that the action A (which s/he is capable of performing) is the adequate means to bring X about, then s/he must want to do A; thus, the attitude of wanting is 'transferred' from X to A (= 'who wants the end wants the means'); then, having this goal and this belief will cause him/her to do A (unless s/he is somehow prevented from doing so); and if all goes well, A will actually bring X about. In ordinary language, these intricate relationships are expressed by the deceptively simple formula 'A in order that X'.[10]

Everything within the curly brackets stands for mental entities. The double arrow represents the ('mysterious') transition from the mind (= cause) to behavior situated in space and time (= effect). RE can be summed up by saying that A occurs now because earlier the agent desired that X should occur and believed that A → X would occur. This formulation reveals the intrinsically teleological nature of RE, which consists in that "when we say A in order that X, the relationship between A and X plays a role in bringing about A" (Wright 1976: 21).[11] More explicitly: "the consequences of goal-directed behavior are involved in its own etiology: such behavior occurs **because** it has certain consequences" (p. 56). By

---

10 Insofar as RE is meant to stand for a many-stage psychological process, one may emphasize some stages at the cost of others, with resulting terminological variation. In the present context goal, purpose, objective, and end are used as synonyms, as are effect and consequence, as well as wanting/desiring/inten-ding to achieve a goal.

11 In this quotation X has been substituted for B.

contrast, causal explanations of the standard 'efficient' type contain no reference to what will (or should) occur afterwards.

For practical purposes, RE may be abbreviated as (G&B) → A, indicating that actions are caused by volitional-epistemic goal-belief combinations. Typically, G&B is called the reason for A.

Although the teleological explanation of A does involve X, it must be clearly understood that here X and A are situated on different ontological levels, namely in the mind and in the space-time, respectively, and in such a way that X precedes A. (To the explanation as such, it is irrelevant whether or not A will actually be followed by X in the space-time.) Therefore, it is of course not being claimed that present events are literally caused by future events. On the other hand, as indicated by the use of *because* above, RE is offered as a causal explanation. It just exemplifies a type of causality different from the efficient (= orthodox) type.

Many different types of phenomena admit of teleological explanations. But it is only to humans (and to higher animals, cf. below) that such terms as goal and belief can be applied literally. Explanations that satisfy these more stringent criteria qualify as rational. Such terms as purposive explanation and intentional explanation are also in use.

Let us clarify the idea that some sort of necessity is involved in the action-explanation. First, it is typically the case that the agent has at his/her disposal not just one action A but several actions A1, A2, and A3, each of which, as far as s/he knows, might serve equally well as a means to achieve X. That s/he then chooses A1 (and not A2 or A3), is due to chance and not to any kind of necessity. But once s/he has chosen A1, s/he must try to do A1 (unless s/he changes his/her mind about wanting X). It is only in this sense that A1 is necessary.

Second, the entailment sign qua sign of necessary connection cannot stand for a transition from one psychological state to another. Why? Because there can be no (genuine) necessity between such temporally distinct occurrences. Necessary relations can obtain only between (non-psychological) concepts. Therefore the only coherent option is to assign to goals and beliefs an ambiguous status which makes them inhabitants both of world-3 and of world-2 (cf. below). It is in their former capacity that they may have conceptual relations (and be shared by several persons) whereas it is in their latter capacity that they may be involved in processes of mental causation.

In addition to its ontological ambiguity, RE performs a double function. On the one hand, it explicates the notion of rational action. On the other, it explicates the notion of rational action-explanation. This is possible because "intentional action is, on causal theory, defined by its causes" (Davidson 1973: 151). This duality is reflected in the fact that in German-language discussions it is *Verstehen* ('understanding') which is opposed to the combination of *Beobachten* ('observing') and *Erklären* ('explaining'). In the physical domain one first observes (or perceives) an event and then explains it. But human actions are understood, not just perceived; and one who understands an action *eo ipso* knows why it occurred, which means that understanding is inseparable from (action-) explanation.[12] To sum up:

> To explain an action as an action is to show that it is rational. This involves showing that on the basis of the goals and beliefs of the person concerned the action was the means he believed to be most likely to achieve his goal (Newton-Smith 1981: 241).

The foregoing condenses to the utmost an argument that was unfolded at considerable length in Itkonen (1983). It is inevitable that in its present form the argument seems less than conclusive. The three most common objections against RE are as follows: i) "Not all actions are rational." ii) "Rationality presupposes conscious deliberation (which is not present e.g. in linguistic change)." iii) "The notion of causality entails a commitment to nomicity but RE contains no reference to laws of any kind."

Ad i) A is rational if it is an adequate means to achieve X. A is irrational either if there is no (realistic) X to be achieved, in the first place, or if there is such an X but A is not an adequate means to achieve it. It is important to understand that RE explains not just rational but also irrational actions. In the latter case the explanatory task consists in showing how the agent has come to believe that what is *de facto* irrational is rational. For instance, Hempel (1965d:464–465) claims that for a person who believes that walking under ladders brings him/her bad luck, walking around a ladder is a rational thing to do, and we can explain his/her action by reference to this rationality. Furthermore, although suicide is the irrational action *par excellence*, Durkheim successfully applies RE to it in his paradigm-creating study from 1897: "Durkheim's notion of cause ... relies on reconstructing the world of the ill-integrated from within so as to make suicide a (semi-) **rational** act" (Hollis 1977: 130; emphasis added). Thus, far from falsifying RE, it is the existence of *prima facie* irrational actions which reveals its true explanatory power. To be sure, different degrees of rationality clearly need to be accepted.

Ad ii) As explained in the previous sections, the majority opinion views use of language (including linguistic change) as goal-directed, problem-solving behavior. It goes without saying that the goals and/or problems involved are taken to be situated at the unconscious level. Now, it makes no sense to speak of achieving

---

12 Actually, the distinction between perceiving and understanding is less sharp because (contra Hume) in simple cases physical cause-effect relations are literally perceived.

goals or solving problems, unless one also endorses some processes of selecting means to achieve the goals or solutions to the problems; and such processes must be unconscious, given the unconscious nature of goals and problems. But this is what it means to endorse the existence of unconscious rationality, however far-fetched such a notion may seem a priori. This view gets independent support from the findings of modern cognitive science:

> There may be – and perhaps there must be – some end to this hierarchy of rational decisions. But the end is not in sight. For all we know, cognition is saturated with rationality through and through (Fodor 1975: 173).

The general argument for the existence of unconscious rationality is of course much older:

> [A]ll the categories which we employ to describe conscious mental acts, such as ideas, purposes, resolutions, and so on, can be applied to [the latent states of mental life] (Freud 1984 [1915]:170).

It is of some interest to note that Freud was anticipated here by Hermann Paul, who pleads for the need to postulate the level of the unconscious between consciousness and physiology:

> If a connection is admitted to exist between earlier and later acts of consciousness, the only viable option is to remain in the domain of the [unconscious] mental and conceive of the mediation on the **analogy** of acts of consciousness (Paul 1975 [1880]:25; emphasis added).

Finally, to vindicate the notion of unconscious rationality, the easiest way is just to point to the fact that experts on animal psychology do not hesitate to characterize the behavior of their subjects as rational: "To explain an action in terms of the agent's [here: rat's] beliefs and desires is to demonstrate that the action is rational with respect to the content of those mental states ..." (Dickinson 1988: 310). "So it turns out that instrumental behavior [by rats] will support an intentional characterization in terms of beliefs and desires after all" (p. 321). I submit that what is true of rats is true of humans as well (cf. Itkonen 2003: 60–64).

Ad iii) Within the theory of action there has been a long and inconclusive debate on whether or not "reasons are causes". As indicated above, I answer this question in the affirmative. It would be disingenuous to deny that A is there because G&B is there; and this means in turn that G&B must be the cause of A. If it is then objected that this cannot be so because causality entails nomicity (which is absent from RE), I conclude that this is a wrong (i.e. too restrictive) notion of causality. Thus I concur with Giddens (1976: 84):

> I shall dogmatically assert the need for an account of **agent causality** ..., according to which causality does not presuppose 'laws' of invariant connection (if anything, the reverse is the case), but rather (a) the **necessary connection** between cause and effect, and (b) the idea of causal efficacy. (Cf. also Itkonen 1983: 35–38).

As is evident e.g. from the discussion of converb constructions, application of RE produces general (rather than nomic) results.

As far as I can see, any objections against RE are futile simply because this is the explanatory schema that the practitioners of typological-diachronic linguistics are utilizing all the time, whether or not they are aware of this fact. Whitney (1979 [1875]) understood this in a way that needs no revision:

> Once more, there is nothing in the whole complicated process of [linguistic change] which calls for the admission of any other efficient force than the reasonable action, the action for a definable purpose, of the speakers of language; ... (p. 144). The work is all done by human beings, adapting means to ends, ... (p. 73).

7 Sense-Perception and Its Complementary Notions: Introspection < Empathy < Intuition

Rational explanations are conjectured on the basis of empathy; and the use of empathy is in turn based on the assumption that there is an analogy between the unconscious goals-cum-beliefs that historical persons (e.g. speakers of L) entertained and the goals-cum-beliefs that the historian (or the linguist) consciously postulates as being those that s/he him-/herself would have entertained if s/he had been in the same situations as the persons s/he is investigating. But what is empathy? This section is devoted to answering this question.[13]

The complement (or contradictory) of 'man' is 'non-man' while the opposite (or contrary) of 'man' is 'woman'. In the present context the most important acts of non-perception are introspection, empathy, and intuition. Cognitive acts are correlative, or interdefinable, with their objects. Sense-perception, introspection, and intuition pertain to three distinct domains, i.e. spatio-temporal entities, contents of consciousness, and norms. These are also known as Popper's world-1, world-2, and world-3, respectively. The nature of introspection and intuition is well-understood (cf. Katz 1981, Itkonen 1981), even if – perhaps – not well-known.

---

13 Some background material that may facilitate the understanding of this section is given in Itkonen (2008b) and Zlatev (2008).

But the nature of empathy, and in particular its relation to the Popperian three-level ontology, has remained unclear.

First, I shall propose a logical reconstruction of the relation between introspection and empathy. Let us for simplicity replace introspection with feeling, with the understanding that feeling subsumes (the awareness of) beliefs, goals, emotions, mental images, and so on. How do I arrive at empathy from what I feel right now? In the following three steps:

I   (i)   I now feel (or am capable of feeling) X >

    (ii)   I would have felt X if I had been in situation Y >

    (iii)   I would have felt X if I had been person Z in situation Y

Here the point (iii) is meant to capture the notion of empathy, identical with Weber-type *Verstehen* or Collingwood-type re-enactment. It can be characterized as vicarious introspection.[14]

Second, I shall propose a logical reconstruction of the relation between introspection, empathy, and (linguistic) intuition. Let us stipulate that 'Y' and X stand for meaning and form, respectively. How do I arrive from introspection to intuition? In the following three steps:

II   (i)   I introspectively know that right now I mean 'Y' by X >

    (ii)   I empathically know that also others can mean or have meant 'Y' by X >

    (iii)   I intuitively know that X means 'Y' (i.e. that one **ought** to mean 'Y' by X)

Empathy turns out to occupy a middle position: on the one hand, its object is no longer purely subjective, as is the object of introspection; on the other, its object is not yet genuinely intersubjective (or social), as is the object of intuition. Therefore, intuition can be characterized as conventionalized empathy.

The move from II-(ii) (= 'somebody means 'Y' by X') to II-(iii) (= 'X means 'Y' *tout court*') is significant because it amounts to a (schematic) account of the emergence of (linguistic) normativity. It follows that before the meaning 'Y' of X has become fully conventional, there is – and must be – a period when it is uncertain whether the X-cum-'Y' combination is (still) known introspectively /

---

14 Schelling (1960: 96) expresses the same idea: "In the pure coordination game, the player's objective is to make contact with the other player through some imaginative process of introspection, of searching for shared clues; ..." (emphasis added).

empathically or (already) intuitively. This uncertainty is integral to the process of linguistic change or, more generally, of conventionalization.

A few qualifications are now in order. First, although introspection constitutes the starting point of I and II, this does not mean that, in conformity with the Cartesian tradition, "knowledge is primarily subjective". Having introspections always takes place in a pre-existent social context that is commonly (= intersubjectively) known to be what it is (cf. Itkonen 2008a as well as the other contributions to Zlatev et al. 2008).

Second, as demonstrated by Frege and Husserl among others, Ought can be neither derived from nor reduced to Is (cf. Itkonen 1991: 283–284). More particularly, it is quite easy to show that, contrary to Lewis (1969), norms (or conventions)   of language cannot be reduced to (non-normative) hearer beliefs/expectations (cf. Itkonen 1978: 182–186); nor can, contrary to Grice (1968), conventional meanings be reduced to (non-normative) speaker intentions (cf. Itkonen 1983: 167–168). Therefore the emergence of normativity must contain a leap from what is non-normative, or II-(ii), to what is normative, or II-(iii).

Third, the logical reconstructions I and II are deliberately schematic. More fine-grained stages and transitions can be postulated, and the psychological mechanisms involved remain to be filled in. I do claim, however, that at least the stages and transitions I-(i) – II-(iii) must be postulated, and exactly in the order introduced here.

Fourth, only the emergence of semantic norms was mentioned above, but analogous remarks apply to the emergence of morphosyntactic and phonological norms.

Fifth, any account of the emergence of norms must be complemented by an account of their disintegration. These are the two aspects of linguistic change. Conceivably, all we need to do is reverse the order of the transitions from I-(i) to II-(iii).

8 In Which Sense Do Typological Explanations Qualify as Functional?

All of the typological explanations adduced so far exemplify RE in one way or another because the explananda are instances of either achieving or maintaining certain goal-states. RE conceptualizes actions as instrumental insofar as any means for achieving goals are *eo ipso* instruments for doing so. Still, it seems fair to say that ephemeral actions like running in order to catch a bus are instruments only in a metaphorical sense.

The form of a genuine instrument is determined by its function, i.e. by how it is meant to be, and is, used. When one entertains the goal of splitting wood, for instance, one chooses an instrument which has such a form as to serve as the means to achieve this goal. These facts are summed up by saying that it is the function of an axe to split wood; and this function is in turn just the first step in several more comprehensive means–ends hierarchies. For instance: why split wood? – in order to have firewood; why have firewood? – in order to make the room warm; and so on.

Speaking may be ephemeral but its results are not insofar as they are sedimented in linguistic structures. These are instrumental in a literal, non- metaphorical sense.[15] When one has the goal of speaking of two successive events E1 and E2, one chooses a linguistic expression so structured as to serve as an adequate means to achieve this goal, i.e. one chooses a complex sentence S1S2. This sentence, i.e. sentence-form, has the function of speaking about E1&E2. This is incidentally the justification of (temporal) iconicity. And, of course, uttering sentences like S1S2 with their characteristic functions is intended to achieve some higher-level goal like informing the audience (which may in turn be intended to achieve some ulterior goal).

Thus, in its primary use, the notion of function is conceptually interdependent with the notion of instrument. From there, the notion of function has secondarily been extended to a host of different and dissimilar entities. This development started with Aristotle:

> [E]verything that Nature makes is means to an end. For just as human creations are the products of art, so living objects are manifestly the products of an analogous cause or principle, ... Again, whenever there is plainly some final end, to which a motion tends should nothing stand in the way, we always say that such final end is the aim or purpose of the motion, ..." (*De partibus animalium*, I,1, 641b: 10–25). If a piece of wood is to be split with an axe, the axe must of necessity be hard; and if hard, must of necessity be made of bronze or iron. Now exactly in the same way the body, which like the axe is an instrument, ... if it is to do its work, must of necessity be of such and such a character, and made of such and such materials" (op. cit., 642a: 10–15).

It is universally agreed today that the Aristotelean analogy between instruments and physical nature is a spurious one. The real question is whether, or to what extent, it is justified to extend the analogy from instruments to living organisms.

---

15 Plato already argued for this view: "Organon ara ti esti to onoma" = "So the name too is some kind of instrument" (cf. Itkonen 1991: 169). Varro continued the same line of thinking: "Ego utilitatis causa orationem factam concedo" = "I admit that language is there for utility's sake" (op. cit., p. 198).

What is at issue, then, is the methodological status of functional explanations as used in biology.

Like most who have dealt with this problem, Hempel (1965c [1959]) refers to the function of the heart. Let us start with the following description:

The heartbeat in vertebrates (= X) has the effect of circulating blood (= Y) through the organism (= Z)

This is a straightforward statement of efficient causation: X causes Y (in Z). A corresponding functional statement results from replacing effect (or consequence) by function: X has the function Y (in Z). But in order to be a plausible functional statement, Y must, in addition, be such as to satisfy some condition necessary for the survival of Z. With this addition, it seems natural to say two things: (i) the heartbeat is there **in order to** make blood circulate in the organism, (ii) the heartbeat is there **because** it makes blood circulate through the organism. Accordingly, functional explanation (= FE) may be formulated in more general terms as follows (cf. also Wright 1976: 81):

FE: As part of Z, X has, and is explained by, the function Y if, and only if, X causes Y which is necessary for the survival of Z

It is important to understand what, exactly, is the relation between RE and FE. They are similar insofar as they are both teleological. In RE the (causal) relation between A and X is involved in the explanation of A, while in FE the same is true of the relation between X and Y. But there are also significant differences: i) The goal–belief terminology does not apply at all to FE, and its (metaphorical) use would only create confusion in connection with FE. ii) The goals of RE need not be actualized whereas the functions of FE are actually there. iii) Most importantly, FE exemplifies nomic causation: it is a matter of (physiological) laws that if Y (as caused by X) ceases to exist, Z dies. By contrast, RE exemplifies non-nomic agent causation.

The differences outweigh the similarities, which means that RE and FE are two different things: "People still confuse functional explanations with purposive explanations, just as Aristotle did" (Woodfield 1976: 212).

As is evident from the Aristotle quotations, applications of FE "represent dead anthropomorphic metaphors" (Wright 1976: 20); and there has been a protracted debate on whether or not FE can be reduced without residue to efficient causation of the orthodox kind. Nevertheless, FE certainly has a legitimate use in the life sciences. Problems arise, however, when the notion of function is further extended from biology to sociology and anthropology.

"Durkheim, in a way characteristic of much nineteenth-century social thought, drew upon 'organic analogies'" (Giddens 1976: 120). His legacy was further developed by Malinowski (1944), Radcliffe-Brown (1952), Parsons (1949), and Merton (1949), among others. The existence of an institution was supposed to be explained by its latent functions, i.e. the unintended consequences of the corresponding institutional behavior, insofar as these were taken to be necessary for the survival of the society as a whole. This indeed exemplifies FE in its purest form. But are such explanations valid? In biology there is a general consensus on what is either functional or dysfunctional for the survival of a given organism. In sociology and anthropology, by contrast, there is no comparable consensus, with the result that each scholar seems to practice his/her own type of FE. Diesing (1972: Ch. 17) offers a sympathetic account of sociological and anthropological functionalism, which certainly deserves to be more widely known. But Hempel (1965 [1959]: 319–325) and Nagel (1961: 520–535) are utterly sceptical about the prospects of functionalism; and Giddens (1976) is blunt in his rejection: its many defects "undermine any attempt to remedy and rescue functionalism" (p. 20) "with its emphasis upon social 'adaptation' to an 'environment'" (p. 111).[16]

Finally, functional explanations are offered in the framework of evolutionary theory. Let us consider the following example. The earlier white variant of butterflies died out in the new grey environment of a mining town because it was easily detected and eaten by birds, whereas the grey mutation survived because it could not be detected.[17] This account contains the two components of any evolutionary explanation, namely random mutation (from white to grey) and natural selection (carried out by birds-cum-environment). The grey colour of the new mutation turned out to be functional for the survival in the new environment, hence the term functional explanation.

How does the foregoing discussion about the different meanings of function bear upon explanation in linguistics? The phenomena discussed in the previous sections are adequately explained by RE. Although RE embodies the notion of instrumental action, which is in turn connected with the notion of function, it would be redundant to call RE functional if this term is not meant to add anything to RE. And it would be wrong to call RE functional if this is supposed to mean that RE should be replaced by FE.

---

16 Functionalism is criticized, among other things, for postulating such dubious entities as needs of a society. Are my expressive needs open to the same kind of criticism? No, because there is the following disanalogy. We have self-knowledge and empathy to fall back upon, in order to grasp what people do or do not need. But no human being is in a position to grasp what a society – an entirely dissimilar kind of entity – needs, at least not by means of empathy.

17 It makes no difference if the enviromental change is supposed to be self-created.

Is there in linguistics a need for FE, in addition to RE? It is tempting to think that if we consider a given language (or its grammar) as a whole, then any of its parts can be explained, if at all, only by referring to how it contributes to the continuing existence of what it is a part of. I do not wish to rule out this type of explanation, but the fate of sociological functionalism should serve as a cautionary example. Functions and dysfunctions must be defined on the basis of generally accepted criteria; and the problem of nomicity needs to be solved or at least skirted. Therefore I prefer to leave this question open.

Finally, is the explanatory schema of evolutionary theory applicable in linguistics? It is reasonably uncontroversial to state that linguistic change consists (at least) of **innovation** followed by **acceptance**. Those who are anxious to apply Darwinism to linguistics argue that these two processes exactly correspond to mutation and natural selection, respectively.

As was seen in above, the problem-solving approach has been widely accepted in typological linguistics. It was also pointed out that this is just an application of RE: to solve the problem is the goal, and the actual solution is the means to achieve this goal. It goes without saying that problem-solving amounts to an **application of intelligence**.

Why is this so important? Cohen (1986: 125) tells us why:

> Hence no evolutionary change of any kind came about through the application of intelligence and knowledge to the solution of a problem. That was at the heart of Darwin's idea. … And that is why Darwinian evolution is so deeply inappropriate a model … for the understanding of [linguistic change].[18]

It is also clear that the meaning of function, as used in Darwinist explanations, has little to do with the original instrumental meaning of this term. The most that can be said is that "biology is a much more realistic metaphor for linguistics than is physics" (Givón 1984: 24) or that "the link between biological and linguistic changes is **metaphorical**" (Itkonen 1984: 209; original emphasis). But metaphors are no substitute for the real thing.

To be sure, if we investigate the phylogenetic evolution of language (and not linguistic change), there is no alternative to endorsing the Darwinist point of view. From the wealth of relevant literature I single out Givón (2002), Sinha (2002), and Zlatev (2002).

In this section I have explained why I in general prefer not to use the term typological-**functional** explanation. Depending on the context, it is either redundant or unjustified.

---

18 In this quotation linguistic change has been substituted for scientific progress.

9 What Other Types of Explanation May Be Needed?

The preceding account does not yet exhaust the gamut of all those explanation-types that may be needed in linguistics. How, for instance, should a given language L1 be explained? Or is such a question meaningless?

As far as I can see, the only reasonable way to explain L1 is to show what, exactly, is its place in an overall framework that is meant to accommodate both the diversity and the unity of the world's languages. Characterizing such a framework as "universal grammar" (= UG) would rehabilitate the use of this venerable term. UG so defined is created by representatives of typological linguistics; it is neither a psychological entity nor a (psychological) theory about such an entity. The explanation-type at issue, originally called "pattern explanation" (= PE) by Kaplan (1964), is described in some detail in Diesing (1972: 157–158). It may be taken to exemplify the so-called coherence theory of truth (cf. Itkonen 1983: 35–38, 123–129, 205–206; Anttila 1989b). PE may be summarized as follows:[19]

PE: X1 as part of Y is explained by Y if, and only if, Y is a coherent whole constituted by PE: X1, X2, X3, etc.

I submit that it is not just RE but also PE that typological linguists have inadvertently been practicing all the time. Therefore PE has an equal right as RE to be called "typological explanation".

PE is "horizontal" or "concatenated" in the sense that linguistic entities are meant to be explained by other such entities. RE, by contrast, is "vertical" in the sense that linguistic entities are meant to be explained by psychological entities. UG can be explained, if at all, in the "vertical sense", for instance, by discovering those categories of **pre-linguistic thought** which, more or less directly, underlie the descriptive categories of UG, such as word class, grammatical role, semantic role, etc (cf. Itkonen 2002b: 153–160).

After discussing those explanation-types that are needed in (typological) linguistics, it may be good to briefly indicate those that are not. Deterministic explanations are not needed, because there are none. Statistical generalizations are very valuable, of course, but they do not qualify as explanations, because their "explanatory necessity" is by far inferior to that of RE. Formal explanations are not needed because, on inspection, they turn out to be functional explanations in

---

19 There is clearly at least a superficial similarity between PE and FE.

disguise. Darwinist explanations have no application within diachronic linguistics. These issues are discussed more exhaustively in Itkonen (2011a).

10 Conclusion

'Function' is both a word of everyday language and a scientific term. In the scientific language, moreover, it has several uses which need to be distinguished from one another. Alternatively, if one use is regarded as paradigmatic, then it is very likely that it does not apply equally well to all contexts. Therefore, if one wishes to fix the exact meaning of 'functional explanation' in linguistics, it is advisable to concentrate on authentic cases where the term 'explanation' has been used within the school of thought designated as 'functional-typological'. This advice has been followed in what precedes.

References

Abondolo, Daniel. 1998. Introduction. In: Daniel Abondolo (ed.), *The Uralic languages*, 1–42. London: Routledge.

Anttila, Raimo. 1989a. Historical and Comparative Linguistics. Amsterdam: Benjamins. [1972]

Anttila, Raimo. 1989b. Pattern Explanation: Survival of the Fit. *Diachronica VI:1*, 1–21.

Arens, Hans. 1969. *Sprachwissenschaft: Der Gang ihrer Entwicklung von der Antike bis zur Gegenwart, Band I*. Frankfurt am Main: Athenäum.

Aristoteles. 1941. *The Basic Works of Aristotle*. Edited and with an introduction by Richard McKeon. New York: Random House.

Bickel, Balthazar and Johanna Nichols. 2005. Exponence of Selected Inflectional Formatives. Inflectional Synthesis of the Verb. *WALS*, 90–97.

Cohen, L. Jonathan. 1986. *The Dialogue of Reason: An Analysis of Analytical Philosophy*. Oxford: Clarendon Press.

Collingwood, R.G. 1946. *The Idea of History*. Oxford: Clarendon Press.

Collingwood, R.G. 1983. The Historical Logic of Question and Answer. In: Preston King (ed.), *The History of Ideas*, 135–152. London: Croom Helm.

Comrie, Bernard. 1986. Markedness, grammar, people, and the world. In: Fred R. Eckman et al. (eds.), *Markedness*, 85–196. New York: Plenum Press.

Corbett, Greville. 2000. *Number*. Cambridge: Cambridge University Press.

Coseriu, Eugenio. 1974. *Synchronie, Diachronie und Geschichte*. München: Fink. [1958]

Croft, William. 2003. *Typology and Universals* (2nd edition). Cambridge: Cambridge University Press.

Davidson, Donald. 1973. Freedom to Act. In: Ted Honderich (ed.), *Essays on Freedom of Action*, 139–156. London: Routledge.

Dickinson, Anthony. 1988. Intentionality in Animal Conditioning. In: L. Weiskrantz (ed.), 305–325. Oxford: Clarendon Press.

Diesing, Paul. 1972. *Patterns of Discovery in the Social Sciences*. London: Routledge.

Dixon, R.M.W. 2002. *Australian Languages*. Cambridge: Cambridge University Press.

Fodor, Jerry. 1975. *The Language of Thought*. New York: Crowell.

Foley, William. 1986. *The Papuan Languages of New Guinea*. Cambridge: Cambridge University Press.

Fortescue, Michael. 1984. *West Greenlandic*. London: Croom Helm.

Freud, Sigmund. 1984. The Unconscious. In: *On Metapsychology: The Theory of Psychoanalysis*, 167–210. The Pelican Freud Library, Vol. 11. Penguin Books. [1915]

Giddens, Anthony. 1976. *New Rules of Sociological Method*. London: Hutchinson.

Givón, Tom. 1984. *Syntax: A Functional-Typological. Introduction, Vol. I*. Amsterdam: Benjamins.

Givón, Tom. 2001. *Syntax: An Introduction, Vol. I*. Amsterdam: Benjamins.

Givón, Tom. 2002. *Bio-linguistics*. Amsterdam: Benjamins.

Grice, P.H. 1968. Utterer's Meaning, Sentence-Meaning, and Word-Meaning. *Foundations of Language 4,* 225–242.

Haiman, John. 1980. *Hua: A Papuan Language of the Eastern Highlands of New Guinea*. Amsterdam: Benjamins.

Haiman, John. 1985. *Natural Syntax*. Cambridge: Cambridge University Press.

Haspelmath, Martin. 1995. The Converb as a Cross-Linguistically Valid Category. In: Martin Haspelmath and Ekkehard König (eds.), *Converbs in Cross-Linguistic Perspective*, 1–56. Berlin: Mouton.

Haspelmath, Martin, Matthew S. Dryer, David Gil and Bernard Comrie (eds.). 2005. *The World Atlas of Language Structures*. Oxford: Oxford University Press.

Hawkins, John A. 1994. *A Performance Theory of Order and Constituency*. Cambridge: Cambridge University.

Heine, Bernd. 1997. *Foundations of Cognitive Syntax*. Oxford: Oxford University Press.

Heine, Bernd. 2002. On the Role of Context in Grammaticalization. In: Wischer and Diewald (eds.), 83–101.

Heine, Bernd, Ulrike Claudi and Friederike Hünnemeyer. 1991. *Grammaticalization: A Conceptual Framework*. Chicago: Chicago University Press.

Heine, Bernd and Tania Kuteva. 2007. *The Genesis of Grammar: A Reconstruction*. Oxford: Oxford University Press.

Hempel, Carl G. 1965a. *Aspects of Scientific Explanation and Other Essays in the Philosophy of Science*. New York: The Free Press.

Hempel, Carl G. 1965b. Studies in the Logic of Confirmation. In: Hempel 1965a, 3–51. [1945].

Hempel, Carl G. 1965c. The logic of Functional Analysis. In: Hempel 1965a, 297–330. [1959].

Hempel, Carl G. 1965d. Aspects of Scientific Explanation. In: Hempel 1965a, 331–496.

Hollis, Martin. 1977. *Models of Man*. Cambridge: Cambridge University Press.

Hopper Paul and Elisabeth Traugott. 1993. *Grammaticalization*. Cambridge: Cambridge University Press.

Itkonen, Esa. 1978. *Grammatical Theory and Metascience*. Amsterdam: Benjamins.

Itkonen, Esa. 1981. The Concept of Linguistic Intuition. In: Florian Coulmas (ed.), *A Festschrift for Native Speaker*, 127–140. The Hague: Mouton.

Itkonen, Esa. 1983. *Causality in Linguistic Theory*. London: Croom Helm.

Itkonen, Esa. 1984. On the 'Rationalist' Conception of Linguistic Change. *Diachronica I:2,* 203–216.

Itkonen, Esa. 1991. *Universal History of Linguistics: India, China, Arabia, Europe.* Amsterdam: Benjamins.

Itkonen, Esa. 1998. Concerning the Status of Implicationl Universals. *Sprachtypologie und Universalienforschung 51:2,* 157–163. [Reprinted in Itkonen 2011b]

Itkonen, Esa. 2002a. Grammaticalization as an Analogue of Hypothetico-Deductive Thinking. In Wischer & Diewald (eds.), 413–422. [Reprinted in Itkonen 2001b]

Itkonen, Esa. 2002b. Analogy: Within Reality; Between Reality and Language; Between Mind and Language; Within Language. In: Anders Hougaard & Steffen Nordahl Lund (eds.), *The Way We Think, Vol. I,* 129–162. Odense Working Papers in Language and Communication, No. 23.

Itkonen, Esa. 2003. *What is Language? A Study in the Philosophy of Linguistics.* University of Turku: Publications in General Linguistics 8.

Itkonen, Esa. 2004. Typological explanation and Iconicity. *Logos and Language V:1,* 21–33 [Reprinted in Itkonen 2011b]

Itkonen, Esa. 2005a. *Analogy as Structure and Process: Approaches in Linguistics, Cognitive Psychology, and Philosophy of Science.* Amsterdam: Benjamins.

Itkonen, Esa. 2005b. *Ten Non-European Languages: An Aid to the Typologist.* University of Turku: Publications in General Linguistics 9.

Itkonen, Esa. 2008a. The Central Role of Normativity in Language and Linguistics. In: Zlatev et al. (eds.), 279–305.

Itkonen, Esa. 2008b. Concerning the Role of Consciousness in Linguistics. *Journal of Consciousness Studies 15:6,* 15–33.

Itkonen, Esa. 2011a. On Coseriu's Legacy. *Energeia 3.* www.energeia-online.de. [Reprinted in Itkonen 2011b]

Itkonen, Esa. 2011b. *Papers on Typological Linguistics.* University of Turku: Publications in General Linguistics 15.

Itkonen, Esa. 2011c. Parataxis and syntactic complexity. In: Itkonen 2011b, 228–244.

Itkonen, Esa. 2013. Philosophy of Linguistics. In: Keith Allan (ed.), *The Oxford Handbook of the History of Linguistics,* 780–813. Oxford: Oxford University Press.

Itkonen, Esa and Anneli Pajunen. 2011. A Few Remarks on *WALS.* In Itkonen 2011b, 102–139.

Jespersen, Otto. 1965. *Philosophy of Grammar.* London: Allen & Unwin. [1924]

Kaplan, Abraham. 1964. *The Conduct of Inquiry.* San Fransisco: Chandler.

Katz, Jerrold. 1981. *Language and Other Abstract Objects.* Oxford: Blackwell.

Lewis, David. 1969. *Convention.* Cambridge MA: Harvard University Press.

Malinowski, Bronislaw. 1944. *A Scientific Theory of Culture, and Other Essays.* Chapel Hill: University of North Carolina Press.

Matisoff, James A. 1991. Areal and Universal Dimensions in Grammatization in Lahu. In: Elisabeth Closs Traugott and Bernd Heine (eds.). *Approaches to Grammaticalization, Vol. II,* 383–453. Amsterdam: Benjamins.

Merton, Robert K. 1949. *Social Theory and Social Structure.* New York: The Free Press.

Mithun, Marianne. 1988. The Grammaticization of Coordination. In: John Haiman and Sandra A. Thompson (eds.), *Clause Combining in Grammar and Discourse,* 331–359. Amsterdam: Benjamins.

Mithun, Marianne. 1997. Lexical Affixes and Morphological Typology. In: Joan Bybee, John Haiman, and Sandra A. Thompson (eds.), *Essays on Language Function and Language Type, Dedicated to T. Givón,* 357–371. Amsterdam: Benjamins.

Mithun, Marianne. 1999. *The Languages of Native North America*. Cambridge: Cambridge University Press.

Nagel, Ernest. 1961. *The Structure of Science*. New York: Harcourt.

Newton-Smith, W.H. 1981. *The Rationality of Science*. London: Routledge.

Pajunen, Anneli (ed.). 2002. *Mimesis, Sign, and the Evolution of Language*. University of Turku: Publications in General Linguistics 3.

Parsons, Talcott. 1949. *The Structure of Social Action*. Glencoe: Free Press.

Paul, Hermann. 1975. *Prinzipien der Sprachgeschichte*. Tübingen: Niemeyer. [1880].

Radcliffe-Brown, A.R. 1952. *Structure and Function in Primitive Societies*. London: Cohen & West.

Rowlands, E.C. 1969. *Yoruba*. London: Hodder & Stoughton.

Schelling, Thomas. 1960. *The strategy of Conflict*. Cambridge MA: The MIT Press.

Silverstein, Michael. 1976. Hierarchy of Features and Ergativity. In: R.M.W. Dixon (ed.), *Grammatical Categories in Australian Languages*, 112–171. Canberra: Australian Institute of Aboriginal Studies.

Sinha, Chris. 2002. Biology, Culture and the Emergence and Elaboration of Symbolization. In: Pajunen (ed.), 69–91.

Whitney, William Dwight. 1979. *The Life and Growth of Language*. New York: Dover. [1875]

Wischer, Ilse and Gabriele Diewald (eds.). 2002. *New Reflections on Grammaticalization*. Amsterdam: Benjamins.

Woodfield, Andrew. 1976. *Teleology*. Cambridge: Cambridge University Press.

Wright, Larry. 1976. *Teleological Explanations*. Berkeley: University of California Press.

Zlatev, Jordan. 2002. Mimesis: The "Missing Link" between Signals and Symbols in Phylogeny and Ontogeny? In: Pajunen (ed.), 93–122.

Zlatev, Jordan. 2008. The Dependence of Language on Consciousness. *Journal of Consciousnes Studies 15:6*, 34–62.

Zlatev, Jordan, Timothy P. Racine, Chris Sinha, and Esa Itkonen (eds.). 2008. *The Shared Mind: Perspectives on Intersubjectivity*. Amsterdam: Benjamins.

Peter Harder
Structure and Function:
A Niche-Constructional Approach[1]

1 Introduction

The relation between function and structure in language remains a contested issue, in spite of efforts from both sides (cf. Croft 1995; Newmeyer 1998; Haspelmath 2000; Boye and Engberg-Pedersen 2010; Langacker 2010). As emphasized by Haspelmath (2000), a key factor in the division between formalist and functionalist approaches is the difference in focal research interests: formalists are interested in language structure and believe it is necessary to start out with structure in order to understand how language functions, while functionalists believe structure can only be understood as embedded in function. Disagreements about concrete issues arise partly from the desire to subsume as much as possible under your own preferred point of view; as in all territorial disputes, a natural tendency is to try to push back the other side as much as possible.[2,3]

In this article, I take up the issue of the precise role of structure in language based on recent developments in evolutionary theory, including a combination of niche construction and cultural evolution. From this position, both groups are right in their main claim: functions of units in human languages as we know them presuppose structure, but the key structural units also presuppose func-

---

1 I am indebted to Esa Itkonen and Shannon T. Bischoff for important comments on an earlier version of this article. Needless to say, remaining errors are my own.
2 This description is meant as a description of the collective state of the field – it is as such not fair to individual authors (cf. below on the ontological difference between individual and collective entities). The generalization is not meant to imply that a formal linguist who breaks new ground by addressing traditionally functionalist issues is merely motivated by imperial expansionism. The point is that for a formal linguist the natural aim is to posit new formal principles and representations. To illustrate this, we may consider the volume *Formal Approaches to Function in Grammar: In Honor of Eloise Jelinek* (Carnie et al. 2003). Eloise Jelinek is introduced as being a self-described avowed formalist, and the 'pronominal argument hypothesis' which distinguishes between languages that take full DPs as arguments and languages that take only pronominal arguments is cited as a major outcome of her work – so even if functional issues are addressed insightfully in her work, this does not bring about a version of linguistics that constitutes an integrated enterprise between formalists and functionalists. (I am indebted to Shannon T. Bischoff for pointing out this volume to me).
3 Among features that have made the debates less fruitful than they might have been, are a number of well-entrenched but fallacious modes of argument charted in Croft (2010).

tional relations. On this point, I argue that linguistic structure differs from biological structure: as pointed out by Stephen J. Gould among others (cf. Gould and Lewontin 1979, Gould and Vrba 1982), anatomical structures in biology should not be assumed to have any functional underpinning; however, because the relation between linguistic structures and their physical substratum is different, the relation between function and structure is also different, cf. the argument below. The position I defend thus belongs on the functionalist side of the divide: it sees structural categories as conventions, underpinned by functional relations, which emerge out of actual usage. However, it accords structure a more clearcut role in a number of respects than certain functionalist accounts.

As suggested above, part of the problem is that one part of the story would like to claim to be the whole story. Examples are the Chomskyan view that performance/E-language is too unsystematic to lend itself to scientific description (Chomsky 1986: 15–46), or when John Taylor (2006: 63) dismisses semantic compositionality in favour of holistic meanings; or when Paul Hopper (1987: 141) claims that grammar exists only in the temporal flow. In spite of such polemical position statements, I take for granted the position that Newmeyer (2010) describes as shared between mainstream functionalists and formalists: that languages have both grammatical properties and usage properties, that these are linked, but that they are not the same – and try to exemplify how such a shared commitment might be cashed out.

One feature of what I propose may be surprising for some linguists on both sides of the divide: hard and structural facts about language are anchored outside the individual mind, as entrenched features of the *environment,* i.e. the sociocultural *niche* – with essentially the same ontological status as hard facts about the structures of business companies and educational systems (cf. Harder 2010). In the panchronic perspective of evolutionary theory, the fact that function presupposes structure while structure also presupposes function reflects a co-evolutionary spiral: patterns of usage give rise to conventionalization of structure – and these structures then form the basis of actual patterns of usage in the next round.

The discussion covers several related but not identical distinctions. The most fundamental distinction is the overall one between a functional and a structural approach; but this distinction is bound up with others such as the distinction between usage and structure, and between grammar and lexicon. On all points, the issue is the tug-of-war between wanting to keep structure distinct and separate, as opposed to wanting to integrate it with other properties (functional properties, usage properties, and lexical properties). Also associated with this pervasive geological fault in the linguistic landscape is the discussion about creativity – an argument that is (misleadingly) linked up with recursion as the final bastion of the innate Chomskyan faculty of language in the narrow sense.

The path of progress in the argument is as follows. First, there is a theoretical section which in addition to presenting the niche-constructional approach tries to show how this framework makes it possible to avoid some of the familiar pitfalls in the discussion between formal and functional linguists (section 2). Based on this foundation, I then suggest an integrated account of the linguistic issues announced in the introduction, focusing on a description of precisely what special status and significance I believe should be assigned to structure in the functionalist approach (section 3).

Although it may appear that I have allowed myself an overly generous amount of anecdotal illustration, this reflects a calculated strategy rather than spontaneous, unbridled verbosity. The overall point of this article is well-defined and simple: to show how function and structure are interdependent, rather than antithetical. The devil, however, is in the details; hence, these been given the space I believe they require.

2 Linguistics and evolutionary theory

In this theoretical section, I begin (2.1) by sketching the background in basic evolutionary theory, which is necessary to make precise the sense in which 'function' is basic to a linguistic theory that also includes structure (cf. also Givón, this volume). I then go on (2.2) to the extension from genetic to cultural evolution, which provides the tools for showing how the characteristic dynamics of evolutionary processes can apply not only to genetic ('intra-organismic') but also to cultural ('inter-organismic') transmission. I then (2.3) present arguments for why the concept of niche construction adds a crucial element to the story: the notion of an evolving *environment* that interacts dynamically with the evolving individuals within it. I conclude (2.4) by arguing that seeing the speech community as an evolutionary niche can provide a framework for understanding the relationship between language as the possession of an individual and language as a shared and collective phenomenon.

2.1 Evolution and functional properties

Ever since Darwin (1871), but increasingly in the last decades, evolutionary biology has been a source of inspiration for understanding the relation between function and structure in linguistics, both from the functionalist and the formalist side (cf.

Pinker and Bloom 1990, Newmeyer 1998, Croft 2000, Givón 2002, 2009, Hauser, Chomsky and Fitch 2002, Pinker and Jackendoff 2005, Deacon 1997, 2009).

In spite of this massive interest, the inspirational potential of evolutionary theory has in my view not been fully realized. Basically, there has been too much imperfectly charted territory between the core issues of linguistics and biology for this to be achieved. To mention one point that has played an important role, the discussion of function and structure has been marred by over-reliance on a parallel with the function and structure of *organs*. This is a key issue in biology, involving the relation between the disciplines of anatomy and physiology, which in biology are naturally treated as interdependent (cf. Givón 1995: 4). But this dependence does not mean that all anatomical features have functional explanations, cf. Gould and Lewontin (1979), and the analogy made it natural for Gould to support (for a while) Chomsky's position as he understood it: elements of 'infrastructure' (whether linguistic or anatomical) may arise as a side effect (the 'spandrel' example) or simply because they are part of the stuff that animals are made of: evolution always has to work with what is there.

Hence, to seek a functional explanation for everything is not fruitful: functional explanations are sometimes there, sometimes not, and if one assumes otherwise, one is at risk of ending up in the position of the mimicry theorist who argued that the pink colour of flamingos could be explained because it enabled them to blend in with the clouds at sunset (Gould 1992: 201).

Yet even if one may be willing to accept Chomsky's metaphor of the 'language organ' in other respects, language does not really constitute an organ in the anatomical sense – it is a skill-based activity (with mental as well as behavioural aspects). Obviously there must be a bodily basis for the activity, but that bodily basis does not constitute an organ with anatomical structure. The input to structural description of language is uncontroversially different from the input to a structural description of the liver – which is the analogy invoked in Newmeyer (1998) in discussing the relation between function and structure: it is necessary to have a good description of the liver as an organ before it makes sense to discuss its functional properties.

Structural links between elements of language are more analogous to structural links between elements of other complex, hierarchically structured skill-based activities like hunting or object manipulation (cf. also Greenfield 1991; Krifka 2007). The relation between function and structure is different from the anatomy-physiology case: structure in complex skills typically presupposes functional relations between sub-elements of the skill. In such cases, structure gets in at a later stage than function. Traffic may serve as an illustration case: only when people are already engaged in the *function* of getting from one place to another does it make sense to consider *structuring* traffic, for instance by separating lanes and imposing right or left hand driving. Putting pure structure first would confound the issue in such cases. With a biological example: you can describe the tongue of a chameleon anatomically without mixing function into it, but you cannot very well describe the chameleon's tongue *skill* without functional issues intruding: it would be weird to describe the act of throwing the tongue forward without including the subsequent act of drawing back the tongue with the prey sticking to it and finally eating the prey. This structural relation depends on behavioural success, not on anatomical properties: the three sub-events are *structurally* integrated into the overarching *functional* whole of getting food; that kind of structure is function-*based* (cf. Harder 1996: 149).

The fundamental reason why this perspective has not played a greater role is the centre-stage position of cognitive infrastructure in the discussion. This is due to the almost hegemonic status of cognitive science in the period, affecting both functionalist and formalist approaches. From around 1960 onwards, overt behaviour smacked of behaviourism. Chomsky's belief that the internal 'thought' function may well be more important than overt communication for understanding language reflects the spirit of the age.

However, the extreme reductionism associated with behaviourism is not the only reason to accord a crucial role to overt behaviour. Also from a non-reductionist point of view, it is necessary to address the question of how inner and outer manifestations of language relate to one another (cf. also Verhagen 2005). Evolutionary biology has a clear answer to this question: whatever the significance of cognitive infrastructure may be, it is only outward, causally effective behaviour that drives evolutionary change. Internal representations are at one remove from the action; to borrow a quote from Michael Tomasello, it is not enough to know that the tiger is coming, you also have to get out of the way. It is only with what I have called the social turn in cognitive linguistics that the causal factors that are at work in the social processes of language use are becoming part of the story, cf. Harder (2010); the argument below continues this line of argument.

The focus on infrastructure has also made it difficult to get beyond a pre-theoretical and intuitive concept of function. In order to avoid the risk of projecting one's own mental understanding of purposes anthropomorphically onto biological processes (cf. the warning in Searle 1992), one has to be very careful to define it strictly as involving relations that are inherent in the process of evolution (cf. Allan, Bekoff and Lauder 1998 on 'nature's purposes'). There must be a hard-core causal element in the understanding of function in order for a functional theory to make contact with evolutionary theory: functions must go beyond the purely cognitive realm.

What I see as the quintessence of an evolution-based concept of function (cf. Harder 2003 for a more detailed discussion) is that function involves a relation between part and whole such that the *function* of that part – e.g. wings – is the *effect* – e.g. powers of flight – that contributes to the selective fitness of the whole – e.g. the bird.[4] Such a theory of functional properties can be tested e.g., by cutting bird wings just enough to eliminate powers of flight in a population without otherwise damaging the specimens and see if that affects selective fitness. In certain birds it might not – but that would then prove that powers of flight had become non-functional for the bird in question (thus water rails occasionally lose powers of flight, especially on isolated islands). As always in evolutionary dynamics, there may be multiple, changing and fuzzy functional relations between a biological or behavioural feature and the organism. An organ whose function is to provide powers of flight may have started off as an organ for regulating temperature, etc ('exaptation', cf. Gould and Vrba 1982).

In order to have a theory of function in relation to a linguistic expression, we therefore have to have a hypothesis about what property (-ies) of that expression constitutes its contribution(s) to making the whole utterance successful (hence worthy of repetition and imitation). The most basic assumption is that the fundamental functional property of a linguistic expression is its conventional meaning. The relation between *signifiant* and *signifié* is functional in nature: What makes the expression *hi* functionally relevant is its meaning as a conventional greeting, just as what makes the definite article *the* functionally relevant is that it signals the definiteness of the expression of which it forms part. This reflects Wittgenstein's famous dictum, 'meaning is use', but in a niche-constructional reinterpretation: not *all* use equals meaning (as also implicit in Wittgenstein's account of meaning as anchored in 'forms of life').

I mention this already in the very general context of what constitutes functional properties in relation to language – because this introduces a level that is much more directly analogous to the dichotomy 'organ/function' than language as a whole: expressions in language are quasi-organs[5] for the speaker who wants to convey meanings to fellow members of the community. We return to the concrete linguistic argument in section 2 below. But first we have to bridge the central part of the gap between linguistics and biology described above: how to capture the basic status of linguistic expressions in the universe of evolutionary biology.

---

4 The question of function is part of a larger issue that also includes teleology and rationality, which is discussed in Itkonen (this volume); cf. also Wright (1973, 1976).

5 'Tool' would be more accurate than 'organ' – but tools share with organs the crucial property of existing as available individuated items, in contrast to language as a whole.

2.2 Cultural Evolution

The gap arises because linguistic expressions like *gargoyle* or *but* do not fit directly into human biology the way livers or knee-jerk reflexes do. Whatever their precise biological basis is, they belong at least partly in the realm of social facts. The question is how evolutionary dynamics can be responsibly applied to the realm of sociocultural facts.

That cultural evolution must enter into language change is sort of obvious, and has been recognized *avant la lettre* ever since Darwin himself (1871) referred to the existence of selection pressures on words. But there have been two main stumbling blocks for developing the idea. One is the form this pattern of thinking took in its first phase following Herbert Spencer (whose social-Darwinist interpretation of the theory is responsible for the phrase 'the survival of the fittest'); Jespersen (1892) is famous for applying the idea to account for the obsolescence of Latin and the superiority of English.

In the cultural domain this gives rise to an abhorrence of being anywhere near the 19th century view of 'primitive' cultures, which also included views on primitive languages (cf. Schleicher 1865), naturally putting Indo-European inflectional languages at the top. These fears surfaced for instance in connection with the discussion of Piraha as an example of a language without recursive syntax, cf. Everett (2005). Therefore it is important to emphasize that 'evolution' does not mean 'progress': since the neo-Darwinist synthesis it has been generally accepted that there is no inherent direction in evolution, and this also applies to cultural evolution. Evolution is the type of development that depends on interplay between individual-level reproduction and aggregate-level differential proliferation – whether or not this is good or bad by any normative criterion.[6]

The other stumbling block has been the specifically linguistic assumption that all languages are equally complex. The assumption is often linked up with an assumption that all languages are *extremely* complex, as testified by the fact that no grammar has yet managed to describe the complete system of any language.

Although cultural evolution is an outgrowth of biology, it might be expected to have implications for the more culturally imbued social sciences as well. However, the notion of evolutionary change in the area of culture collides with social constructionism, the dominant paradigm in this area. The crucial assump-

---

6 As pointed out in Trigger (1998), however, the cost of outright rejection of the concept of cultural evolution includes the loss of any possibility of aiming to achieve social progress by learning from our mistakes.

tion in social constructionism is defined by its opposition to positivism. Instead of assuming that apparently solid structures are part of objective reality, social constructionists see them as founded merely in socially shared interpretations backed up by powerful vested interests. Cultural evolution as an attempt to account for aspects of social change would come into this picture as a new version of objectivism, now in sociobiological guise. Any attempt to introduce causal explanations is subject to a suspicion of reintroducing discredited absolutes.

In linguistics, the argument against social constructionism (under the name of the 'blank slate' or 'standard social sciences model') has been most saliently conducted by key generativist figures such as Fodor and Pinker (cf. Pinker 1994, 2002), enlisting biology on the generative side against the unconstrained scope of social processes. Just as social constructionists see themselves as the chief alternative to determinism and positivism, so adherents of an innate language capacity view themselves as the chief alternative to the completely blank slate.

The pioneers in bringing back the issue of cultural evolution in a scientifically sanitized version are Richerson and Boyd (cf. Richerson and Boyd 2005). Their key addition to evolutionary theory is the case where information that impinges on the shaping of organisms is transmitted not via genes, but via other members of the social group. As a striking introductory example, they point to an investigation of the incidence of violence in the American South. With a murder rate at ten times the national average, twice that of inner cities, an explanation is called for. The investigation rules out genetic and direct environmental impact as likely explanations, and they line up a body of empirical evidence including statistics as well as psychological and behavioural experimental findings to support the conclusion that the key factor is a cultural code of honour that is specific to the southern subculture. A salient finding is that Southern violence is no higher when it comes to random aggression or rapacity – it ties in specifically with situations where there is a question of personal honour involved, such as insults or acts of aggression targeting women.

When information is transmitted as part of the sociocultural process, a more peaceful example being when fathers pass on their craftsmanship and the family business to their offspring, it remains an evolutionary process because it conforms to the basic format: at the individual level, there is reproduction going on from one generation to the next; at the population level, there is differential proliferation in that selection pressures favour some types of family occupations at the expense of others, leading to different types of economies and societies over time. Similarly, Richerson and Boyd suggest that a strong code of honour may be selectionally advantageous in sparsely populated country with law enforcement officers being also thin on the ground.[7]

In recent years a number of treatments of historical change in language have appeared which are clearly compatible with the notion of cultural evolution (MacWhorter 2005, Dahl 2004, Heine & Kuteva 2007, Givón 2009). Plausible suggestions for the broad outlines of certain developmental trajectories towards the kind of complexity that characterizes human languages as we know them have also appeared: Nominal and verbal elements are candidates for the primeval bottom level (Heine and Kuteva 2007), non-linear morphology must be seen as a development from linear (Dahl 2004); syntactic subordination must be seen as a development from paratactic relations (Givón 2009), etc. This does not provide a royal road of cultural evolution towards human languages as we know them, however. What precisely the concept of cultural evolution may entail for the primal development from a stage where no culturally entrenched language existed to modern languages is thus not by any means well-established and consensual knowledge. However, an impetus towards a more differentiated understanding of evolutionary trajectories in sociocultural space has been provided by a new twist on evolutionary theory: the notion of niche construction.

2.3 Niche construction

The concept of 'niche' denotes an environment that offers a specific set of 'affordances' (cf. Gibson 1979) that certain organisms are adapted to. Part of the dynamics of evolution consists in mutations that create beings with coping skills that fit into hitherto unoccupied niches – as when life conquered dry land by means of hard egg shells. In this case the process can be divided into the biological part

---

7 Richerson and Boyd do not point to direct implications for the understanding of language, beyond opening up a new space of possibilities; the generative point of view remains one possibility, even if others offer themselves:

> While many animals have rudimentary capacities for social learning, these are uniquely hypertrophied in humans...These capacities might underlie language, though an important school of linguists insists that language learning is a special-purpose capacity. (Richerson and Boyd 2005: 240)

Although social learning is an important part of the picture as illustrated above, which is in harmony with one aspect of social constructionism, Richerson and Boyd see culture, and cultural evolution, basically as a new dimension of biology ("Culture is as much a part of biology as walking upright", 2005: 7), rather than as an interface phenomenon.

and the environmental part: the environment (dry land) was there first, with the relevant set of affordances for life; the biological change (producing hard egg shells) came later.

Such a division becomes impossible with niche *construction,* which occurs when there are processes of feedback between organism and environment that go both ways: the species changes its environment in certain ways which in turn influence the selection processes in the species. As a result of that altered selection, in the next round the population has a different impact on its environment than before, thus reshaping the environment to which it is concurrently adapting. Deacon (1997, 2009) illustrated this mechanism with the case of the beaver. Over the years, beavers have adapted to living in an environment with ponds (cf. their flat tails, for instance). Simultaneously, however, they have developed a behavioural repertoire that includes building dams – thus creating ponds. Beavers are thus adapted to environments with dams built by beavers. This makes the nature-nurture dichotomy inapplicable. If you ask whether the explanation for the beaver's overall 'pond competence' is in the beaver's nature or in influence from the environment, there is no sensible answer – and the reason is in the causal spiral that is the defining characteristic of niche construction.

Niche construction has been suggested by Deacon (1997, 2009) as a scenario for the process that gave rise to language: at some point certain hominids came into a causal spiral that created both a new niche for the species and a new set of behavioural skills – language skills – that matched this niche. Paramount among the environmental changes is the fact that human habitats are *speech communities*; matching this inside the organism there must be the necessary genetic underpinning to function as speakers. Deacon suggests that this is the only plausible explanation for the set of otherwise unconnected features that enable language: in addition to the facility for language learning, features like lowered larynx, cortical control of vocalizations, etc.

Niche construction has been criticised for trying to get mileage out of already familiar features of evolution (such as the fact that living organisms change their environment). From the point of view argued here, however, the special emphasis in niche construction serves a crucial purpose: to include the trajectory of evolutionary changes that occur *outside* the organism as part of the explanatory mechanism. Richerson and Boyd define culture as an individual/psychological feature, motivating this choice (2005: 259 note 4) with the absence of a consensual definition of culture based on "a body of socially transmitted traditions". Without providing a consensual definition of culture-in-the-environment, niche construction nevertheless offers a crucial step in that direction: once we accept that cultural niche construction is real, we also have to accept that culture exists in the environment – otherwise the evolutionary spiral would be unable to get off the ground.

Another significant feature about niche construction as opposed to cultural evolution is that cultural transmission in the form of tradition from one generation to the next may get lost – if the parent generation for some reason fail to transmit their craft to enough offspring, skills may get lost for no other reason (as when boat-building was lost in the Tasmanian population). In contrast, information that is built into the cultural niche cannot get lost in the same sense (although it may no longer exert selection pressure that is sufficient to drive adaptation). As a third distinguishing factor, cultural evolution and niche construction do not always coincide: there can be cultural evolution without niche construction, when a culture gradually learns to adapt better to the same environmental niche affordances – as Inuit cultures did, in contrast to the Greenland Norse (cf. Diamond 2005), and there can be niche construction without cultural evolution (as in the case of the beaver)[8].

The most interesting case, however, is the one in which we have both at the same time. Although cultural evolution can accommodate also changes due to niche construction, it does not highlight the co-existence of *two* add-ons to 'classic' neo-Darwinism in these cases: in addition to the role of cultural transmission of information in shaping organisms, there is also the ongoing construction of new cultural *environments*. The role of this third channel can throw light on the cultural anchoring of human language.

To begin with, cultural niche construction renders obsolete the discussion between a Chomskyan innateness position and a blank-slate type of social constructionism. Chomsky's position on innateness essentially asserts that there can be no meaningful research into the *why* of the human capacity for structured language (because it simply arose by accident); the blank slate position asserts that there can be no meaningful research into the *nature* of the language capacity (because like any other capacity it simply arises as a result of social pressures). Neither of these positions is either credible or scientifically fruitful once the existence of cultural niche construction is available. It is obvious that the rise of modern languages involves a form of cultural evolution (the only alternative is that one day a community woke up and spoke a full-fledged language). It is also obvious that human beings adapt to the languages of the communities in which

---

8 The emphasis on cultural evolution and niche construction in this article does not constitute a rejection of the genetic side of language evolution: clearly both elements must be part of the full story. Since no other animal is genetically equipped for full mastery of a human language, there is a genetic dimension, and since differences between languages cannot be explained by reference to genes, there is a dimension involving sociocultural niches. The controversy is about the link between the two sides, with Chomsky, Deacon and Tomasello taking different positions.

they grow up. Linguistics needs to capture the nature of those processes rather than pretending they do not occur.

2.4 Speech communities as evolutionary niches

The most significant result of invoking cultural niche construction as the explanatory context for linguistics is that it provides a framework for understanding language as a feature of the environment. Although it is obvious from a commonsense-perspective, this insight has generally been located in the theoretical periphery, marginal in relation to the centre-stage concern of how language arises in the individual. Because of the contested character of social facts and well-established cautionary principles of methodological individualism, it has been difficult to reach a consensual account of the status of language as a collective property.

In view of this situation, below I offer a somewhat laborious account of the ontological underpinning of collective, community-level facts – including linguistic facts. I approach them in three narrowing-down stages. First I address the basic ontological distinction between properties of individuals and properties of collectives; secondly, the role of populations as crucial collective objects in evolutionary biology; and finally the status of the sophisticated type of population that constitutes *communities* as a factor in the human habitat.

The point of departure for this whole exercise is an intuitively appealing form of reductionism that asks: if all properties of collective entities must be manifested by individuals, how can it be that there are collective properties that are not properties of individuals? After all, as quipped somewhere by Roland Barthes, we do not have a science of flower *posies*, only a science of individual plants.

The distinction between properties of individuals and collectives was first made a focal issue by Bertrand Russell in his theory of types (Russell 1908): even if a class has only one member, the logical properties of the class are different from the logical properties of the members. A linguistic example, pointed out by Dahl (2004), is that the class of Indo-European strong verbs has been historically more stable than the members – i.e., individual verbs have come and gone but the class has remained relatively intact. Stability as predicated of the *individual* verbs would thus be more misleading than stability as predicated of the conjugational *class* of verbs. Commonsense awareness of the distinction is manifested in the proverbial phrase: *he cannot see the wood for trees*. Things that you can say about woods but not about trees include the property of being dark and being the habitat of large predators such as tigers.

In evolution, the key form of collective is the population. As stressed both by Richerson and Boyd (2005) and by Croft (2000), the central element in applying evolutionary thinking to new domains is to introduce a population level of analysis[9]. In Croft's theory of language change, the population level is crucial in being the locus of selection (or differential proliferation), and by the fact that species are (a special kind of) populations: the spreading of a mutation takes place not in the individual (which either has or does not have the mutation) but as a result of differential reproductive success among individuals depending on whether or not they have the mutation. Without interaction between individual-level processes (pre-eminently reproduction) and population-level processes (pre-eminently proliferation), evolution cannot occur. Thinking about language in evolutionary terms thus entails thinking about alternative variants and their differential distribution in a population – which may be a population of speakers, or (as argued by Croft) a population of utterances. In either case, an ontology that contains only individuals does not allow us to explain the proliferation (or extinction) of particular linguistic forms.

This brings us to the third level, the human community. What enables human beings to form communities is an innate property investigated from an evolutionary point of view by Tomasello (1999, 2008) and from the point of view of language use by Herbert Clark (1996): the capacity for joint attention and action.

Joint attention is the crucial evolutionary novelty because it brings a special intersubjective relation into being. Participants who are capable of *jointly* attending to an object (rather than merely having a *shared* object of attention, as when a group of ducks are looking at the same hunting eagle) can do things together in ways that other organisms cannot. When mum and dad pay joint attention to their child, this complex mental state is not reducible to the sum of two simple mental states, mum paying attention and dad paying attention – the felt qualities of the two states are clearly distinct. Thus, a joint mental state by definition cannot be reduced to the sum of mental states in individual minds. I regard this as providing an anchoring for an essential feature of linguistic facts that has been pointed out over the years by Itkonen (1978, 2008): linguistic facts have the status of *norms*, they are not facts about individuals.

This means that a new type of relationship between members of a group becomes possible. It can be expressed as the capability of forming a 'we'. A 'we' that is engaged in joint activity is not reducible to the sum of separate individu-

---

9 The distinction between the individual and the population level is well-entrenched in diachronic linguistics, independently of evolutionary thinking, cf. Coseriu 1975 [1952], 1974 [1958] – cf. Andersen (2006) for a critique of the reductionist fallacies of importing a biological version of evolutionary theory into linguistics.

als that happen to enter into each other's affairs; a new and more powerful distinction has come into being between individual and group. Tomasello (2008: 6) shows how this provides an underpinning for Searle's concept 'collective intentionality', the building block of his theory of social reality. Paper money HAS value; horse MEANS 'horse' – this is not something that is a characteristic of the mental content of individual people, it is part of the way the world works. It could not be part of the way the world works if it were not in individual minds also, but its joint aggregate force is ontologically different from the piecemeal status as part of individual minds.[10]

Finally, a crucial element in going from a purely cognitive position to viewing language as a social fact is a simple change of perspective: it consists in viewing mental content as a feature of other people rather than a feature of the self. The most crucial feature of the human niche is that it makes a difference what goes on in *other* people's minds. In the passage where Croft argues against understanding meaning as a feature of the environment, he says (2000: 111) that "thoughts and feelings cannot go anywhere outside of the minds of humans, whether it is "into" words or "into" an external space" – but the distinctive fact about the human environment is precisely that thoughts and feelings do not stay locked into the individual mind: because of joint understanding, it does in fact break out into the social space that we inhabit, thus creating an environment to which we human beings adapt. In the rest of the animal kingdom, mental events matter only to the extent they underlie outward behaviour – but to human beings the thoughts and feelings of others are part of the world we live in and respond to.

It follows directly from this feature of human subjectivity – or rather intersubjectivity, cf. Sinha (1999: 232) – that mental content is a crucial feature of the social environment, not only as a feature of individual-level relations, but also as

---

10 This does not provide an answer to the most concrete question about social facts: in what special place do they exist? The reason there is no convincing answer to that question, however, is that it is not the right question to ask. What makes certain meaning-imbued facts social rather than individual is not their concrete location. It is true that mental facts can only exist inside the minds of individuals, which makes collective mental facts non-distinct in terms of location from individual facts – but this is so basically for the same reason that there is no difference in terms of location between the wood and the individual trees. Collective mental facts are aggregates underpinned by the existence of individual mental facts, just as woods are aggregates underpinned by the existence of individual trees. What makes them different is not location, but the property of being collective as opposed to individual, which as argued makes a difference in terms of the way the world works.

A familiar way of getting at this property is to refer to common knowledge, and this is indeed a key feature – but I think it needs to be based on a description that focuses on the collective fact that has to exist in order for there to be something that can be commonly known.

a feature of relations between individuals and the group. If there is a 'we' around in the social environment with thoughts and feelings, it is of crucial existential interest to the individual to be able to strive to position herself optimally (or at least satisfyingly) with respect to this collectivity of mental content.

It is this perspective that is at the core of language as a social entity. Language is a mentally imbued feature of social groups which is of crucial importance for individuals as they relate to those groups. An illustration of the relation between social structures in general and the structures of language that form part of them is the fact that in terms of the patterns discussed by Dahl 2004, there is a relationship between events that cause the breakdown of sociopolitical structures, like wars and invasions, and events that cause changes in language structures: when the social niche collapses, so does the language that is an integrated part of it (cf. the fate of Old English after 1066).

3 The structuralist-functionalist dichotomies – in the light of niche-constructional evolution

This second half of the paper discusses a series of the intertwined issues that enter into the discussion between formal and functional linguists of how function relates to structure. They form a series of contrasting pairs, with the structural dimension on one side, and on the other side various functionalist positions which I think go too far in the direction of reducing the role of structure. Since the most basic of the dichotomies involved is the pair 'structure vs. function', I begin (3.1) with that. I then go on to the structure-usage pair (3.2), which in turn is closely linked to the structure-variation pair (3.3). Finally, I address the most structure-internal part of the agenda, the grammar-lexicon dichotomy (3.4). I conclude this section by discussing an illustration case, that of subject-auxiliary inversion in English (3.5). In the end, I draw the threads together (section 4).

3.1 Structure and function

Two basic prerequisites for understanding the relation between function and structure in evolutionary terms have been specified in the introduction: First, function has to do with the contribution of parts to the success and reproduction of the larger units of which they form part, and secondly, the structure of complex hierarchically organized skills does not exist prior to functional relations – rather, structure emerges from functional relationships between the component parts of the skill.

Before spelling out what that implies for linguistic structure, it should be pointed out that language also has components (like organs) and these enter into what I have called *component*-based structures. Component-based structure is the only kind that exists in inorganic nature, an example being atoms that combine into crystals (cf. Harder 1996: 152). In biological and social structures function-based structure co-exists with component-based structure.

A crucial difference is that component-based structure arises bottom-up, as elements are combined into larger units, while function-based structure presupposes a higher unit (in relation to which the element has its function). To take an artefact as an example, the division of a knife into the structural units of handle and blade presupposes the overall 'cutting' function: blades and handles do not lie around separately, before being accidentally combined into knives – but naturally knives also have components, including atoms and molecules.

As examples of component-based structural units in language one may mention the formants of speech sounds, which exist regardless of the functions of the sounds they enter into. On reflection, however, it will be obvious that the core type of structural relations in language are not the purely component-based ones but rather those that are function-based – including hierarchical relations in the sentence. For instance, it is impossible to describe an expression as a 'modifier' without considering the larger whole to which it belongs, and to whose success it makes a contribution (in combination with the head). What makes the structural roles of clause constituents function-based is that they exist as contributions to such a larger whole: just as in the case of a knife, it is inconceivable that there should have been modifiers and heads lying around before some bright person chose to combine them into larger expressions.

The blade/handle and modifier/head examples are chosen because the function-based nature of their structural relations is fairly obvious and transparent. But what about those cases where 'formal' categories do not match functional relations so transparently?

This question is what more than anything else has kept the structure/function argument going, and section 2.5 will go through a recent case. The problem is due to the nature of *conventionalization*, the process whereby 'cultural laws' (also describable as operational *norms*) arise, imposing 'status functions' on behaviours and artefacts in a cultural niche. This process has a naturally occurring input, which is assigned additional properties that do not follow from and may interfere with its pre-conventional "nature". In a human group collaborating about a task, there may be no need for formal, conventional structure, but one may also at one point find it practical to choose to appoint a formal, conventional boss. Once that happens, the 'boss' role comes on top of what the relevant person as an individual might have done in a given situation. One would hope that there is a good match with the person's natural responses and the actions expected of a leader – but as we all know, there is no guarantee of that. Conventionalization thus presupposes natural properties, but introduces an extra level of complexity.

In the case of language, the relative role of conventional properties is greater than in most other cases. Collaboration (as in hunting) can take place without any conventional structure – but without conventionalization we would not have a human language at all. Needless to say, this does not eliminate the role of spontaneous, situation-specific purposes – but when one chooses linguistic communication (rather than e.g. brute force) as the causal instrument for serving these purposes, one has to channel them through existing linguistic conventions.

This means that conventions acquire more of a life of their own in language than in other behaviours. A conventional pattern such as structuring sentences with a syntactic subject may be generalized not because its specific functional motivation (such as reserving a slot for the clausal topic) is necessarily always motivated, but because it fits into the overall system in other ways. Something similar is at work in the case of the formal hierarchy in business companies. Making do with an informal group of people may not be feasible in the long run. Discrepancies between formal structure and real life tend to arise in both cases: there may be subject expressions that are not really topics, and there may be CEOs who do not really know how to manage the company. Such cases, however, do not demonstrate that you can understand what CEOs are without presupposing the function of managing the company, or that you can understand syntactic subjects without presupposing the function of being clause-level topics.

Most linguists probably to some extent accept the existence and role of conventionalization as described above, with the possibility of gaps between conventional and occasion-specific properties. But under the conditions of polarized debate they veer away from the middle ground – and then functionalists tend to overemphasize the correspondence between formalized structure and actual function, while formalists tend to overemphasize the possible absence of correspondence.

Much of the discussion about function and structure, also in relation to subjects, has been about whether a uniform, invariant function could be ascribed to structural units such as grammatical subjects – and if not, it is often assumed that it can be regarded as purely structural, rather than describable in functional terms. But to be precise about the relation between function and structure requires that the two are investigated together: the conditions under which subject choice has a transparent and independent functional role need to be part of an account of exactly what function subject choice has under what structural conditions. To take an obvious example of why it is necessary to have recourse to function when describing syntactic subjects: the existence of symmetric pairs such as *Joe resembles Jack* and *Jack resembles Joe*, which serve different communicative functions even if they are truth-conditional equivalents, means that there are cases where subject choice is the minimal difference; other cases need to be accounted for together with the factors that interact with subject choice.[11] As a special case, it has sometimes been assumed that the existence of 'empty' subjects, as in atmospheric predicates (such as *it* in *it is raining*) undermines the possibility of having a role for functional description of subjects. But there are two reasons why this reflects a simplistic view of functional properties. First of all, functional principles may be applied more or less widely across the board. Sometimes they are applied only in clearly motivated cases, sometimes they are generalized in ways that are often felt to be superfluous; children will recognize the experience of mother forcing them to wear warm clothes even in cases when children deem it unnecessary. Such experience do not show that a functional motivation is absent – in fact the whole situation can only be understood within a functional universe, as (over)generalization of an inherently functional measure beyond the cases for which the functional motivation applies.

But more interestingly, perhaps, it also shows the need to have a 'systemic' understanding of functional organization, rather than the simplistic one-to-one hypothesis that is used to argue against function-based description whenever functions are not invariant. The standard cases of languages where overt subjects are said to be obligatory (such as English and Danish), actually only have obligatory subjects in indicative sentences – and in these, the order of subject and verb plays a role for distinguishing between interrogative and declarative mood. I have frequently asked audiences if they knew an example of languages with obligatory overt subjects where the subject did not have such an extra functional role, and I have yet to be offered a counterexample.

The rise of syntactically structured languages can also be understood in terms of function-based structure, as the result of a process whereby a conventional division of labour emerges out of usage patterns. When language acquired structure, phylogenetically speaking, speakers went from using only holophrastic utterances, complete in themselves, to syntactically structured utterances. This entailed that 'linguistic function' went from being a relation between a linguistic expression and a whole act ('external function') to acquiring also utterance-internal variants (such as a proto-subject function and a proto-predicate function). In

---

11 This coincides in part with the basic rationale for construction grammar, cf. Croft (2001) on construction-specific subjects – but for reasons discussed below, section 2.4, (cf. also Harder 2010: 259), function-based and construction-based structure do not in general coincide.

syntactically complex utterances, each part does not have its function directly in relation to the situation – it has its (sub)function in relation to the whole linguistic act. That act in turn has a function analogous to that of the whole but unstructured utterance: the alternative utterances *Yes!* and *I will be there* may have the same utterance function (e.g. of accepting an invitation), but the constituents of the latter have sub-utterance functions that only in combination manage to achieve the whole situational purpose.

As I have argued previously (e.g. Harder 2004, 2010), this development is analogous to the change from a one-man company to a company with an internal division of labour: all people working for the company have *internal* subfunctions, which must be described in relation to the *external* function served by the company as a whole – and this simultaneously defines their position in the *structure* of the company. As pointed out by Givón (2010: 167), arguing against Bickerton (2008), the mechanism whereby two linguistic elements begin to collaborate syntactically cannot solely be a formal 'merge' operation – they have to interact *functionally* in order for this to happen. To pursue the analogy above, a business 'merger' in which the two companies are merely formally united but have no functional interaction is unlikely to provide the parent company with heightened *external* functionality.

The understanding of structure and function as being intertwined, because functions can be both internal and external, is the traditional view in European linguistics. In American linguistics, the dominant understanding of the term 'functionalist' is one who believes that linguistic properties can be derived solely from its *external* function.[12] I suggest that the European approach, which assumes that functions of linguistic expressions can have both internal and external dimensions, is better suited for fostering a more fruitful interaction between the structural and the functional approaches.

The key conclusion of the argument in this section is that linguistic structure presupposes function and comes into being by the conventionalization of certain functional relations. Conventions are social facts, with the status of norms or cultural laws that are causally efficacious in the niche. Because evolutionary function depends on consequences of overt behaviour, the existence of functional relations in the niche environment is ontologically primary in relation to their

---

12 I was reminded of this by editors and reviewers of *Language* in connection with Boye and Harder (2012): our article was originally entitled "A functional theory of grammatical status and grammaticalization", but since the sense in which it was functional depended on functional relations between linguistic expressions, we were warned that an American audience would understand this as claiming that grammatical status could be explained by external function alone, so we changed the title to a usage based account.

mental, cognitive representations: if *calda* did not work – in the Italian 'niche' – so as to point members to the hot rather than the cold tap, it would not be cognitively *represented* as meaning 'hot'. The motivation for having conventions is also social: as pointed out by Lewis (1969), conventions serve to enable and facilitate social collaboration.

The crucial contribution of cultural niche construction to this account of the role of conventions for structure is to make it possible to go beyond the unfruitful dichotomies (mental/environmental, nature/nurture) by offering a credible account of how mental, cognitive structuring can acquire normative status as part of a community environment to which members adapt.

3.2 Structure and usage

As pointed out above, a purely internalist cognitive approach to language cannot make contact with evolutionary accounts. However, in the last decade and a half (cf. Harder 2010) a development has been going on towards a usage based linguistics (cf. Barlow and Kemmer 2000) that integrates the description of social patterns of usage with the description of cognitive, conceptual properties. This is simultaneously a fusion between older functionalist and newer cognitivist strands of linguistics. Usage, being overt action, is better positioned to link up with an evolutionary notion of function. However, here, too there is a risk of one part of the truth wanting to be the whole truth. A too exclusive focus on usage – a tendency I have termed usage fundamentalism – would sever the link between the level of concrete online action and the level of the 'cultural laws', the conventionalized functional relations to which actual usage is adapted.

Two examples may be offered to illustrate this risk. One pertains to the notion of linguistic meaning, i.e. the semantic side of the linguistic sign; the other to the understanding of syntactic relations as opposed to usage frequencies.

Linguistic meaning is central to the notion of compositionality in the formal (Fregean) tradition, and the scepticism towards such semantic building blocks in the usage based approach is partly a matter of scepticism towards the idea of precise truth-conditional contributions from each linguistic element. To replace this conception of meaning, two suggestions have been that in my view go too far towards eliminating the role of 'cultural laws'. One is to reserve the term 'meaning' for the usage level alone (cf. Croft 2000: 111):

> A less obvious problem that follows directly from the primary one is that linguistic expressions do not contain meanings. Meaning is something that occurs in the interlocutors' heads at the point of language use.

This is partly a terminological issue, since Croft does not deny the existence of conventions; but it is important to a key point discussed in section 1.4 above, the status of human mental constructs as joint property in communities. From a niche-constructional point of view, it is essential that expressions that are entrenched in the community are understood as having meanings which constitute affordances for members, and where it is therefore a matter of selection pressure that you know what words mean – as in the case of *calda* in Italian. If we decide to say that words only mean something "at the point of language use", it follows that speakers cannot know what words mean before they use them. I think this is both counterintuitive and misleading.

Another attack on word meaning is based on the same desire to put as much as possible into acts of usage and leave as little as possible for the level that I call 'cultural laws'. An example of this is when Taylor (2006) rejects what he calls the 'dictionary + grammar model' and the compositional approach to meaning. Echoing familiar cognitive linguistics assumptions about partial compositionality, he suggests that the whole idea of starting with word meaning is wrong. Instead, meanings essentially belong in "multi-word expressions" which speakers have learned 'as such', i.e. in concrete usage situations, and once that is realized *the semantic contribution of component words will become less and less of a concern* (Taylor 2006: 63).

I think Taylor's examples are persuasive, as far as they go: one would not want to base a description of the expression *all over* on its component parts, for instance. But the issue of 'semantic contribution' also applies to the whole multi-word expression *all over*, and larger expressions such as *all over the paddock* (Australian/New Zealand usage). The only way you can avoid the 'semantic contribution' issue is by going all the way to whole utterances with fully contextually specified meanings – a list of actual utterances, in other words. This would amount to usage fundamentalism, denying the role of speakers knowing what contribution a specific expression can make to the utterance.

The positions of Croft and Taylor as discussed above (cf. also Harder 2010: 112 and 290–297) illustrate the position quoted from Richerson and Boyd (cf. note 7) involving the purely individual definition of culture: there has been an absence of consensual definitions of how cultural knowledge can be a collective property. Niche construction, however, offers a way to understand meaning in the social environment as part of the way the world works. What happens is that human communities create cultural laws that change the causal structure of life in the niche. Just as the laws of nature cause adaptive evolutionary change, so do the cultural laws that are the result of niche construction.[13]

The obvious objection is, why do we need to have anything else than the actual flow of usage as a cultural factor? Is not actual usage the only manifestation of language that we come across in real life?

The answer has to do with the causal structure of selection pressures as they work in relation to linguistic utterances. To say that selection pressure only consists in responding appropriately to individual acts of usage would be to underestimate the complexity of community life. Speakers at the same time respond to selection pressures exerted by linguistic expressions. It is especially obvious in the case of young children: they need at the same time to achieve their situational goals and to achieve a better grip on language. The fact that *calda* means 'hot' rather than 'cold' in Italy is a 'cultural law' that it is to your advantage to get your head around once and for all – treating it only as an ever-surprising property of a scattered series of individual events is not a good coping strategy.

The second type of issue where the risk of usage fundamentalism raises itself is in connection with the relationship between syntactic constructions and usage instances of such constructions. The problem arises when facts about actual usage events are taken as definitive of the properties of the construction as a conventional linguistic item, without considering the independent role of the cultural laws without which usage events would not be causally efficacious. The case of complementation as analysed by Thompson (2002) illustrates this risk: she argues that because the most frequent role of matrix clauses is to be an epistemic-evaluative 'appendix' to the formally subordinate clause, this is the 'real' function of matrix clauses (rendering structural subordination much less significant than formalists think). As argued in Boye and Harder (2007) and vigorously pursued by Newmeyer (2010), this type of argument is not valid: although frequency may give an indication of functional relations, it is never definitive.

This part of the conclusion strictly speaking does not depend on the rationale of the 'cultural niche construction' argument; it already follows from the distinction between individual-level events and population-level selection patterns. The same principle applies in biology: the penis has two uses, one of which typically occurs more frequently than the other, but it does not follow that the other use is functionally irrelevant. The complexity of functional systems is such that there are inherently two levels of description which cannot be reduced to one another:

---

[13] They may even, as exemplified by the rise of lactose tolerance (cf. Laland at al. 2003), trigger adaptive genetic change: In a cattle-keeping culture, being able to digest milk gives a selective advantage. But for language, the relevant type of adaptation is the sociocultural adaptation to meaning assignments in the niche.

descriptions of actual usage/behaviour cover one level, while both structural and functional description depend on the causal mechanisms that apply at the population level. Meaning-imbued conventions are special cases of such causal mechanisms.

3.3 Structure and variation

The role of variation is an aspect of the relationship between usage and structure. However, it deserves a section of its own, because it is the focal point of a cultural divide in the macro-linguistic community. Mainstream 'core' linguists understand their task as predicated on the description of linguistic structure. If a linguist is working on a particular language, her goal is to write a grammar of the language, and that means to describe how speakers of the language structure their utterances in ways that reflect the 'cultural laws' in the community. It is only natural if they may understand variation as noise, as something that may undermine the laws they are trying to capture.

Sociolinguists, on the other hand, have their identity bound up with the description of variation. The more variation, the merrier. A recent trend is to stress the phenomenon of multilingual ('multiethnolectal') variation in inner cities, where the whole idea of referring to the structures of national languages such as Danish and German becomes lost from sight (cf. Jørgensen 2010). They have natural allies in the usage based approach and its focus on the variability of actual usage as opposed to the structural laws embodied in grammatical descriptions

In terms of the theory I am proposing, however, the apparent head-on collision between the two approaches on closer inspection will reveal itself as two rivalling perspectives on the same complex phenomenon rather than as a disagreement about the facts. As rightly stressed by Croft (in continuation of Labovian sociolinguistics), variation is not an impediment to the evolution of conventions – it is a prerequisite for it. Variation is the basic condition of all evolutionary systems. Function enters into the equation because functional relations are what endow some variants with higher selective fitness than others. Keller's (1990) example of *engelhaft* driving out *englisch* in the sense of 'angelic' in 19th century Germany can be used as an example of the greater selective fitness of the first word in a period where the ambiguity became more and more potentially intrusive because of the rise of England to being the dominant power in Europe.

As in evolutionary biology, variation is everywhere in language use. The mistake is not to stress its foundational status, but to understand it as contradicting the existence of structural categories. In the case of cultural niche constructs

such as languages, the opposite is in fact the case: if there were no structural categories, it would not even make sense to speak of variants. If there were not a presupposed category of postvocalic –r, it would not make sense to describe 'zero'
as a possible variant of postvocalic –r. If that category was taken out of linguistic
theory nothing would remain (in this case, quite literally!).

Expressed as a property of the cultural laws of *langue*, the same fact can be
expressed by saying that linguistic laws that determine what expressions 'count
as', and how to express certain meanings in the community include scope for
variation, just as the laws of the legal system permit scope for variable legal consequences, depending on the circumstances. If there were no cultural laws for
specifying how a given meaning could be expressed (or interpreted), there would
be no mechanism for assigning two interpretations the status of variational alternatives. They would just be different in the sense that everything is different from
everything else – the way the sound of a door closing is different from the colour
of the sunset. In the absence of laws, there would be nothing to describe either
for the student of variations in legal practice, or for the variational linguist (cf.
Harder 2010: 292 for a discussion of Croft's views on the issue of variation).

The bottom line is that variation presupposes structure. The more variation
there is, the harder it will be for learners to 'crack the code', i.e. to figure out the
laws that specify what it counts as in the community to use certain expressions,
or conversely, how to convey intended meanings to other members of the community. But a learner who gives up on figuring out what those laws are will not
be able to join the community. And if there are no structural laws, there can be no
speech community.

3.4 Structure and the lexicon

The last of the contested contrasts differs from the others in pertaining to language as such – i.e. it takes for granted that we can describe what 'a language' is
like. However, it is related to the other contrasts in that the more of the description you move into the lexicon understood as a list of individual expressions, the
less you leave for what is traditionally understood as grammatical structure.

This tendency is an aspect of 'construction grammar', which is currently
reconfiguring syntactic theory. Construction grammar does not eliminate traditional grammatical entities, such as categories that are abstract and relational.
They are, however, subsumed under the constructional format. Thus we can have
a 'subject-predicate' construction, viewed as an 'item' that enters into the aggregate of combined constructions that constitute a complete utterance. A grammar
is a list of items that enter into a relational matrix, such that complex construc-

tions 'inherit' the semantic, syntactic and phonological properties of the simpler constructions that enter into them, while adding properties of their own.[14]

From a functional point of view, the most striking fact about the descriptive format of construction grammar is that it is fundamentally oriented towards highlighting *components* rather than functional relations. In this it contrasts both with functional and formal syntax. The functional tradition that includes Foley and Van Valin (1984), Dik (1989), Hengeveld and Mackenzie (2008) describes how sentences are built up by layers with different functions, with verbs and arguments at the bottom and interpersonal (in cognitive grammar terminology, "grounding") elements at the top.

It is striking that this functionally based 'layered' structure has clear analogies to the hierarchical levels of generative grammar, cf. Siewierska (1992). This is not accidental: one would expect semantically and distributionally motivated categories to show a considerable degree of overlap, since linguists of all persuasions agree that meaning has a role to play in motivating the distribution of linguistic expressions. In section 2.1 above, I argued that what created syntactic structure (phylogenetically speaking) was the rise of functional relations *within* the utterance – in contrast to holophrastic utterances, where there is only a functional relation between the (a-syntactic) utterance and the (non-linguistic) *context*. From this perspective, formal syntax (to the extent distribution and semantics match up) is really a formalization of functional relations. This underground correlation between the two approaches is also reflected in the label of 'functional heads' as applied to the supra-lexical levels of the syntactic hierarchy.

The ideological thrust of construction grammar involves an assertion of the importance of the lexicon, cf. Goldberg's (1995) critique of the generativist description of the lexicon as the lunatic asylum of all irreducible irregularities. What you get up front in construction grammar is a list where *all* the syntax has been relocated so as to belong inside the items. This is illustrated in the diagrams in Croft and Cruse (2004: 227, 247 and 256), where the movement towards construction grammar is reflected in the fact that the levels gradually fade away as superordinate frames of description, leaving only the individual items.

The point here is to recognize that although this is an entirely valid description – the syntactic categories of the language are stamped into the properties of expressions at all levels from morphemes up to clause-length constructions – it

---

14 Let me point out also in this section that I think the constructional attack on the simplistic dichotomy (totally general-totally idiosyncratic) makes a valuable point. However, just as in the case of other new approaches that have pitted themselves against structure as traditionally understood, there is a danger that part of the truth may want so badly to be the whole truth that too little room is left over for a modified version of the other side.

would be misleading to let this be the whole story. Functional relations could not very well exist in items alone: if they did not also have a life of their own, it is inconceivable that they would be engraved in the items themselves.

What is left out, or backgrounded, in this description can be described in relation to the metaphor of 'cracking the code'. To the extent the code can be understood as a list, there is really no cracking to be done – there is only the task of mastering one construction at a time. That would be okay if the task of combining them was trivial. It can indeed be viewed like this, as 'simply' a matter of unification. But that would abstract away from the speaker's capacity to estab-lish functional relations between items; it is no accident that unification is an operation conceived within a purely mathematical, formal frame of reference. Functionally speaking, the task of cracking the code is a matter of figuring out how elements collaborate ('co-function') in bringing about a complete utterance meaning. Although a functional syntax can be distilled out of constructional descriptions (the information is there, although distributed over the individual constructions), it should also be given a separate place in the description so as to be recognized as a part of language that is inherently *non*-item-like.

In a *langue* perspective, functional relations exist as cultural laws saying that if you combine items of certain kinds in certain ways, you get an utterance with certain causal powers. To crack the code means to develop an internal procedural competency to handle (produce/understand) utterances that tap the affordances that such laws constitute. That competency depends on two abilities – in other words a dual mechanism, *pace* Dabrowska (2011): (1) the ability to retrieve the stored items from the mental 'constructicon', and (2) the ability to make them collaborate (co-function) in the right way. This last constitutes the competency that is specifically associated with functional syntax, which is effectively back-grounded in a constructional format.

Competencies constitute adaptations to *langue* as part of the way the world works in the niche. The verb 'internalize' is misleading about this process – because it does not necessarily follow that the laws as such are represented in the (adapted) mind/brain. It is too intellectualist in its associations, as it were – a procedural competency is about finding a way forward that works, not about intellectual categories. Combining linguistic expressions requires a procedural competency that (as pointed out by Pawley and Syder 1983, Sinclair 1991) is more taxing than mere retrieval.

This principle can also throw light on the last bastion of the innateness hypothesis, recursion (cf. Hauser, Chomsky and Fitch 2002 and the following debate). As pointed out by many authors (e.g., Givon 2009, and contributions to van der Hulst 2011), the specific rise of the morphosyntactic apparatus for clausal subordination will hardly support the dramatic significance assigned to this property in itself: recursive processes of understanding can also be triggered by paratactically organized sequences of sentences. Nevertheless, I believe there is something about recursive reapplication of linguistic operations that is significant as a feature of the human language ability also from a functional point of view. This feature can be described in continuation of the argument about constructions – about the distortion in putting all of syntax inside individual stored items.

Recursion offers the clearest contrast between the constructional approach and what I have called functional syntax. Its crucial functional dimension (cf. Harder 2011) is not the formal property of 'discrete infinity', but its affinity with the 'successor function' (cf. Hauser, Chomsky and Fitch 2002). The core of the ability to master the successor function is, as argued in Harder (2011), not in the upper reaches of the ability, marching on towards infinity – it is in taking the first step beyond what is entrenched: if a speaker can take the first step, the ability can be used again. Subitizing, cf. Chafe (this volume), is the skill of assigning a cardinality to small groups without going through a counting process – recognizing pairs up to e.g. 'fivesomes' when you see them. Subitizing thus involves building up entrenched routines, one for each number. But learning how to keep counting involves openness towards new cardinalities – just as open-ended combination of linguistic structures affords communication that goes beyond what is routinized and entrenched.

The possible step beyond entrenched routines that is the defining feature of the successor function may be regarded also as a key feature in the basic concept of cultural niche construction – the theoretical underpinning of the argument in this article. Reconstructing the cultural niche entails that existing routines are exposed to change – if the environment changes, the routines are not going to work in the same way as in the old environment where they arose. (An obvious example is the updating operations applied to computers and the havoc they may wreak on one's work routines). Functional feedback as an agent of change would not work unless there was an option of going a step beyond routines – responding to new selection pressures by recombining existing options in new ways. All functional options in language systems should be understood in the light of this 'successor function': they offer themselves as recombinable in unforeseen ways. Again, this approach shows what may be gained by aligning structure and function in the appropriate ways, and using them to show the untenability of the polarized opposition: Reduction to eternal unchangeable structure and reduction to entrenched routines are equally misguided as ways of describing languages.

Let me illustrate what I mean by an analogy. The Lego factory – one of the main success stories in Danish manufacturing history – went through a bad spell not so long ago. One explanation that was put forward was a new line of products, which consisted in models of modern and fascinating constructions such as space shuttles, formula 1 racing cars, etc. Like earlier products, they were built out of lego-style blocks – but they were designed so that there was a specific building routine associated with each product. Once you had managed to build the spacecraft, that was essentially it. You could take it to pieces and build it again, of course – but there was no obvious way to use the pieces to produce anything new. There was just the same routine.

This contrasted with the concept on which classic Lego was predicated, appealing to the ability to build an open-ended range of products – of the kind where you could always add another instalment if you wanted. Whether this was the explanation of the period of losses or not, the company reinvigorated the classic strategy and is now doing well again.

Issues like frequency and entrenchment have rightly figured prominently as part of the functionalist agenda; as epigrammatically expressed by Du Bois (1985), "grammars do best what speakers do most". The point I am making here, however, is that this, too, is a case where it is important not to try to push part of the truth into being the whole truth. Functionalists should reserve a visible space in their theory also for going beyond the frequent and entrenched. It is important what language makes it *possible* to do, not just what speakers as a matter of fact do most of the time. The fact that formal recursivity does not capture this property makes it all the more important that the option of combinatory creativity – which cannot be understood in terms of a list of items – is recognized explicitly in a functional theory of language.

3.5 Subject auxiliary-inversion: an illustration case

All the issues discussed above are designed to show that while all interesting structural relations must be understood and described in relation to function, functionalists also need to recognize the role of structure within a functional, usage based theory of language. I am going to illustrate this shared point by reference to an issue that has recently revived the 'tug-of-war' type of discussion between the two positions: subject-auxiliary inversion in English (=SAI).

The two main protagonists are Goldberg and Newmeyer. On several occasions Newmeyer (e.g. Newmeyer 1998, Borsley & Newmeyer 2009) has used SAI to argue for the need to recognize purely formal generalizations, regardless of functional properties – since there is no unitary function associated with it. From the functionalist side, however, Adele Goldberg (Goldberg 2006, summarizing Goldberg and del Giudice 2005), has argued that there is a functional dimension that a purely formal description would overlook. Rejecting the 'necessary-and-sufficient' conditions requirement, she suggests an account that has the same radial category structure as certain lexical items (cf. Lakoff 1987: 83), with the most general feature being that SAI clauses are 'nonpositive', i.e. deviate from the positive, pattern that is associated with classic assertive declarative sentences. Against this Borsley & Newmeyer (2009), citing Jackendoff (2007) for a similar position, point out that none of these properties, including non-positivity, are reliably associated with the SAI. In fact, there is double dissociation between the two: sentences without SAI also have those properties, and SAI sentences do not always have them.

The disagreement illustrates several issues that divide the two approaches, and which an account based on the premises of this article can hopefully help to clear up. The key point is the causal dimension of the evolutionary concept of function, which entails that in order for a meaning to be conventionally associated with an expression, the expression must be capable of *signalling* that meaning – it must reliably cause the meaning to be evoked in the minds of other members of the community. On that criterion 'non-positiveness' cannot be part of the general meaning of SAI. It is not the case in general that you can take non-inverted positive clauses and make them non-positive by inverting subject and auxiliary, or that hearing SAI one is entitled to infer non-positivity. What you can do is to infer non-positivity as part of the meaning of a *particular* construction – including, as one case where it occurs on its own, SAI used to signal yes-no interrogatives. In other cases, SAI is part of different constructions that also contains e.g. fronted negative adverbials (as in *Only then will he understand...*), the modal verb *may* (as in *may a million flies infest his armpits*, cf. Goldberg 2006: 172), etc. So in each of the different constructions it is the combination of this other feature with SAI that has 'a function' – not SAI in itself (cf. also Borsley & Newmeyer 2009: 141).

It may appear as if the argument tacitly accepts classical all-and-only categories as the touchstone of meaning-assignment. But that is in fact not the case. Goldberg invokes an analogy with a polysemous item such as *baby*, whose meaning varies polysemously between 'new-born child' and 'sexy partner' (and other meanings) – but there is a crucial difference here. The choice of the word *baby* with different variations is not constrained by co-occurrence with other items. Even though *yes sir, she's my baby* invokes a song in which it means 'partner', there is nothing in the language that prevents a proud father from presenting his new-born daughter with just that phrase. In other words, the variation in *baby* is a feature of the meaning potential of that particular expression, and whenever the speaker uses it, he brings that *same* variational potential to bear on the utterance meaning – and this constitutes the function of the lexical item.[15] Thus in my view Goldberg has not shown that "the set of constructions that exhibit SAI naturally form a coherent functional category" (Goldberg 2006: 167); I will return below to the question of what her argument *does* show.

This naturally raises the question: Does that mean that Newmeyer is right in saying that SAI proves the untenability of a functional approach to syntactic categories?

The answer is: not according to the logic of function-based structure. The apparent problem is due to the unfortunate ambiguity of the linguistic term *form*: it can mean both 'expression side' (as in "form vs. meaning") and 'structure' (as in "categories of form vs. categories of usage"). The crux of the matter is that SAI is inherently an *expression-side* feature of linguistic structure – not a content-side or semantic feature. It is uncontroversial from a functional point of view that there can be expression-side features that have no reliable content-side correlate. The syllable *be-* as in *behaviour, besides*, and *believe* has no reliable semantic function and therefore does not constitute a linguistic sign or conventional unit – and the same is true of SAI.

In terms of the topic of this article, the important thing is that what I have just provided is a *functional* description: only within a functional theory does it make sense to distinguish between those expression-side features that have a designated uniform function and those that only have functions in combination with other items. In terms of function-based structure this also has implications for how to understand their *structural* position: those which have their own content have a structural independence not shared by expressions that mean something only in combination with other items (thus *be-* as well as SAI are only *structural* units of English on the expression side). Thomsen (2003: 241) has described a gradual diachronic development in Danish compound verbs from one expression-side syntactic mechanism to another (roughly from German-style

---

15 To address a potential objection, let me show how this applies to the generalized syntactic subject construction, in spite of the variation in topicworthiness, including the existence of empty subjects. The answer has to do with the special conditions that obtain when a feature becomes obligatory. When speakers choose to express themselves by means of an indicative sentence type, subject obligatoriness means that they simultaneously undertake to nominate the most topic-worthy constituent as syntactic subject. In construction-grammatical terms, this constructional choice 'unifies' with other constructional choices, including verbs with zero valence (in which case there is no topic argument available) and presentational constructions (in which case the topic role is vacant because it is incompatible with the presentational function). The absence of topicworthy subjects in such cases can be explained by a clash between constructional specifications. There is no analogous logic that can explain the absence of non-positiveness in SAI cases like so can they!

compounding, as in *nedsætte,* to English-style 'satellite' constructions, such as *sætte ned*, both meaning 'lower' as in 'lower the price'). Here we have two syntactically distinct expression patterns, and it would be absurd also from a functional point of view to assume in advance that one pattern must by decree share a particular meaning which contrasts with a different meaning shared by instances of the other pattern. (It would be an instance of the same logic that may induce scientists to attribute a function to the pink colour of flamingos).

This does not imply that Goldberg's description of the semantic similarities is wrong – only that is has a different status than she claims. The pattern of semantically related SAI constructions has the same status as similarities between a group of different *lexical* items in a semantic field (which is clearly a usage-level category, not a structural category).[16]

From a panchronic evolutionary perspective one might go a step further: the non-structural, scatterplot relations between SAI constructions are partly the result of diachronic developments that have moved English away from a language state in which inversion was a more general feature of constituent order relations in English (associated with its development away from being a V2 language). Danish, which is a full-blown V2 language, has a very general distinction between assertion and non-assertion in which inversion plays a role (cf. Hansen & Heltoft 2011: 316); and thus the synchronic situation in English can to some extent be described in terms of what developments have *disrupted* the more general structural role that inversion previously had in English (just as the erstwhile unity of leg structure may be discernible in a panchronic evolutionary description of the different anatomies of horses and cows). The point in the context of this article is that functionalists also need to be clear about what constitutes a synchronic structural relation.[17]

---

16 There is an important point of principle about the strong and weak points of construction grammar which it would take us beyond the scope of this article to pursue: the extent to which it promotes a conflation of lexical and combinatorial properties. The main and important point in Goldberg (2006) is to stress the need for generalization that may get overlooked in a 'one-construction-at-a-time' approach. But the case of SAI as discussed above shows that it may not be obvious how construction grammar maintains the distinction between lexical and syntactic similarities.

17 The distinction is fully compatible with the existence of a cline between more or less productive cases – it points to the need to be clear about the extent of productivity in all cases. It is also compatible with the existence of cases where the same mechanisms apply to usage frequency and to categorical differences between grammatical and ungrammatical sentences. A case in point is Hawkins' (1994) theory of constituent order as reflecting processability, which provides motivation both for structural patterns (such as the fact that clausal objects cannot be clefted, cf *it is that it is cold that she claimed) and for usage patterns (the infrequency of that-clauses in subject position).

4 Conclusion

Niche construction is central to the argument in this paper, because it introduces a crucial component for the evolutionary understanding of structure and function in language: an evolving sociocultural environment. The co-evolutionary spiral of speakers and environment makes it possible to specify how it can be that language function is basic in relation to structure, while at the same time functional properties of linguistic utterances cannot be described without understanding their structure. On this story, the structure of a language such as Danish is primarily a property of a particular sociocultural niche: the Danish speech community. It is constituted by the set of cultural laws that specify what it 'counts as' to use and combine linguistic expressions in those particular ways that are covered by the laws.

Like other laws for cultural activities, such as the laws of soccer football, of neighbourly interaction or of bank transactions, these laws presuppose functional relations between the items that they structure. This does not mean that all of them are functionally optimal or even have a clearly identifiable function. It means, however, that each item should be investigated in terms of what contribution – if any – it makes to the successful execution of a larger process, and its structural position – if any – depends on the result of that investigation.

If the structure of language is entrenched in a set of cultural laws, this explains why it is not a property of any actual usage event, any more than the laws of football are the property of any actual football match – or even a property of the whole aggregate of usage events or football matches. This reflects a complexity that is built into human societies. They arise and undergo historical changes because cultural laws are superimposed upon natural laws, adding extra sets of causal relations to those provided by the physical laws of the universe.

Laws do not say everything there is to say about acts of usage, any more than criminal laws say everything about human behaviour. Describing language as it works in the social life that is channelled through acts of usage involves much more than describing the laws of language that are invoked. From an evolutionary point of view, the basic level is not that of the laws, but that of the actual variational spectrum of activities: they are what give rise to the continuing process of emergence of new laws out of the flow, and the obsolescence of old laws.

The overall structure of the argument above has been to show *first* that in language the most interesting kinds of structure are inherently part of a universe that includes functional relations – and *subsequently* show how, within such a function-imbued universe, structural and functional description need to go hand in hand. The view proposed goes against three other positions in the academic landscape: One is the classic generative position, whereby structure comes first and should be described independently of function; another is the cognitivist position whereby language structure is all in the head; the third is the 'usage fundamentalist' position whereby structure has no existence beyond individual acts of actual usage. But most of all, it is opposed to the kind of argument in which any concession to structure is regarded as one down for the functionalist position, and any concession to function is seen as a step towards denying the reality of structure.

References

Allen, Colin, Marc Bekoff, and George Lauder (eds.). 1998. *Nature's Purposes*. Cambridge, MA: MIT Press.

Andersen, Henning. 2006. Synchrony, Diachrony, and Evolution. In *Competing Models of Linguistic Change*, ed. by Ole Nedergaard Thomsen. Amsterdam: John Benjamins. 59–90.

Barlow, Michael and Suzanne Kemmer (eds.). 2000. Usage Based Models of Language. Stanford: CSLI Publications.

Bickerton, Derek. 2008. How central is recursivity? Symposium on the Genesis of Complex Syntax, Rice University, Houston, March 2008.

Borsley, Robert D. and Frederick I. Newmeyer. 2009. On Subject-Auxiliary Inversion and the notion "purely formal generalization". *Cognitive Linguistics* 20–1 (2009), 135–143

Boye, Kasper and Peter Harder. 2007. Complement-taking predicates: usage and linguistic structure. *Studies in Language* 31. 3, 569–606.

Boye, Kasper and Peter Harder. 2012. A usage-based theory of grammatical status and grammaticalization. *Language* 88, 1, 1–44

Boye, Kasper and Elisabeth Engberg-Pedersen (eds.). 2010. *Language Usage and Language. Structure*. Berlin/New York: De Gruyter Mouton.

Carnie, Andrew, Heidi Harley, and Maryann Willie (eds.). 2003. *Formal approaches to function in grammar: In honor of Eloise Jelinek*. (Linguistik Aktuell 62.) Amsterdam: John Benjamins.

Chomsky, Noam. 1986. *Knowledge of Language: Its nature, Origin and Use*. New York: Praeger.

Clark, Herbert H. 1996. *Using Language*. Cambridge & New York: Cambridge University Press.

Coseriu, Eugenio. 1974. [1958] *Synchronie, Diachronie und Geschichte: Das Problem des Sprachwandels*. München: Wilhelm Fink Verlag. Translated by Helga Sohre from *Sincronia, diacronia e historia: El problema del cambio lingüístico*. Montevideo: Universidad de la Republica.

Coseriu, Eugenio. 1975. [1952] System, Norm und Rede. *Sprachtheorie und Allgemeine Sprachwissenschaft*. München: Wilhelm Fink Verlag. Translated by Uwe Petersen from Sistema, norma y habla. *Revista de la Faculdad de Humanidades*, 9.113–177, Montevideo 1952.

Croft, William A. 1995. Autonomy and functionalist linguistics. *Language* 71, 490–532.

Croft, William A. 2000. *Explaining Language Change. An Evolutionary Approach*. London: Longman.

Croft, William A. 2001. *Radical Construction Grammar. Syntactic Theory in Typological Perspective*. Oxford: University Press.

Croft, William A. 2010. Ten unwarranted assumptions in syntactic argumentation. Kaspe Boye & Elisabeth Engberg-Pedersen (eds.) . 313- 354.

Croft, William A. and D.Alan Cruse. 2004. *Cognitive Linguistics*. Cambridge etc: Cambridge University Press.

Dahl, Östen. 2004. *The Growth and Maintenance of Linguistic Complexity*. Amsterdam & Philadelphia: John Benjamins.

Darwin, Charles. 1871. *The descent of Man, and selection in relation to sex*. Concise edition 2007. Selections and commentaries by Carl Zimmer; foreword by Frans de Waal.

Deacon, Terrence. 1997. *The Symbolic Species. The co-evolution of language and the human brain*. Harmondsworth: Penguin.

Deacon, Terrence. 2009. A role for relaxed selection in the evolution of the language capacity. *PNAS (=Proceedings of the National Academy of Sciences)* vol. 107, suppl. 2, pp. 9000–9007.

Diamond, Jared. 2005. *Collapse. How societies choose to fail or survive*. New York: Viking Penguin.

Dik, Simon C. 1989. *The Theory of Functional Grammar. Vol 1: The Structure of the Clause*. Dordrecht: Foris.

Du Bois, John. 1985. Competing motivations. In: Haiman, John (ed.) *Iconicity in syntax*. Amsterdam: John Benjamins, 343–365.

Everett, Daniel L. 2005. Cultural Constraints on Grammar and Cognition in Pirahã. *Current Antropology* 46, 4, 621–645.

Foley, William A. and Robert D. Van Valin. 1984. *Functional Syntax and Universal Grammar*. Cambridge: Cambridge University Press.

Fortescue, Michael, Peter Harder and Lars Kristoffersen (eds.). 1992. *Layered Structure and Reference in a Functional Perspective*. Amsterdam: John Benjamins.

Gibson, James J. 1979. *The Ecological Approach to Visual Perception*. Boston: Houghton Mifflin.

Givón, T. 1995. *Functionalism and Grammar*. Amsterdam: John Benjamins.

Givón, T. 2002. *Bio-linguistics: the Santa Barbara lectures*. Amsterdam: John Benjamins.

Givón, T. 2009. *The Genesis of Syntactic Complexity*. Amsterdam/Philadelphia: John Benjamins.

Givón, T. 2010. Where do simple clauses come from? In Kasper Boye and Elisabeth Engberg-Pedersen (eds.), 167–202.

Goldberg, Adele. 1995. *Constructions: A Construction Grammar Approach to Argument Structure*. Chicago: Chicago University Press.

Goldberg, Adele. 2006. *Constructions at work. The Nature of Generalization in Language*. Oxford: Oxford University Press.

Goldberg, Adele E. and Alex Del Giudice. 2005. Subject-auxiliary inversion: A natural category. *Linguistic Review* 22, 411–428.

Gould, Stephen Jay. 1992. *Bully for Brontosaurus*. Harmondsworth: Penguin

Gould, Stephen Jay and Richard C. Lewontin. 1979. The Spandrels of San Marco and the Panglossian Paradigm: A Critique of the Adaptationist Programme. *Proc. Roy. Soc. London* B 205 (1979), 581–598

Gould, Stephen Jay and Elisabeth S. Vrba. 1982. Exaptation–A Missing Term in the Science of Form. *Paleo biology* 8:4–15. Also in Colin Allen, Marc Bekoff and George Lauder (eds.) 1998, 519–540.

Greenfield, Patricia M. 1991. Language, tools and brain: The ontogeny and phylogeny of hierarchically organized sequential behavior, *Behavioral and Brain Sciences* 14: 531–595.

Hansen, Erik & Lars Heltoft. 2011. *Grammatik over det Danske Sprog*. København: Det danske sprog- og litteraturselskab.

Harder, Peter. 1996. *Functional Semantics. A Theory of Meaning, Structure and Tense in English*. Berlin: Mouton de Gruyter.

Harder, Peter. 2003. The Status of Linguistic Facts. Rethinking the Relation between Cognition, Social Institution and Utterance from a Functional Point of View. *Mind and Language* 18, 1, 52–76

Harder, Peter. 2010. *Meaning in Mind and Society. A Functional Contribution to the Social Turn in Cognitive Linguistics*. Berlin/New York: Mouton de Gruyter

Harder, Peter. 2011. Over the top. Recursion as a functional option. In Hulst, Harry van der (ed.). 233–244

Haspelmath, Martin. 2000. Why can't we talk to each other? Review of Newmeyer (1998). *Lingua* 110, 235–255.

Hauser, Marc D., Noam Chomsky and W. Tecumseh Fitch. 2002. The Faculty of Language: What Is It, Who Has It, and How Did It Evolve? *Science* 298. 1569–1579

Heine, Bernd and Tania Kuteva. 2007. *The genesis of grammar: A reconstruction*. Oxford: Oxford University Press.

Hengeveld, Kees and J. Lachlan Mackenzie. 2008. *Functional Discourse Grammar. A Typologically-Based Theory of Language Structure*. Oxford: Oxford University Press.

Hopper, Paul. 1987. Emergent Grammar. In: Aske, Jon, Natasha Beery, Laura Michaelis and Hana Filip (eds.), Proceedings of the Thirteenth Annual Meeting of the Berkeley Linguistics Society. Berkeley: Berkeley Linguistics Society.139–157.

Hulst, Harry van der (ed.). 2011. *Recursion and Human Language*. (Studies in Generative Grammar 104). Berlin/New York: De Gruyter Mouton.

Itkonen, Esa. 1978. *Grammatical Theory and Metascience*. Amsterdam: John Benjamins.

Itkonen, Esa. 2008. The central role of normativity for language and linguistics. In J. Zlatev, T. Racine, E. Sinha, & E. Itkonen, *The Shared Mind: Perspectives on Intersubjectivity*. Amsterdam/Philadelphia: Benjamins. 279–305.

Jackendoff, Ray. 2007. Linguistics in cognitive science. The state of the art. *The Linguistic Review* 24, 347–402.

Janssen, Theo and Gisela Redeker (eds.). 1999. *Cognitive Linguistics: Foundations, Scope, and Methodology*. (Cognitive Linguistics Research 15). Berlin/New York: Mouton de Gruyter.

Jespersen, Otto. 1892. *Studier over Engelske Kasus, med en Indledning: Fremskridt i Sproget*. University of Copenhagen.

Jørgensen, Jens Normann. 2010. *Languaging: Nine years of poly-lingual development of young Turkish-Danish grade school students*. Vol. 1, Copenhagen studies in bilingualism.The Køge series, vol. K15. København: Københavns Universitet, Det Humanistiske Fakultet.

Keller, Rudi. 1990. *Sprachwandel. Von der unsichtbaren Hand in der Sprache*. Tübingen: Francke

Krifka, Manfred. 2007. Functional Similarities between Bimanual Coordination and Topic/Comment Structure. *Interdisciplinary Studies on Information Structure* 08 (2007), ed. by S. Ishihara, S. Jannedy, and A. Schwarz, 61–96

Kristiansen, Gitte, Michel Achard, Rene Dirven, and Francisco J, Ruiz de Mendoza Ibàñez (eds.). 2006. *Cognitive Linguistics: Current Applications and Future Perspectives*. Berlin: Mouton de Gruyter.

Lakoff, George. 1987. *Women, Fire and Dangerous Things*. Chicago: University of Chicago Press.

Langacker, Ronald W. 2010. How not to disagree. The emergence of structure from usage. In
    Kasper Boye and Elisabeth Engberg-Pedersen (eds.), 107–143.
Lewis, David. 1969. *Convention: A Philosophical Study*. Cambridge, MA: Harvard University
    Press.
McWhorter, John H. 2005. *Defining Creole*. Oxford: Oxford University Press.
Newmeyer, Frederick J. 1998. *Language Form and Language Function*. Cambridge, MA: MIT
    Press.
Newmeyer, Frederick J. 2010. What conversational English tells us about the nature of grammar:
    A critique of Thompson's analysis of object complements. In Kasper Boye and Elisabeth
    Engberg-Pedersen (eds.), 3–43.
Pawley, Andrew K. and Frances H. Syder. 1983. Two puzzles for linguistic theory: nativelike
    selection and nativelike fluency, in: Jack C. Richards and Richard W. Schmidt (eds.),
    Language and Communication. London and New York: Longman, 191–226.
Pinker, Steven. 1994. *The Language Instinct. How the Mind Creates Language*. New York:
    William Morrow and Company.
Pinker, Steven. 2002. The Blank Slate. The Modern Denial of Human Nature. Harmondsworth:
    Penguin
Pinker, Steven and Bloom, P. 1990. Natural Language and Natural Selection. *Behavioral and
    Brain Sciences,* 13, 707–784.
Pinker, Steven and Ray Jackendoff. 2005. The Faculty of Language: What's Special about it?
    Cognition 95.2, March 2005, 201–236
Richerson, Peter J. and Robert Boyd. 2005. *Not by genes alone. How culture transformed human
    evolution*. Chicago and London: University of Chicago Press.
Russell, Bertrand. 2008. Mathematical Logic as Based on the Theory of Types. *American Journal
    of Mathematics* .Vol. 30, No. 3, Jul., 222–262. Also in Russell, Bertrand. 1956. *Logic and
    Knowledge,* London: Allen and Unwin.
Schleicher, August. 1865. *Über die Bedeutung der Sprache für die Naturgeschichte des
    Menschen*. Weimar: Hermann Böhlau.
Searle, John R. 1992. *The Rediscovery of the Mind*. Cambridge, MA.: MIT Press
Siewierska, Anna. 1992. Layers in FG and GB. In: Fortescue et al. (eds.), 409–432.
Sinclair, John McH. 1991. *Corpus, concordance, collocation*. Oxford: Oxford University Press.
Sinha, Chris. 1999. Grounding, mapping and acts of meaning. In Janssen and Reder (eds.),
    223–255.
Taylor, John R. 2006. Polysemy and the Lexicon. In Kristiansen et al. (eds.). 51–80.
Thomsen, Ole Nedergaard. 2003. Danish. In *Variationstypologie. Ein sprachtypologisches
    Handbuch der europaischen Sprachen in Geschichte und Gegenwart/Variational Typology.
    A Typological Handbook of European Languages Past and Present*, ed. by Thorsten
    Roelcke. Berlin/New York: Walter de Gruyter. 199–249.
Thompson, Sandra A. 2002. 'Object complements' and conversation. *Studies in Language* 26.1.
    125–164.
Tomasello, Michael. 1999. *The cultural origins of human cognition*. Cambridge, Mass: Harvard
    University Press.
Tomasello, Michael. 2008. *Origins of Human Communication*. Cambridge, MA: MIT press.
Trigger, Bruce G. 1998. *Sociocultural Evolution*. Oxford: Blackwell.
Verhagen, Arie. 2005. *Constructions of Intersubjectivity*. Oxford: Oxford University Press.
Wright, Larry. 1973. Functions. *The Philosophical Review*, Vol. LXXXII, 2: 136–68.
Wright, Larry. 1976. *Teleological Explanations*. Berkeley: University of California Press.

Wallace Chafe
Toward a Thought-Based Linguistics

An oversimplified view of current linguistics may see it as split into two major camps, often labeled "formalism" and "functionalism". Practitioners within each of these camps certainly do not agree on everything, but most formalists agree at least that there is some kind of formal syntactic system at the heart of language, that it can be represented with rules of some kind, and that a major task of linguistics – perhaps *the* major task – is to discover the nature of that system and the rules that generate it.

Linguists who find this way of understanding language limited, deficient, or misguided may all be called functionalists, but there is little else that unifies them. Their major interest may lie in cognitive linguistics, anthropological linguistics, sociolinguistics, psycholinguistics, pragmatics, discourse studies, corpus linguistics, language documentation, or elsewhere. There is no coherent answer to the question of what functionalism is, but its broad scope has the advantage of opening the door to a range of issues that can lead to a richer understanding of language in all its complexity.[1]

1 Language function

There are two ways of addressing the question of how something "functions". One way is to examine how it is used. A car, for example, is used for driving to the store or going on a trip. The other way is to examine how it performs that function: to investigate, for example, how a car is constructed by connecting an internal combustion engine to four wheels. When it comes to language and asking, first, how it is used, the most general (and seemingly obvious) answer is that language allows one individual to know something of what another individual is thinking. That use can be summarized by saying that language functions as a vehicle of communication. Sharing thoughts through language lets humans interact in a variety of productive ways that are unavailable to other living organisms.

How, then, does language make this communication possible? The most general (and again seemingly obvious) answer is that it associates thoughts with sounds, which, unlike the thoughts themselves, can pass through the air and in that way connect one mind with another. To be sure, the sounds may be repre-

---

1 This chapter is a digest of a longer work in progress titled How Thoughts Shape Language (and Vice Versa).

sented with written symbols like those you see before you now, and may even be replaced with hand movements, but the thought-sound association has been at the center of language throughout its history. At the same time, that association would not be possible if thoughts were not organized or structured in some way, and thus language functions not only to communicate thoughts but also to impose on them a structure they would not otherwise enjoy. The thought-sound association, in short, allows language to function as a complex means of communication while simultaneously organizing how we think.

2 Looking through the wrong end of the telescope

In 1982 the Swedish linguist Per Linell published a book titled *The Written Language Bias in Linguistics*. It was not widely circulated and had little influence on those whose bias he described, but it is worth recalling his insistence on the extent to which linguistics has relied on writing. The very term "grammar" is derived from the Greek for "letter". From Panini to the present, linguistics has been concerned above all with language as it is written. Behind this written language bias, however, lies another bias that is even more insidious. If language associates thoughts with sounds, the bulk of linguistic effort has tilted toward the sounds and away from the thoughts. Linguistics has for the most part been sound-based, not thought-based. It is not that all linguists are phoneticians, but that most linguists direct the bulk of their attention to elements of language that are, in the end, ways of organizing sounds.

In the comic strip "Pickles" of April 5, 2009 the protagonist Earl, while playing checkers with his friend Clyde, keeps repeating the word "plinth". He explains, "It's my word of the day. Every day I learn a new word. I read an article that said learning a new word every day will help your mind stay sharp." "So," asks Clyde, "what does 'plinth' mean?" "Oh, I have no idea. The article didn't say anything about learning what they mean." Linguistics today is less narrowly focused than Earl, but postulated components of language like sentences, words, prefixes, suffixes, and the rest have generally begun with their sounds and not their meanings. No one would deny, of course, that a word "has a meaning." But putting it that way implies that its meaning is something attached to it, something a word *has*, not something it *is*.

Linguists who have worked with unwritten languages may have noticed a problem when they try to teach the speakers of such languages to write them. It is ironic that the first step typically taken toward "revitalizing" an endangered language is to find a way to write it. There is an understandable wish to prepare language lessons in a written format, along with a tacit belief that written languages enjoy greater authority and prestige. Nevertheless, and especially for adults, the task of learning to write a language one has spoken all one's life but has never written turns out to be difficult and frustrating, with little chance of complete success. Writing forces one to pay attention to how a language *sounds*, but in the absence of writing one's attention is naturally directed toward the *thoughts* a language conveys. Shifting attention to its sounds can be an unfamiliar and difficult task.

But thoughts and sounds hardly play equivalent roles. Language begins with thoughts in the mind of a speaker and ends with an imperfect replica of those thoughts in the mind of a listener. The sounds are the medium through which communication is achieved, but they function only in service to the thoughts, where language begins and ends. Devoting the bulk of one's attention to sound-based elements, catching sight of thoughts only in the distance, is like looking through the wrong end of a telescope. If linguistic attention were commensurate with the relative importance of these two poles of language, thoughts would far outweigh sounds in the distribution of linguistic effort.

The bias toward sounds is of course fully understandable. Sounds are easy to observe and we understand them reasonably well. Their overt physical manifestations give us a good handle on them, and modern advances in electronic analysis let us investigate them in considerable detail. Thoughts are not like that at all. Their subjectivity places them well beyond the public observability that gives so much of an advantage to sounds. But if thoughts have the functional priority just described, as linguistics progresses in fits and starts toward a fuller understanding of language complexity, sooner or later it will be forced to shift more of its attention to the nature and fundamental role of human thinking.

3 What are thoughts anyway?

Because thoughts and language are so inextricably intertwined, language can contribute substantially to our understanding of the nature of thoughts. There may even be a temptation to equate the flow of thoughts with the flow of inner language, but it is important to realize that language is not the whole story. The lack of equivalence between thoughts and language can be observed in a variety of ways. People often experience difficulty "turning thoughts into words," explicitly recognizing the difficulty with statements like "I don't know quite how to say it" or "that's not exactly what I meant." One well-known scholar described this experience cogently in the following way:

> Now what seems to me obvious by introspection is that I can think without language. In fact, very often, I seem to be thinking and finding it hard to articulate what I am thinking. It is a very common experience at least for me and I suppose for everybody to try to express something, to say it and to realize that is not what I meant and then to try to say it some other way and maybe come closer to what you meant; then somebody helps you out and you say it in yet another way. That is a fairly common experience and it is pretty hard to make sense of that experience without assuming that you think without language. You think and then you try to find a way to articulate what you think and sometimes you can't do it at all; you just can't explain to somebody what you think (Chomsky 2000: 76).

This divide between thoughts and language is also observable in the hesitations, false starts, and rewordings that are scattered throughout much of ordinary speech. Interestingly enough, both introspection and disfluencies show that people routinely compare what they are thinking with how they are expressing it verbally, or how they might express it. Evidently people monitor their verbal options for organizing and expressing their thoughts, weighing the possibilities. Separately aware of what they are thinking and ways of verbalizing it, they may identify and evaluate discrepancies. Further evidence for this lack of equivalence between thoughts and their verbal expression is available when the same or similar thoughts are verbalized differently on different occasions (Chafe 1991, 1998, 2012). If thoughts were identical with language, verbalizing them would be a more straightforward task than it obviously is.

To what extent and in what form are thoughts themselves available to conscious inspection, apart from the way they are verbalized? Certainly much of thinking is pervaded by inner language, which parallels overt language in possessing both a thought-based and a sound-based component. The sound of language is experienced as auditory imagery, and it may be tempting to believe that auditory imagery is all that inner language is (cf. Jackendoff 1987: 291). But, just as with overt language, the auditory component is tied to thoughts. The fact that we are independently conscious of the thoughts is convincingly demonstrated by the familiar "tip-of-the-tongue" experience, first investigated systematically by Roger Brown and David McNeill (1966) and then in a number of other studies surveyed by Alan S. Brown (1991). During that mildly stressful experience we may be fully conscious of a thought, perhaps accompanied by visual or other nonverbal imagery and perhaps by an emotion as well. We know that the thought is associated with a sound, but for a greater or lesser period of time we cannot bring to consciousness what the sound is.

Other thoughts lack an association with sound altogether. An example might be the small sheath on the end of a shoelace that allows the lace to be passed easily through a small hole. A few people associate their thought of that object with the sound "aglet", but probably most who are totally familiar with the thought are ignorant of that sound. There is a resemblance to the tip-of-the-tongue experience, but the thought-sound association is not just temporarily lost, it never existed in the first place.

The independence of thoughts and auditory imagery is demonstrated in the opposite direction by rote learning: knowing the sounds of a song or poem, for example, with little awareness of their meaning. As a child I learned to sing "America the Beautiful" while giving no thought to the meaning of a "fruited plain". Often in the course of working with a language only partially familiar to me, I have recognized words as sounds alone (like Earl's "plinth"), failing to associate them with the thoughts that would dominate the consciousness of a native speaker. The biggest step in learning a new language is learning to hear sounds and associate them immediately with thoughts, bypassing the sounds themselves. These experiences illustrate the fragility of the thought-sound association on which language depends, an association that is disrupted in the tip-of-the-tongue experience and, in the opposite direction, in rote learning. Its fragility, alas, increases with age.

Can one be conscious of nothing more than a thought when it fails to be accompanied, not just by auditory imagery, but by imagery of any kind? There are differences in the extent to which people experience imagery at all (e.g., Poltrock and Brown 1984), opening the possibility of wholly imageless thought, a topic that was actively investigated before behaviorism discarded it as irrelevant (Humphrey 1951). When William James asked people about the images they had of their breakfast table, he reported that:

> an exceptionally intelligent friend informs me that he can frame no image whatever of the appearance of his breakfast-table. When asked how he then remembers it at all, he says he simply '*knows*' that it seated four people, and was covered with a white cloth on which were a butter-dish, a coffee-pot, radishes, and so forth. The mind-stuff of which this 'knowing' is made seems to be verbal images exclusively (James 1890, p. 265).

Was his friend experiencing imageless thought? The answer depends on how we interpret James's phrase "verbal images". James may have believed that his friend experienced nothing more than the sounds of language, or auditory imagery. More interesting, however, is the possibility that his friend was conscious of thoughts that for him lacked imagistic accompaniments of any kind. That is the more interesting possibility because it implies that those imageless thoughts were enough to let James's friend "know" what was on his breakfast table. The possibility of totally imageless thought is surely worth further study, now that the hold of early twentieth century prejudices has been loosened.

4 Two views of language design

Figure 1 summarizes two contrasting perspectives on the design of language, with the currently more popular view on the left. Language is centered there on syntax, which functions as the driving force for semantics (organized thoughts) and phonology (organized sounds). The view on the right sees language driven by the thoughts that are consciously experienced by both speakers and listeners. A sound-based linguistics settles on syntax as its chief object of study. If one takes a thought-based perspective, the determining function assigned to syntax on the left seriously distorts language's true nature.

For thoughts to be verbalized by a speaker they must first be structured in accordance with a language's unique semantic resources. But before the resulting semantic structures are passed on to sounds, they in turn must be modified in several ways that combine to yield a syntactic structure. The meanings of idioms and grammatical constructions that have arisen in the course of a language's history must first be replaced by their literal and historically earlier counterparts, because those (rather than the semantic elements behind them) are the structures expressed by sounds. The resulting "quasi-semantic" structures must also be ordered in temporally linear constructions that are required by the linearity of sounds, and probably also by a human need to operate in terms of a relatively small number of combinatory patterns. These processes of "literalization", "linearization", and "patterning" yield a syntactic structure that can be submitted successfully to a language's phonology.

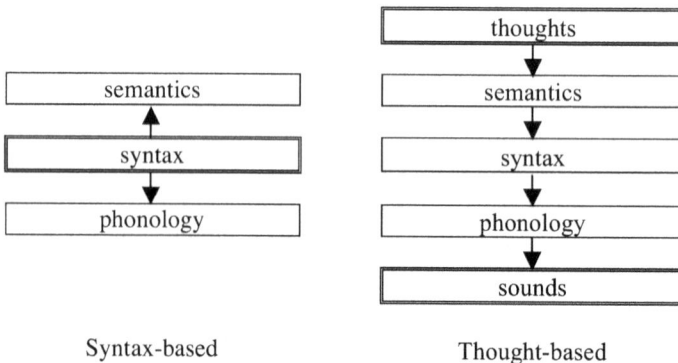

Figure 1: Two views of language design

Now, entertain conjecture that discovering the structure of a language is like climbing a mountain. In most of linguistics the summit, thoughts, is so enshrouded in fog that nearly everyone is satisfied with establishing a base camp farther down. Focusing on sounds lets one keep both feet on the ground of physical observations, where disagreements can be resolved in objective terms. But many linguists are bold enough to continue upward at least to phonology, where they can explore what different languages do with sounds. They may be content at that level, and ascending to syntax does call for greater risks and disagreements. Those who proceed to that level are usually willing to accept it as their final goal. There are others, however, who struggle on to semantics, hoping for a view that is more revealing. The air is thinner and the fog thicker and there is more disagreement on what is there, but the potential rewards are enticing. Few are foolish enough to venture still further into the realm of thoughts, where the air is so thin and the fog so thick that one easily falls victim to vertigo and hopeless confusion. This chapter samples a few forays in that direction, hoping for glimpses that are otherwise unobtainable, when and if the fog lifts, if only momentarily.

Details of the thought-to-sound progression summarized on the right side of Figure 1 present a topic far too large and far too complex to be explored here in detail, and of course there is a huge amount left to be discovered. Here we can simply note why each stage has its own validity – the nature of thoughts themselves, why thoughts and semantic structures differ, why syntax intervenes before semantic structures are passed on to phonology, and what separates phonology from sounds themselves. These stages do not constitute an ordered series that speakers actually follow as they speak, either consciously or unconsciously. Rather, they help to *explain* how it is that a language expresses a particular thought with a particular sound. The explanation necessarily includes historical changes responsible for a particular thought-sound association. Obviously those changes are not themselves part of a speaker's knowledge, which only operates with their results. Conscious awareness is limited to the thoughts and the sounds, not to the processes that bring them together.

5 Thought structure

| thoughts | ⟵ | ? |

Figure 2: How are thoughts structured?

How can we describe thoughts without simply falling back on whatever language might be used to express them? Thoughts are so tied to language that it is easy to despair of representing them in any other way. Nevertheless, by identifying components of thought that are expressed by all languages in some way, we may succeed in discovering constant properties of thoughts themselves, properties that are independent of whatever constraints are imposed on them by a particular way of expressing them in a particular language at a particular time.

This approach suggests that thoughts are built on what can appropriately be called "ideas" – basic units of mental experience. They include ideas of "events" (things that happen) and "states" (the way things are), and they are nearly always accompanied by ideas of persons, objects, or abstractions that participate in those events and states. The latter are sometimes called "referents" or "entities", but here, following Langacker (2008: 105), I will call them simply "things". Various linguists have noticed the impossibility of experiencing the idea of a particular event or state without including within it the idea of one or more participants – one or more things (cf. Givón 2001: 53, Croft 2001: 87, Langacker 2008: 1004). In the other direction, however, it *is* possible to experience the idea of a thing without associating it with any particular event or state.

It always helps to be able to refer to an example, and even better an example derived from actual talk. The brief phrase in (1) may seem ridiculously simple, but it is enough to provide an initial basis for discussion. In the course of a certain conversation, a woman who will here be called Gloria focused her attention on what she remembered of a coherent series of events in which she had been a participant – a coherent "topic" (Chafe 1994: 120–136). The events included in this topic occurred while she was on her way home from work one evening. Her memory of those events was stimulated by a question from her interlocutor, but that larger context need not concern us here. We can notice simply that Gloria introduced her topic by establishing a temporal orientation for what followed.

(1) I was working late,

Still within the realm of thought, ideas of events, states, and their participants can be visualized as situated within a multidimensional thought space, a space whose dimensions include time, space, epistemology, emotions, interaction with an interlocutor (an interpersonal orientation), and placement in the surrounding context (a textual orientation; cf. the "metafunctions" of Halliday 1985). The event verbalized in (1) was oriented as *remembered* and *in progress*. Gloria thought, furthermore, that the idea of this event was not already active in her hearer's consciousness, while the idea of herself *was* already active for her hearer because, after all, she was the person speaking.

We need to realize in addition that thoughts include both imagery and emotions. Gloria's image of working after hours must have included perceptual details unavailable to her interlocutor, who may well have formed her own idiosyncratic image of the event as she listened to what Gloria said. The same can be said of emotions. Gloria must have experienced her own attitude toward the event, while her listener may have felt differently about it.

In short, the thought with which Gloria began was focused on the idea of an event that was remembered as having been in progress. She was introducing it to her listener as something new, but the idea of herself, its agent, was already "in the air." How these ideas and these orientations came to be represented, first semantically and then syntactically, is discussed in the two sections to follow.

6 From thoughts to a semantic structure

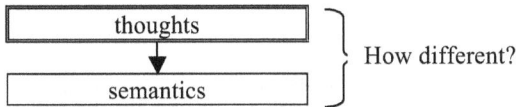

Figure 3: Thoughts versus semantics

Each language structures thoughts in accordance with its own semantic resources, although there may be significant overlap from one language to another. But how and why is this semantic structuring different from the thoughts themselves? Two anecdotes from my own past are worth mentioning.

In my early work with the Seneca language I recorded and transcribed several renditions of a ceremonial speech that the speaker and his listeners regarded as the same speech each time it was performed (Chafe 1961, Foster 1974). To be sure, there were places in the speech where established formulas were repeated, but transcriptions made it clear that the language of the speech as a whole was by no means the same from one rendition to another. Those who performed and listened to it, however, were not concerned with verbatim wording but with the thoughts the words conveyed, and it was those thoughts that were experienced as the same each time.

Turning to language of a different kind, in the 1970s a group of us in Berkeley produced a short film that has come to be known as the Pear Film (Chafe 1980). Our principal aim was to see how different people and speakers of different languages would verbalize their memories of what happened in the film. Of interest here is the fact that some people told their narratives on more than one occasion, following a technique resembling Frederic Bartlett's "method of repeated reproduction" (Bartlett 1932: 63–94), except that the language was spoken and not written (Chafe 1986). To verbalize her thoughts of a man who was picking pears in a tree and failed to notice that a boy was stealing his pears, one woman spoke as follows on three separate occasions, using markedly dissimilar words to express thoughts that were similar if not the identical (Chafe 1991):

(1) a. and [the boy] looks up at ... at the man who's up the ladder,

b. and the man doesn't know that the little boy is there.

(2) a. ... and ... the man is still up in the tree,

b. ... oblivious to ... to ... the this boy stealing his pears.

(3) a. ... but the man up in the tree,

b. ... didn't notice this boy down here at all.

The Seneca speeches, the pear stories, and other observations of this kind clearly showed a distinction between people's thoughts and how they were verbalized, with the same thoughts related not only to different syntax but also to different semantic structures at different times. But are semantic structures different in kind from thoughts themselves? There are several reasons why a thought as such cannot be represented directly by sounds, but especially important is the impossibility of assigning a different sound to each particular idea experienced by a particular speaker at a particular time. A century ago Franz Boas remarked:

> Since the total range of personal experience which language serves to express is infinitely varied, and its whole scope must be expressed by a limited number of phonetic groups, it is obvious that an extended classification of experiences must underlie all articulate speech (Boas 1911: 18).

What a language does, of course, is assign a particular idea to a *category*, where the idea is interpreted as an instance of something already familiar. The category then makes it possible for the idea to be associated with a sound, thus solving Boas's problem, while at the same time relating the idea to others that are instances of the same category. Edward Sapir summarized this need for categorization as follows, using "concept" for what is here called an "idea":

> We must cut to the bone of things, we must more or less arbitrarily throw whole masses of experience together as similar enough to warrant their being looked upon – mistakenly,

but conveniently – as identical. This house and that house and thousands of other phenomena of like character are thought of as having enough in common, in spite of great and obvious differences of detail, to be classed under the same heading. In other words, the speech element "house" is the symbol, first and foremost, not of a single perception, nor even of the notion of a particular object, but of a "concept," in other words, of a convenient capsule of thought that embraces thousands of distinct experiences and that is ready to take in thousands more (Sapir 1921: 13).

Three points are important to mention. First, a categorized idea retains a direct relation to a thought, not to a sound. It is a prime example of language-imposed thought-structuring. I will indicate the thought-related status of a category by labeling it in italics: Gloria categorized her idea as an instance of the event category we can label *work-late*. Second, every language offers its own unique collection of semantic resources, and prominent among them is a huge inventory of categories. This inventory may overlap to a greater or lesser extent with that of other languages, but no two languages are identical in this respect. Third, it is not unusual for a category to combine formerly separate elements into familiar "collocations" – elements that have occurred so often and so usefully together that they have coalesced into a single semantic unit, as with *eat-breakfast*. I will indicate the unitary status of a collocation with a hyphen, as with *work-late*.

In addition to categorized ideas, there are some that are contextually identifiable in a way that allows them to enjoy their own, already established association with a sound, as with a proper noun or pronoun. The idea of Gloria might variously be verbalized with "Gloria", "Mrs. Jones", or in some other way. In the present case, because she was the speaker, she could communicate the idea of herself with the first person pronoun. We can thus distinguish the *categorization* of the event with *work-late* from the *identification* of its participant with *I*.

The thought-related orientations of this event and its participant find counterparts in semantic features that often have traditional linguistic labels. Thus, we can say that the thought orientation as being *remembered* was represented semantically as *past*, the orientation *durative* as *progressive*, the orientation *not active for the hearer* as *new*, and the orientation *already active for the hearer* as *given*. These may appear to be nothing more than different labels for elements of thought, the only real difference being the assignment of the idea of the event to the category *work-late*, and the assignment of the idea of its participant to the pronoun *I*. All the semantic labels, however, are no longer informal descriptions of elements of thought, but choices from the semantic resources of English.

There is an important issue here. The parallelism between the semantic structure and the thought suggests that the thought itself was a mirror of what English semantics made available – that Gloria's thinking, in other words, was shaped by her speaking. This feedback from language into thought has been convincingly demonstrated by Dan Slobin (1996) and Melissa Bowerman (1996), and it has been well labeled with Slobin's phrase "thinking for speaking". But what of thinking that has not been organized for speaking?

Another personal anecdote may be revealing. In the Seneca language there are four ways to translate the English pronoun "we". The individuals involved may number two ("dual") or more than two ("plural"), but in addition they may include the hearer ("inclusive") or not ("exclusive"). I have never fully integrated this four-way distinction into my own thinking, where my native language does not require it. Attempting to speak Seneca, I find myself falling back most often on the plural exclusive form and being corrected, perhaps with the dual inclusive. The unavoid-ability and automaticity of these distinctions for Seneca speakers suggests that the dual-plural and inclusive-exclusive distinctions are an integral part of their think-ing, whether they are speaking or not. They are absent from my own thinking and require a conscious effort to apply. If asked, I know of course whether there are two or more than two people, and whether the hearer is one of them or not. But I do not normally think that way. For Seneca speakers, in contrast, they are evidently distinctions that extend beyond thinking for speaking alone.

Against this background, we can look back at the pear narrative excerpts quoted above, spoken at different times by the same person:

(1) a. and [the boy] looks up at ... at the man who's up the ladder,

     b. and the man doesn't know that the little boy is there.

(2) a. ... and ... the man is still up in the tree,

     b. ... oblivious to ... to ... the this boy stealing his pears.

(3) a. ... but the man up in the tree,

     b. ... didn't notice this boy down here at all.

The speaker interpreted her idea of the man ignoring the boy as an instance of three semantic categories: *not-knowing*, *being-oblivious to*, and *not-noticing*. These choices were applied to the same thought, or something close to the same thought. The choice in (3) was the negation of the *event* of noticing, in contrast to the *states* in (1) and (2): *not knowing* and being *oblivious to*. If the event-state distinction is present in the realm of thought, we have here another case of feed-back from semantics into thinking. Thoughts, we can say, are easily influenced by how they are "semanticized". We will see below how syntax may feed back into thoughts as well.

7 From semantics to syntax

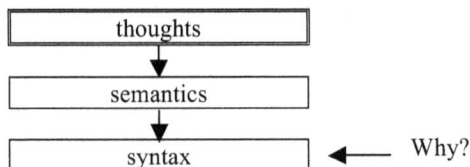

Figure 4: Why syntax?

Why is it that semantic structures are not represented directly by phonology and sounds? Why does syntax intervene? This question is seldom asked, but it has always hung over my own understanding of language. As outlined above, I would suggest that an uninterrupted passage from semantics to phonology is impossible for at least two reasons and probably a third. First, languages are significantly affected by "lexicalization", a term covering the diachronic formation of idioms and grammatical constructions (Chafe 2008). The passage to sounds demands that the output of those processes be replaced by their historical origins, a process we can call "literalization". Second, sounds are unavoidably linear in time to an extent that surpasses the linearity of semantic elements, and thus unordered elements of a semantic structure must be temporally ordered. We can speak of "linearization". As a probable third factor, there are likely to be mental processing limitations that confine syntax to a restricted number of combinatory patterns, although these patterns differ radically across languages.

As an example, a semantically unitary collocation must be expanded or "literalized" into its historically earlier constituent elements: separate words or word parts. To return to Gloria's phrase, the unitary collocation *work-late* is represented in its syntactic structure by the words "work" and "late", linearized in that order, and in this case preceded by the subject "I".

More complex is the literalization of the *progressive* orientation into the discontinuous "be ...-ing" construction, which reflects several layers of English language change. Its history is discussed in the Middle English Grammar of Mustanoja (1960). In Old English there were two constructions: one a participial construction with an "-end" ending (Nickel 1966), the other a gerundial construction with an "-ing" ending and a preceding preposition "on". In the thirteenth century "-end" fell together with "-ing" and the distinction between the two constructions was blurred. The "on" was later reduced to "a-", as in "he was a-coming". When this last usage became archaic, English was left with "he was coming" as its way of verbalizing the semantic element *progressive*.

Students of idioms have observed that people are often conscious of the literal meanings of idioms (e.g., Gibbs 1994), a phenomenon I have characterized in terms of "shadow meanings" (Chafe 2008: 265). The idiom "spill the beans" has been a favorite example. It expresses the idea of prematurely disclosing a secret, but while that idea occupies the foreground of consciousness, one might also experience a mental image of beans being spilled, including the kind of beans, the container they were spilled from, and the direction of the spill (Lakoff 1980). In the present case, if Gloria had verbalized her thought, not with "I was working late" but "I was burning the midnight oil," one might experience a shadow image of an oil lamp at night. The presence and nature of a shadow meaning may vary from person to person, and surely oil lamps were more salient at an earlier time, but the point here is that syntactic elements have the potential to feed back into thoughts themselves.

In Gloria's "I was working late," the copula combined the semantic orientation *past* and agreement with the first person subject in the word "was". Less obvious was the attachment of the copula to the preceding word in "I was", a change that would be more obvious if Gloria had said "I'm working late", contracting "I am" to "I'm" The result is the syntactic sequence of words and word parts in Figure 5, which includes the relevant constituent structure.

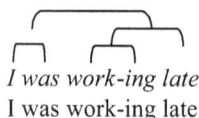

I was work-ing late
I was work-ing late

Figure 5: A syntactic representation

Figure 5 raises another question of interest. In the sequence of stages from thoughts to sounds, at what point are thought-based elements directly symbolized by sound-based elements? That the brain recognizes a disconnect between thought-based and sound-based elements is well demonstrated by the tip-of-the-tongue experience discussed earlier. The progression from thoughts through semantics to syntax aims at structures amenable to direct symbolization by sounds, and thus it is realistic to regard syntax as Janus-faced, pointing one way toward thoughts, the other toward sounds. The elements included in Figure 5 have allegiances in both directions, as suggested by spelling them both with italics (for thought-based elements) and without (for those that are sound-based). In the Pickles cartoon described in section 2, Earl repeated "plinth" with no awareness of *plinth*.

8 From syntax to phonology and sounds

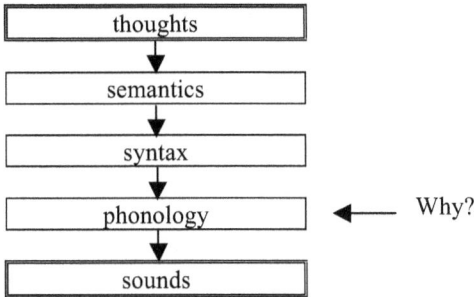

Figure 6: From syntax to sounds

We can ask finally why an intermediate stage of phonology needs to be recognized between the sound-based face of syntax and sounds themselves. Here too the answer lies in language change, as when Gloria pronounced *working* as *workin*. In this less elegant or more casual register, English has introduced a phonological change from "ng" to "n". It is an example of language change in progress, captured by distinguishing phonology from sounds themselves.

Superimposed on this result was a prosodic structure imposed by the interpersonal given-new orientation, combined with the textual orientation of more to come. The entire phrase moved from low to increasingly higher prominence, with a lengthened rising pitch at the end. The resulting pitch contour is suggested by the tracing of fundamental frequency in Figure 7, where a possible transcription is shown as well.

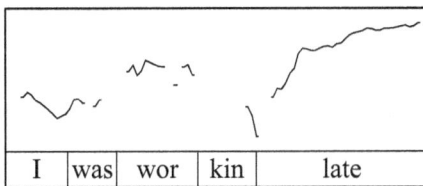

I was WOR-kin LATE ↗

Figure 7: Addition of prosody

9 Thought and language as a continuous flow

This suggested thought-based explanation of a simple English phrase aimed for a fuller understanding of the relation between thoughts and sounds. Several implications are worth adding, and we can begin by noticing that syntactic structures are customarily represented as isolated and invented samples of language devoid of context. Although space has limited the discussion here to this brief example, I have tried to embed it in the ongoing flow of thoughts and language. In a more detailed study it would be desirable to represent the flow itself, something impossible with isolated tree diagrams confined to two dimensions within a very small space. Modern technology opens the possibility of enjoying representations that are more detailed and constantly changing. A suggestive comparison is a musical score, where constantly changing, multidimensional sound is represented on separate staves that are not confined to a single page. As a further advantage, computational representations need not be confined to pages at all. One can hope eventually to arrive at ways of representing the flow of thoughts and language that are fuller and more realistic.

10 Does language shape thoughts?

The question of whether people who speak different languages think differently goes back at least to German scholars like Johann Gottfried von Herder, Wilhelm von Humboldt, and Heymann Steinthal. It was brought back into the foreground with the writings of Benjamin Lee Whorf from 1927 to 1941 (Whorf 1956). Strong opinions continue on both sides of this question. Those who are convinced that Whorf was totally misguided often express their opinions emotionally and ad hominem. Geoffrey Pullum described Whorf as a "Connecticut fire prevention inspector and weekend language-fancier" (Pullum 1991: 163), and Pieter Seuren wrote of "an amateur linguist who, as a mature student, took courses with Sapir during his years at Yale and, for some time, gained popularity with the American anthropological establishment" (Seuren 1998: 189). Steven Pinker wrote that Whorf's suggestion "is wrong, all wrong! The idea that thought is the same thing as language is an example of what can be called a conventional absurdity: a statement that goes against all common sense but that everyone believes because they dimly recall having heard it somewhere and because it is so pregnant with implications" (Pinker 1994: 56–57).

In the context of this chapter Whorf can be seen as prescient in his concern for relating language and thought. If he sometimes went too far, that is hardly surprising and is not an issue here. What is worth noting is that suggestions regarding the thought-language relation have been widely and deliberately misunderstood. To suggest that language influences thought is not at all to say that "thought is the same thing as language" as in the quote from Pinker. In section 3 above we saw some obvious reasons for distinguishing the two.

It has been particularly misleading to see this question as asking whether "differences in thought ... can be conditioned by differences of grammatical structure" (Jackendoff 1994: 186). If one accepts the view of language advocated here, it is clear that the issue is the relation between thoughts and *semantic*, not *syntactic* ("grammatical") structures. The latter by their very nature – by definition – are removed from a direct relation to thoughts. We have seen how lexicalization and linearization distort syntactic structures to increase their distance from thoughts. Asking whether *syntactic* structures influence thoughts is pointless. If the question, on the other hand, is whether different languages provide their speakers with different *semantic* resources, it is apparent that they do. No one doubts that different languages organize *sounds* in different ways, and surely they differ at least as much and probably much more in the ways they organize *thoughts*, despite the commonalities that do exist.

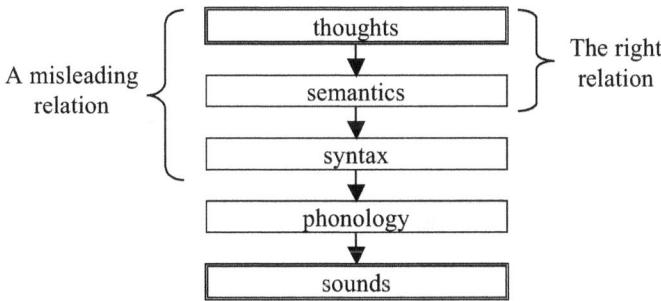

Figure 8: Where language and thoughts do and don't relate

If the way one thinks as one is speaking does differ across languages (Slobin's "thinking for speaking"), we are left with the question of the extent to which all of thinking – not only its verbal component – is affected by the different semantic resources of different languages. If an important component of thinking is verbal – inner language – certainly that much of thought cannot avoid being affected by language differences. Aspects of thought that are not verbal but, say, imagistic and emotional may be freer to go their own ways regardless of one's language. In all probability the influence of verbalized thought on the totality of thought differs with different situations, different individuals, and different cultures, with some cultures encouraging either verbal or nonverbal thinking to different degrees. Language necessarily influences how we think when we speak aloud and also when we speak to ourselves, but that can be only part of the full story.

Implicit in the above is the distribution of universality and particularity among the stages of language production. Because syntax is the product of highly specific, language-particular diachronic changes (lexicalization, linearization, pattern formation), it is obviously the place where languages can be expected to differ the most. It is thus ironic that it should be the place where so many have searched for "universal grammar". Surely semantics should take priority in this search. While there are important differences in the semantic structures of different languages, they are multiplied considerably in syntax. In the end one wonders whether thoughts are not the place where speakers of different languages agree the most. Although differing semantic structures surely feed back into those thoughts, that is a matter of feedback and only when one is overtly or covertly verbalizing. When it comes to universals, they may be maximally present in thoughts, a bit less in semantics, and much less in syntax.

11 Interdisciplinary convergence

Finally, it would seem that thoughts are the place where disciplines outside of linguistics can contribute the most. Semantic, syntactic, and phonological structures are primarily the concerns of linguists, but thoughts offer themselves eagerly to interdisciplinary convergence, as suggested in Figure 9.

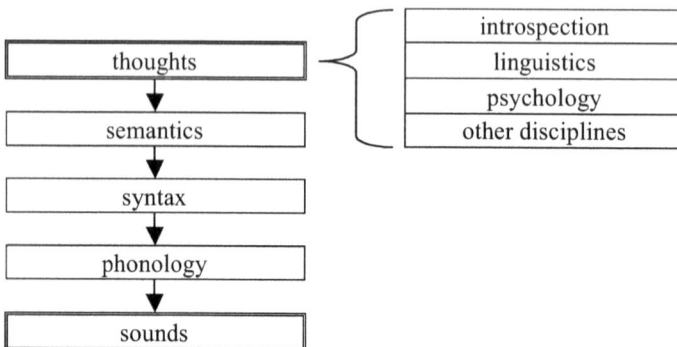

Figure 9: Interdisciplinary convergence on thoughts

As a simple and easily appreciated illustration of this convergence, we can consider how thoughts deal with very small numbers of things. To begin with introspection, when you look at Figure 10 you undoubtedly know immediately, accurately, and confidently that the rectangle on the left contains three happy faces. You may also know that the rectangle on the right contains eleven, but only because you counted them. The two experiences are very different.

Against the background of those introspective observations, we can turn to linguistic typology and particularly the comprehensive study of number marking by Greville Corbett (2000). Languages range from marking number optionally if at all, through marking a singular-plural distinction, or singular-dual-plural, or singular-dual-trial-plural. Corbett examined evidence for a quadral marking in several Austronesian languages and concluded that the forms in question were not restricted to precisely four, but were rather a type of "paucal".

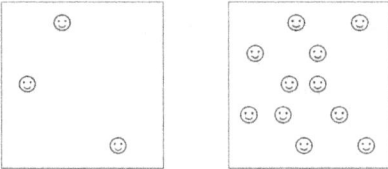

Figure 10: Collections of Happy Faces

It is worth asking whether this special way of thinking about very small numbers relates to human needs. People do frequently need to think and behave differently depending on whether there are one, two, or three of something, whereas they seldom need to think or behave differently depending on whether there are twenty-six or twenty-seven. The widespread importance of *two* reflects a wide range of real-world circumstances favoring that number: the symmetry of the human body (two eyes, two hands, and so on), the frequent salience of dyadic relations in society (men and women, parents and children, Democrats and Republicans), and more abstract oppositions like good and bad, large and small. When it comes to three, the special salience of that number in folklore and music has been discussed, for example, by Alan Dundes (1980), and for music by Rozin et al. (2006).

The observation that we have a special way of processing very small numbers has intrigued psychologists since the nineteenth century. W. Stanley Jevons wrote in *Nature* in 1871 about 1,017 trials, during each of which he threw some black beans toward a white box in such a way that anywhere between one and fifteen beans landed randomly in the box. Each time, he immediately guessed at the number in the box and found that he was always accurate up to four, but that with five he already made an occasional error. Somewhat later, working with two subjects in addition to himself and with a more complex apparatus, Howard C. Warren concluded that "except under special stress of attention, or with subjects especially apt in this direction, the function of perceptive counting [as he called it] is limited to the numbers One, Two and Three" (Warren 1897: 589). The term "subitize" was introduced for this phenomenon in the 1940s by psychologists at Mount Holyoke College (Kaufman et al. 1949). Subitizing and counting rely on entirely different mental processes, and some psychologists have tried to identify what those processes are and how they relate to more general mental abilities. A useful review of relevant research has been provided by Trick and Pylyshyn (1993, 1994).

We saw earlier how a particular thought is interpreted as an instance of a semantic category, thereby acquiring the sound of a word and at the same time associating the thought with other instances of the same category. We might interpret our idea of a particular animal as an instance of a category that allows us in English to associate it with the sound "dog", while also raising expectations that the animal may bark, chase squirrels, and make a good pet. Suppose, then, that we also possess categories of twoness and threeness that lead us to interpret particular groups of objects as instances of those categories. Categorization, in other words, may apply to both examples in Figure 11: on the left an instance of the dog category, on the right an instance of threeness. The latter, of course, does not necessarily lead to an overt marking of trial number, but in any case it offers this category as an immediate thought-organizing device.

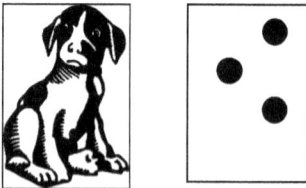

Figure 11: Instances of the dog and threeness categories

If we operate with small number categories, why should they be limited to two or three? Might not some language somewhere offer a *seventeenness* category that would create immediate recognition of that many items? Such a category seems unlikely, of course, and we might see it as excluded by capacity limitations on focal consciousness, limitations that would be far exceeded by a display of seventeen items. If the latter were categorized at all, it might be as an instance of a texture.

This has been a relatively simple example of how introspection can be supported by evidence from both linguistics and psychology to bring us to a fuller understanding of a frequently encountered and easily observable mental phenomenon. Introspection alone is suggestive and may even be ultimately determining, but it benefits from support by more systematically accumulated and publicly observable evidence. In the end all these observations and more need to be incorporated within a more comprehensive theory of mental processing. Linguistics shows how such phenomena affect the ways languages organize thoughts, while psychology aims to specify their precise nature and relate them to processes of greater generality.

We may regret that linguistic typologists are unaware of research on subitizing, while the relation of the latter to number-marking in languages is not something that has occurred to psychologists. A similar situation exists with the desirability of relating the ways languages mark tense to the psychology of memory, but that is a topic for another day. Potential convergences like these and many more offer a vast field for future exploration. Obviously there are countless aspects of human experience that are manifested in both thought and language. Understanding them better can profit immeasurably from explanations that allow evidence of many kinds to converge on a richer result.

12 Summary

We began with the obvious observation that language enables one person to know what another person is thinking, a function it accomplishes by (1) associating thoughts with sounds and (2) giving organization to those thoughts. There are several observations that clearly distinguish thoughts from language itself: difficulties "turning thoughts into words," verbal disfluencies, and disparate reverbalizations of the same thought on different occasions. Inner language, often associated with thinking, has both sound-based and thought-based components, and the independence of the latter from the former is well demonstrated by the "tip-of-the-tongue" experience in which a thought and sound are no longer immediately connected.

The process of associating thoughts with sounds was seen to pass through stages of semantic structuring, syntactic structuring, and phonological structuring before the final output in sounds is achieved. Thoughts themselves were seen as organized as ideas of events and states and their participants, oriented in time, space, epistemology, emotions, social interaction, and context. Each language structures thoughts with its own semantic resources, including the categorization of particular ideas and the choice of language-specific orientations. The need for a separate syntactic stage was seen as arising in part from historical processes of lexicalization and grammaticalization, in part from the sound-imposed need for linear organization, and probably also from a general human need to operate with a limited number of combinatory patterns. A further stage of underlying phonology, again the result of language change, provides the final link to sounds.

The familiar controversy surrounding the ideas popularized by Benjamin Lee Whorf was seen as misdirected to the extent that it focuses on the relation between thoughts and *syntax*, when the question should concern the relation between thoughts and *semantics*. A focus on universals of syntax was seen as misguided too if syntax is the place where languages can be expected to differ the most. It is in fact in thoughts that universality can be most productively sought. It was suggested, finally, that thoughts are the place where disciplines outside of linguistics can contribute the most, as was illustrated with the special treatment of very small numbers in linguistic number marking and its reflection in psychological studies of subitizing, two manifestations of a single mental phenomenon.

References

Bartlett, Frederic C. 1932. Remembering: A Study in Experimental and Social Psychology. Cambridge, UK: Cambridge University Press.

Boas, Franz. 1963. [1911]. *Handbook of American Indian Languages.* Bureau of American Ethnology, Bulletin 10, Part 1. Reprinted by Georgetown University Press. Date and page number from that publication.

Bowerman, Melissa. 1996. The Origins of Children's Spatial Semantic Categories: Cognitive versus Linguistic Determinants. In John J. Gumperz and Stephen C. Levinson, *Rethinking Linguistic Relativity*, pp. 145–176. Cambridge: Cambridge University Press.

Brown, Alan S. 1991. A Review of the Tip-of-the-Tongue Experience. *Psychological Bulletin* 109: 204–223.

Brown, Roger, and David McNeill. 1966. The "Tip of the Tongue" Phenomenon. *Journal of Verbal Learning and Verbal Behavior* 5: 325–337.

Chafe, Wallace. 1961. *Seneca Thanksgiving Rituals.* Smithsonian Institution, Bureau of American Ethnology Bulletin 183. Washington, D.C.: United States Government Printing Office.

Chafe, Wallace. 1986. Beyond Bartlett: Narratives and Remembering. In E. Gülich and U. Quasthoff (eds.), *Narrative Analysis: An Interdisciplinary Dialogue*, 139–151. Special issue of Poetics, Vol. 15.

Chafe, Wallace. 1991. Repeated Verbalizations as Evidence for the Organization of Knowledge. In Werner Bahner, Joachim Schildt, and Dieter Viehweger (eds.), *Proceedings of the Fourteenth International Congress of Linguists, Berlin 1987*, 57–68. Berlin: Akademie-Verlag.

Chafe, Wallace. 1994. Discourse, Consciousness, and Time: The Flow and Displacement of Conscious Experience in Speaking and Writing. Chicago: The University of Chicago Press.

Chafe, Wallace. 1996. How Consciousness Shapes Language. *Pragmatics and Cognition* 4: 35–54.

Chafe, Wallace. 1998. Things we Can Learn from Repeated Tellings of the Same Experience. *Narrative Inquiry* 8: 269–285.

Chafe, Wallace. 2008. Syntax as a Repository of Historical Relics. In Alex Bergs and Gabriele Diewald (eds.), *Constructions and Language Change*, pp. 259–266. Berlin: Mouton de Gruyter.

Chafe, Wallace. 2012. From Thoughts to Sounds. In James Paul Gee and Michael Handford (eds.), *Routledge Handbook of Discourse Analysis*, 357–365. London and New York: Routledge.

Chafe, Wallace (ed.). 1980. The Pear Stories: Cognitive, Cultural, and Linguistic Aspects of Narrative Production. Norwood, NJ: Ablex.

Chomsky, Noam. 2000. *The architecture of language*. New York: Oxford University Press.

Corbett, Greville. 2000. *Number*. Cambridge, UK: Cambridge University Press.

Croft, William. 2001. Radical Construction Grammar: Syntactic Theory in Typological Perspective. Oxford and New York: Oxford University Press.

Dundes, Alan. 1980. The Number Three in American Culture. In Alan Dundes, *Interpreting Folklore,* 134–159. Bloomington, IN: Indiana University Press.

Foster, Michael K. 1974. *From the Earth to Beyond the Sky: an Ethnographic Approach to Four Longhouse Iroquois Speech Events*. National Museum of Man Mercury Series, Canadian Ethnology Service Paper No. 20. Ottawa, Canada: National Museums of Canada.

Gibbs, Raymond W., Jr. 1994. The Poetics of Mind: Figurative Thought, Language, and Understanding. Cambridge: Cambridge University Press.

Halliday, M.A.K. 1985. An Introduction to Functional Grammar. London: Edward Arnold.

Humphrey, George. 1951. Thinking: An Introduction to its Experimental Psychology. London: Methuen.

Givón, T. 2001. *Syntax: An introduction. Volume 1*. Amsterdam/Philadelphia: John Benjamins.

Jackendoff, Ray. 1987. Consciousness and the Computational Mind. Cambridge, MA: MIT Press.

Jackendoff, Ray. 1994. Patterns in the Mind: Language and Human Nature. New York: Basic Books.

James, William. 1890. *The principles of psychology*. New York: Henry Holt. Reprinted 1950 by Dover Publications.

Jevons, W. Stanley. 1871. The Power of Numerical Discrimination. *Nature, 3,* 281–282.

Kaufman, E. L., M. W. Lord, T. W. Reese, & J. Volkmann. 1949. The Discrimination of Visual Number. *American Journal of Psychology, 62,* 498–525. [have]

Lakoff, George. 1980. Getting the Whole Picture: The Role of Mental Images in Semantics and Pragmatics. *Proceedings of the Sixth Annual Meeting of the Berkeley Linguistics Society,* 191–195.

Langacker, Ronald W. 2008. *Cognitive Grammar: A Basic Introduction*. Oxford and New York: Oxford University Press.

Linell, Per. 1982. *The Written Language Bias in Linguistics*. Studies in Communication 2. Department of Communication Studies, University of Linköping, Linköping, Sweden.

Mustanoja, Tauno F. 1960. A Middle English Grammar. Part 1. Parts of Speech. Helsinki: Société Néophilologique.

Nickel, Gerhard. 1966. Die Expanded Form im Altenglischen: Vorkommen, Funktion und Herkunft der Umschreibung beon/wean + Partizip Präsens. Neumünster: Karl Wachholtz.

Pinker, Steven. 1994. *The Language Instinct.* William Morrow.

Poltrock, Steven E., & Polly Brown. 1984. Individual differences in visual imagery and spatial ability. *Intelligence, 8,* 93–138.

Pullum, Geoffrey. 1991. *The Great Eskimo Vocabulary Hoax and Other Irreverent Essays on the Study of Language.* Chicago: The University of Chicago Press.

Rozin, Paul, Alexander Rozin, Brian Appel, & Charles Wachtel. 2006. Documenting and Explaining the Common AAB Pattern in Music and Humor: Establishing and Breaking Expectations. *Emotion, 6,* 349–355.

Sapir, Edward. 1921. Language: an introduction to the study of speech. New York: Harcourt, Brace.

Seuren, Pieter A.M. 1998. Western Linguistics: An Historical Introduction. Oxford: Blackwell.

Slobin, Dan I. 1996. From "Thought and Language" to "Thinking for Speaking." In John J. Gumperz and Stephen C. Levinson, *Rethinking Linguistic Relativity*, pp. 70–96. Cambridge: Cambridge University Press.

Trick, Lana M., & Zenon W. Pylyshyn. 1993. What Enumeration Studies Can Show Us About Spatial Attention: Evidence for Limited Capacity Preattentive Processing. *Journal of Experimental Psychology: Human Perception and Performance, 19,* 331–351.

Trick, Lana M., & Zenon W. Pylyshyn. 1994. Why Are Small and Large Numbers Enumerated Differently? A Limited-Capacity Preattentive Stage in Vision. *Psychological Review, 101,* 80–102.

Warren, Howard C. 1897. The Reaction Time of Counting. *Psychological Review, 4,* 569–591.

Whorf, Benjamin Lee. 1956. Language Thought, and Reality: Selected Writings of Benjamin Lee Whorf. (John B. Carroll, ed.) Cambridge, MA: MIT Press.

Michael P. Kaschak and Morton Ann Gernsbacher
Changing Language

1 Introduction

One of the central questions facing researchers interested in language is why languages are structured the way that they are. Based on Chomsky's influential research (e.g., Chomsky, 1965; 1981), many scholars have approached this question starting from the assumption that there are universal principles governing the structure of naturally occurring human languages, and that these principles may be a part of the genetic heritage of the human species (see Pinker, 1994, for a well-known explication of this view). The existence of such universal principles, often referred to as innate Universal Grammar, explains why languages have similar structure across the globe and provides a theoretical basis for exploring questions regarding the acquisition of language in children (e.g., Pinker, 1989) and the evolution of language in our species (e.g., Pinker & Bloom, 1990). Universal Grammar (and the broader generativist approach to linguistics) has been useful in setting the terms of many debates surrounding the acquisition of language (e.g., Chomsky, 1965; Seidenberg, MacDonald & Saffran, 2002) and the ways that languages change across historical time (e.g., Lightfoot, 1991; 1999). A side effect of this theoretical approach, however, has been to grant language a special, unique status within the more general cognitive apparatus, and therefore to divorce examination of linguistic structure (and the acquisition of that structure) from examination of other aspects of the cognitive apparatus: memory, attention, categorization, social cognition, and the like.

Functionalist approaches to linguistics take a different tack in explaining why languages are structured the way they are. Rather than treating linguistic knowledge as special and unique within the cognitive apparatus, functional approaches embrace the idea that knowledge of language does not hold special cognitive status. Thus, for example, the acquisition and use of linguistic categories should follow the same principles that govern the acquisition and use of categories in other domains of knowledge (e.g., Taylor, 1998). An oft-repeated phrase in functionalist linguistics captures this notion succinctly: Knowledge of language is knowledge (e.g., Goldberg, 1995). The functionalist perspective posits that languages are structured as they are because of the interplay between linguistic input, human cognitive processing, and the social factors that impact the processing and production of language as they occur in real time. Christiansen and Chater's (2008) approach to language evolution represents an example of such a view, suggesting that the brain was not shaped by the need to acquire language; rather, language was shaped by our brains' ability to learn from linguistic input. Young children have certain limitations on their learning abilities (e.g., Newport, 1990; Saffran & Thiessen, 2003; Hudson Kam & Newport, 2009). Based on these limitations, linguistic structures that are more difficult to learn are less likely to be transmitted across generations of language users, and over time this learning bottleneck constrains the possible forms that a language can take to include only those forms that are comparatively more learnable.

The position advocated by Christiansen and Chater (2008), among others, suggests that understanding how languages are shaped, and how they work, requires attending to events and changes that have occurred over multiple timescales. These include long-term changes, such as those that have occurred over the course of the evolution of the human species, and linguistic changes of the sort that historical linguists have detailed as occurring over the course of decades and centuries (e.g., Labov, 1994; 2001). These events also include relatively short-term changes, such as the behaviors that develop as we use language across the lifespan and the comparatively minor adjustments to the comprehension and production of language that occur every time we have a conversation (e.g., Clark, 1996; Giles, Coupland & Coupland, 1991). Rather than assuming that linguistic knowledge crystalizes at some point early in one's life and that the structures of a language are unchanging within the individual, this perspective highlights the malleability of linguistic behavior. The linguistic behavior of individual people and the patterns of usage within a language community are in a constant state of flux. Some of these changes may reflect temporary adaptations to a given circumstance (e.g., adjusting one's perceptual representations to accommodate an unfamiliar accent; Sumner & Samuel, 2009). However, under the right circumstances, local changes that occur when speakers make contact with each other can spread through a linguistic community and produce language change on a broader scale (e.g., Labov, 2001).

Understanding why languages are structured the way that they are, then, requires considering not only the kinds of changes in linguistic behavior that occur over broad stretches of time (years, decades, centuries), but also the way that local adaptations of linguistic behavior contribute to these broader changes. The past decade has witnessed rising interest in studying the adaptations in linguistic processing that occur on comparatively short timescales (minutes, hours, and days). Research in this area has largely focused on changes to phonological representations (e.g., Kraljic & Samuel, 2005; Sumner & Samuel, 2009) and to syntactic patterns (e.g., Kaschak & Glenberg, 2004; Wells et al., 2009). The flexibility in performance demonstrated by these studies confirms that adult language use remains open to change (as suggested by the functionalist perspective), and this research has begun to answer questions about how linguistic knowledge is acquired, stored, and changed.

The purpose of this chapter is to present an overview of recent work demonstrating learning and adaptation effects in phonological and syntactic representations. We have two goals. First, in reviewing these two strands of research from the past decade or so, we hope to highlight the commonalities and differences between adaptations that occur within the phonological and syntactic domains. This will help us to extract more general principles that govern how linguistic behavior changes as a function of experience. Second, we will also look at cases where the linguistic adaptations appear to follow principles that have been advanced in the study of other domains of cognitive performance, particularly memory. Such demonstrations will bolster the case for the functionalist claim that knowledge of language is just like other sorts of knowledge, and that learning within language follows the same general patterns that govern learning in other domains.

2 Syntactic Adaptations

Psycholinguistics was born as a branch of cognitive science in the fallout of the famous Chomsky-Skinner interchange. Chomsky's (1959) evisceration of Skinner's (1957) behaviorist approach to language acquisition helped to propel the rising cognitive revolution by demonstrating the need to consider internal mental representations when thinking about how languages are learned and subsequently used. From the start, then, psycholinguists have focused on the notion that there is a fixed internal grammar (the "rules" of language), and the question of how linguistic input was processed in order to recover the syntactic structure of a sentence was a question of major interest. Along the way, there were some doubts about the necessity of positing a fixed internal grammar (e.g., Haviland & Clark, 1974), but it was not until the later development of theoretical approaches such as the Competition Model of Bates and MacWhinney (1989) and constraint-based theories of sentence comprehension (e.g., MacDonald, Pearlmutter & Seidenberg, 1994) that accounts admitting of the possibility of flexibility in syntactic representations were pursued with much vigor.

Constraint-based theories of sentence processing posit that language users track the probability of a range of linguistic events (e.g., How often do certain words co-occur? How often do certain syntactic structures occur? How often do particular verbs appear in a given syntactic structure?, and so on), and use this probabilistic information to make real-time decisions about the most likely interpretation of an incoming sentence. The representation of grammatical knowledge was probabilistic, opening the possibility that as the probabilities of certain events in one's linguistic input changed, the representation of grammatical knowledge would also change. Although this was a straightforward prediction of the constraint-based approach to sentence processing, early work in this domain focused largely on how the long-range probabilistic structure of language (e.g., estimates of the relative frequency of different syntactic structures that were derived from large corpora of language use; see Jurafsky, 1996) affected sentence comprehension. Exploring learning and adaptation effects within experimental paradigms has been a comparatively recent development.

Kaschak and Glenberg (2004) report one of the earliest studies of syntactic adaptation in language comprehension. In a series of experiments, they explored what happened when participants were exposed to a novel syntactic construction. The novel construction was dubbed the *needs* construction, and is exemplified by sentences such as, *"The meal needs cooked* before the guests arrive." This construction is a feature of the dialect of American English spoken in the midlands region (most famously around Pittsburgh), but was unfamiliar to the upper Midwestern participants in the experiments. Within a handful of exposures to this novel construction, participants trained on the new construction were able to process it as quickly as control participants process the version of the construction used in their dialect (*The meal needs to be cooked* before the guests arrive"). That is, participants quickly adapted to the new syntactic feature.

It is important to note that participants trained on the *needs* construction were able to generalize their ability to process it beyond the input presented during initial training. Kaschak and Glenberg (2004) demonstrated that participants generalized the construction to at least one additional verb (*wants*, as in, *"The dog wants walked* before it gets too late"), as evidenced by the fact that they processed sentences with the new verb as readily as they processed sentences containing *needs*, and that they were doing so from the very first encounters with the new verb. Kaschak (2006) further showed that learners generalized the *needs* construction to a pseudo-cleft form ("John thinks that *what the meal needs is cooked* before the guests arrive). The fact that participants are readily able to process the *needs* construction with a novel verb and in a different syntactic context helps to strengthen the conclusion that participants in these studies were learning a new syntactic feature (as opposed to simply learning a new use of the verb *needs*).

Kaschak and Glenberg (2004) report one further finding of interest. They were concerned with how the learning of sentences such as, "The meal needs cooked before the guests arrive" would affect the processing of more familiar sentences such as, "The meal needs cooked vegetables to make it complete" (dubbed the *modifier* construction, since *cooked* serves as a modifier in this case). One possibility was that learning the *needs* construction would impair processing the *modifier* construction (since participants had learned that *cooked* was not being used as a modifier in these experiments). However, Kaschak and Glenberg (2004) report the opposite finding: Learning the *needs* construction facilitated processing of the *modifier* construction. This facilitation was found only when processing the *needs* construction early in the experiment involved considering the *modifier* construction. Upon reading, "The meal needs cooked...," participants were expecting *cooked* to be used as a modifier (as evidenced by slower reading times on the subsequent words of the sentence, in which the modifier interpretation was shown to be wrong). This consideration of the modifier interpretation, although it ultimately turned out to be the wrong interpretation of the *needs* construction sentences, was remembered and available to facilitate the processing of the *modifier* construction when it appeared later in the experiment. Participants who did not consider the *modifier* construction earlier in the experiment showed no such facilitation. Thus, the nature of the processing work that was done while initially learning the novel *needs* construction affected the participants' subsequent patterns of language processing.

Casenheiser and Goldberg (2005; Boyd & Goldberg, 2011) have also shown that adults are capable of learning novel syntactic forms. They created a construction in which "approach" events are described using a new syntactic form. Across several studies, Goldberg and colleagues found that adults could readily learn the new construction, could retain their learning over a delay of a week (Boyd, Gottschalk & Goldberg, 2009), and could produce novel utterances with the construction. These data complement Kaschak and Glenberg's (2004) study by indicating that syntactic adaptation can extend beyond modifications of familiar structures to entirely novel forms.

Wells, Christiansen, Race, Acheson and MacDonald (2009; see also Farmer, Fine & Jaeger, 2011) provide another demonstration that changes in one's linguistic environment can change the way that syntactic structures are processed. Wells et al. (2009) explored the processing of sentences with object relative clauses («The reporter that the senator attacked admitted the error»), which are considerably more difficult to understand than subject relative clauses («The reporter that attacked the senator admitted the error»). However, after extensive training on relative clauses, the difference between processing object and subject relatives was greatly attenuated. The finding that the processing of the less-frequent object relative clauses benefited more from the relative clause training than the processing of the more-frequent subject relative clauses is an example of the *inverse frequency effect* (e.g., Ferreira, 2003), wherein lower-frequency forms tend to show larger learning or priming effects than higher-frequency forms.

Luka and Choi (2012; Luka & Barsalou, 2005) provide another demonstration of syntactic adaptation effects. Across a series of studies, Luka and colleagues examined grammaticality ratings for sentences such as, "Debbie ought to buy a car as reliable as that fireman had." These sentences are rated as marginally grammatical at the beginning of the experiments. But after repeated exposure to this type of sentence, grammaticality ratings of sentences with this structure increased. Luka and Choi (2012; Luka & Barsalou, 2005) thus show that participants' assessment of the grammaticality of particular sentence structures can be improved via exposure to more tokens of the structures. There are parallels between this finding and the *mere exposure effect* (e.g., Zajonc, 1968), where it is found that liking of a particular stimulus increases as a function of exposure to that stimulus (see Luka & Barsalou, 2005, for a discussion of this point). Interestingly, Luka and Choi (2012) show that these adaptations can persist for a long time; even a week after exposure to the target structures, participants assessment of the sentences' grammaticality remained elevated. The long-lasting syntactic adaptation effect parallels the long-lasting perceptual learning effect reported by Kraljic and Samuel (2005; see discussion below). In both cases, the adaptations persisted even when participants were presented with more normative patterns of language experience between the training phase of the studies and the subsequent assessment of the adaptation effects.

Syntactic adaptation effects have also been demonstrated in language production. These demonstrations come mainly from studies exploring structural priming, or the tendency for speakers to repeat syntactic constructions across utterances (Bock, 1986; Pickering & Branigan, 1998; Pickering & Ferreira, 2008). For example, a person who has just produced a double object dative (DO; *The boy gave the girl a valentine*) is more likely to subsequently produce a double object to describe another transfer event (*The teacher sent the students a note*) than to produce a prepositional object dative (PO; *The teacher sent a note to the students*) to describe the same event. Hartsuiker and Kolk (1998) were among the first to report long-range adaptations within a structural priming paradigm. They elicited production of dative constructions in Dutch, and found that repeated production of datives over the course of the experiment led to higher rates of usage for those constructions at the end of the experiment compared to the beginning of the experiment. Hartsuiker and Westenberg (2000) report a similar finding in an experiment examining priming of the ordering of auxiliary verbs and past participles. They also report that the accumulation of priming across the course of the experiment was stronger for the less-preferred word orderings, providing another example of the inverse frequency effect.

To better understand the syntactic adaptions that occur across the production of multiple utterances, Kaschak and colleagues (Kaschak, Loney & Borreggine, 2006; Kaschak, 2007; Kaschak, Kutta & Jones, 2011) followed up on these initial reports by systematically manipulating the production of DO and PO dative constructions. In the first phase of these experiments, participants are induced to produce a certain proportion of DO and PO constructions (ranging from 100% DO constructions to 100% PO constructions). In the second phase, participants are given the freedom to choose the DO or PO construction in their productions. These studies show that participants are sensitive to the relative frequency with which they have produced each construction within the experiment. As the initial training phase of the experiment moves from being 100% DO to 100% PO, production of the DO construction declines (Kaschak, 2007; Jaeger & Snider, 2008). These studies also show an inverse frequency effect, with stronger adaptations in behavior being shown when participants are biased toward the lower-frequency PO construction than when they are biased toward the higher-frequency DO construction (e.g., Kaschak, Kutta & Jones, 2011; Jaeger & Snider, 2008).

Speakers are not only sensitive to how frequently they produce particular syntactic constructions, they are also sensitive to how frequently individual verbs are used within those constructions. Coyle and Kaschak (2008) held the frequency of producing DO and PO constructions constant across participants who produced each construction an equal number of times throughout the experiment. But Coyle and Kaschak (2008) also assigned individual verbs to appear only in one construction or the other (e.g., *give* would appear only in the DO, and *send* would appear only in the PO). Subsequent productions involving the target verbs showed that participants were sensitive to this bias – that is, participants were more likely to use the DO construction with verbs that had been biased toward the DO construction, and more likely to use the PO construction with verbs that had been biased toward the PO construction. Taken together, this set of results suggests that language producers are sensitive to the rates of production for given constructions within the confines of an experiment, and that their linguistic choices are shaped by this information.

As is the case in the grammaticality judgment experiments reported by Luka and Choi (2012), the syntactic adaptations that arise in language production experiments seem to be long lasting. Kaschak, Kutta and Schatschneider (2011) replicated the design of Kaschak (2007), in which participants were first biased toward either the DO or PO construction and are then given the freedom to choose either construction in generating subsequent productions. In this study, the two phases of the experiment were separated by one week. The results were clear: the syntactic adaptation that was produced in the first phase of the study was still present a week later. Kaschak, Kutta and Coyle (in press) extended this finding by investigating whether the adaptations that occur in the training phases of these studies transfer across language production tasks (e.g., a written stem completion task versus a picture description task) and whether the transfer would be similar when the tasks occurred in the same session or were separated by a week. The results suggest that syntactic adaptations transfer across task within the same session, but not when separated by a week. Syntactic adaptations were seen after a delay of a week only when the same language production task was used in both sessions. Kaschak et al. (in press) interpret these findings to suggest that the processing that goes into producing sentences – the task demands of completing a sentence stem, or describing a picture – are an important part of what is remembered from a particular episode of language production. Thus, the match between the circumstances of production during the establishment of the syntactic adaptation and during the assessment of that adaptation will determine in part how strongly the adaptation effect is observed. The overall pattern observed here is consistent with findings from the memory literature, particularly demonstrations that the importance of matching encoding and retrieval conditions for memory performance increases as the delay between encoding and retrieval increases (e.g., Read & Craik, 1995).

The literature reviewed above makes the case that syntactic representations continue to change with experience. Syntactic adaptations most likely occur very quickly, requiring only a small number of exposure sentences. Kaschak and Glenberg's (2004) participants learned the *needs* construction after 10 training sentences, and Kaschak et al.'s (2006) language production experiment produced strong adaptation effects with 10 training sentences. Syntactic adaptations are quite durable, persisting for at least a week. Syntactic adaptations are also sensitive to trial-by-trial changes across an experiment. Kaschak, Kutta and Jones (2011) found that beyond the general adaptation effects that occurred within their experiment, the immediate context – whether a participant had produced one or more DO or PO constructions on the immediately preceding trials – was a strong predictor of syntactic choice. Kaschak et al. (in press) and Kaschak and Glenberg (2004) discuss at length the ways that the syntactic adaptations that were observed in their studies fit with the larger body of studies concerning learning and memory, and how their findings are consistent with patterns that have been observed across many paradigms that have been used in the memory literature.

One issue that deserves additional comment is the presence of inverse frequency effects in many of the studies reported here. The finding that lower-frequency structures get more of a boost from exposure during training is interesting in that it represents a possible explanation for why low frequency options do not disappear from languages entirely. Repeated exposure to the higher-frequency syntactic choices in studies such as these does not seem to increase rates of usage for those choices too much above the baseline (see Reitter et al., 2011; Kaschak, Kutta & Jones, 2011), suggesting why higher-frequency choices do not snowball and push lower-frequency choices out of the picture. In contrast, use of the lower-frequency choice does produce a change in rate for that construction, thus serving to strengthen the place of that choice in the language. Frequency-sensitive learning of the sort described here is characteristic of connectionist models (e.g., Chang et al., 2006), providing another indication that general-purpose learning mechanisms may underlie patterns of language use.

3 Phonological Adaptations

A primary obstacle faced during the processing of speech is the amount of variability that is present in the input. The acoustic properties of a given word or speech sound can vary across speakers, and can vary within a single speaker across time. This is a recurrent problem for language users, as we are constantly faced with sub-optimal listening conditions (e.g., noisy rooms), speakers with unfamiliar dialects and speech patterns, and other sources of variability. The question of how listeners "hear through" this variability to perceive speech accurately has driven a good deal of research into speech perception over the last several decades. Early efforts to address this question focused largely on the idea that listeners have invariant, abstract representations of speech sounds, and that the variability present in the input is somehow normalized to the abstract representations (e.g., Liberman, Cooper, Shankweiler & Studdert-Kennedy, 1967; Kuhl, 1991). In short, the variability caused by differences in speakers, listening conditions, and so on, is stripped away during the perceptual process and recognition of speech sounds in terms of the stable underlying phonetic representations of one's language could proceed. This approach to speech perception fits within the general suggestion that linguistic representations become relatively stable after a certain point during one's formative years.

The idea that abstract phonetic representations are stable through adulthood, and are not changed by exposure to different sources of variability (such as having a conversation with someone with an unfamiliar dialect), can be called into question based on at least two sets of data. First, a number of studies in sociolinguistics have demonstrated that shifting patterns of speech behavior in young adults is responsible for sound change within linguistic communities (see Labov, 2001, for an extensive treatment of this issue). It seems plausible that these changes in production are accompanied by changes in the underlying perceptual representation of the sounds in question. Second, and more germane to the thrust of this chapter, a series of recent studies has documented the adjustments in perceptual representations that occur when listeners are exposed to different varieties of speech input (e.g., Kraljic & Samuel, 2005; Kraljic & Samuel, 2011; Sumner & Samuel, 2009; Norris, McQueen & Cutler, 2003). These studies fit within a growing body of literature (e.g., Nygaard & Pisoni, 1998; Bradlow & Bent, 2003; Trude & Brown-Schmidt, 2011) suggesting that speaker variability and other such "noise" in the speech signal may be more integral to construction of speech representations than previously thought.

Kraljic and Samuel (2005) conducted a series of experiments in which participants were exposed to normative /s/ or /sh/ sounds, or to sounds that were ambiguous, being somewhere between /s/ and /sh/. Participants performed an auditory lexical decision task in which ambiguous /s/-/sh/ sounds were heard. Previous work (Norris et al., 2003) had shown that lexical information would be used as the basis for deciding whether the ambiguous sound was an /s/ or /sh/. For example, an ambiguous sound heard in "eraser" would be perceived as an /s/, but the same sound heard in "official" would be perceived as /sh/. Subsequent to the lexical decision task, participants were tested with a range of sounds on the /s/-/sh/ continuum and indicated whether the sound was more like /s/ or /sh/. Consistent with previous demonstrations that listeners can adjust to the features of the speech that they are hearing (e.g., Norris et al., 2003; Bradlow & Bent, 2003; Maye, Aslin & Tanenhaus, 2008), Kraljic and Samuel (2005) found a perceptual learning effect: When the lexical decision task involved hearing ambiguous /s/-/sh/ sounds in places where an /sh/ would normally appear, participants were more likely to hear an ambiguous test sound as an /sh/ than as an /s/ (and vice versa for participants who heard the ambiguous sounds where an /s/ would normally appear during the lexical decision task). Interestingly, the perceptual learning effect persisted across time. There was no difference in the size of the perceptual adaptation effect between a group of participants who were given the /s/-/sh/ discrimination test immediately after the lexical decision training task and a group of participants who were given the discrimination task after performing a silent visual discrimination task for 25 minutes. Subsequent experiments showed that the perceptual learning effect persisted across time even when participants were presented with unambiguous "correcting" productions of /s/ and /sh/ from the same speaker that had produced the lexical decision items between the initial training phase and the test phase. The perceptual learning effect appears to be quite robust.

A further issue regarding the perceptual learning effect described by Kraljic and Samuel (2005; Norris et al., 2003; Maye et al., 2008) is that of speaker specificity: Is the learning specific to individual speakers, or does it generalize across speakers? The answer to this question is that the degree of generalization appears to depend on the particular contrast that is used for the perceptual learning study. Kraljic and Samuel (2007) performed two learning experiments, one employing a contrast between stop consonants (/d/ and /t/) and one employing a contrast between fricatives (/s/ and /sh/). Participants generalized their perceptual learning of the stop consonants across speakers, but did not do so for the fricatives. Kraljic and Samuel (2007) suggest that this difference is driven by the fact that fricatives are a useful source of speaker-specific information (i.e., variation in fricative production is diagnostic with respect to speaker identity), but stops are not. The perceptual learning effects will therefore extend as far as is licensed by the generality of the information presented in the particular phonetic contrast.

There are two things to note about the literature reviewed in the preceding paragraphs. First, the perceptual learning that has been demonstrated appears to interact with different levels of linguistic representation. Norris et al.'s (2003) initial demonstration of perceptual learning using the lexical decision task as a training paradigm showed that perceptual adaptation occurred only when the ambiguous speech sounds were presented within words; no learning occurred when the speech sounds were presented in non-words. This suggests that lexical representations play a role in the adaptation process. Beyond this, Kraljic and Samuel's (2007) data demonstrate that perceptual learning reflects sensitivity to particular dimensions of a given speech sound (e.g., voice onset time, or place of articulation). Idemaru and Holt (2011) propose that *dimension based statistical learning* (i.e., learning of the statistical regularities corresponding to particular dimensions of speech sounds) may be a mechanism that drives both long-range learning of phonological categories and the comparatively shorter-range learning demonstrated in experiments such as those reported by Norris et al. (2003) and Kraljic and Samuel (2005). Second, Kraljic and Samuel's (2007) finding that learning of contrasts that contain speaker-specific information generalizes differently than learning of contrasts without speaker-specific information suggests that learners are sensitive to the dimensions of speech sounds on which speakers differ, and this information is used as the speech perception system adapts to individual speakers. Given that adapting to individual speakers is a valuable skill for listeners, it is perhaps unsurprising that listeners would be sensitive to the dimensions of speech that should be attended to for accomplishing that adaptation.

Adaptation to individual speakers functions to shape phonological representations and facilitate speech perception. There is also evidence that adaptation to individual speakers can have consequences for language comprehension. Geiselman and Bellezza (1976, 1977; see also van Berkum, van den Brink, Tesink, Kos & Hagoort, 2008) proposed that listeners use acoustic information to recover information that is likely to be true of the speaker, and that this information plays a role in generating an interpretation of the linguistic input. As one example, van Berkum (2008) asked participants to listen to sentences such as, "If I only looked like Britney Spears," or "I have a large tattoo on my back." Measurement of event-related brain responses indicated that participants rapidly noted the incongruity when the voice characteristics of the speaker did not match the content of the sentence (e.g., the "Britney Spears" sentence being spoken by a male, or the "tattoo" sentence being spoken by someone with a refined upper-class accent). Speaker identity was rapidly taken into account when generating an interpretation of the sentences. Goldinger (1996, 1998; see also Church & Schacter, 1994) demonstrated the role of speaker information in memory performance. When participants are given a running old/new distinction task (wherein they must decide whether each word presented to them is "old," i.e., a repeated word from the list, or "new"), the odds of a participant correctly noting that a word is repeated are increased when the second token of the word is produced by the same speaker who produced the first token of the word. Nygaard and Pisoni (1998) further showed that speech perception performance in sub-optimal conditions (e.g., when listening to speech under noisy conditions) is improved when the listener has prior experience listening to that speaker.

More recent studies employing the visual world paradigm pioneered by Tanenhaus and colleagues (e.g., Tanenhaus, Spivey-Knowlton, Eberhard & Sedivy, 1995) have demonstrated that speaker information is used to guide speech perception and language processing from the very earliest stages of processing. For example, Trude and Brown-Schmidt (2011) presented participants with visual displays containing pictures of a target word such as *back* as well as pictures of a phonological distractor such as *bag*. In the visual world paradigm, the participants' eye position is monitored from the onset of the target word (back). The questions of interest in this paradigm are a) how often, and how far into the spoken target word, do the participant's eyes fixate on the distractor word (which begins the same as the target word, and is disambiguated from the target word at some point after the onset of the speech stimulus), and b) which variables affect the degree to which participants fixate on the distractor item. Trude and Brown-Schmidt (2011) found that speaker-based information was likely accessed at the very onset of the presentation of the target word, and that this information was immediately used to determine the identity of the word in question. Using a similar eye-tracking method, Creel & Tumlin (2011) confirm the finding that speaker-based information is accessed almost immediately upon hearing speech input, and that this information is rapidly deployed in the service of language comprehension.

Thus far, we have observed that perceptual learning occurs quite readily in listeners, that the learning process is sensitive to both low-level dimensions of speech sounds and higher-level lexical and semantic representations, and that the changes that result from perceptual learning are a durable component of the memory traces left by experiences with a given set of speech input. An important next step will be to explicate the exact nature of the memory mechanisms that are at work in these studies. Kraljic and Samuel (2011) begin to tackle this issue in a set of experiments that explore conditions under which perceptual learning had previously been found to be blocked: when the learner first heard the speaker produce standard tokens of a speech sound before producing the ambiguous variants of that sound, and when the learner saw the speaker producing the ambiguous variants of the sound with a pen in his or her mouth. Kraljic, Samuel and Brennan (2008) suggested that the blocking of perceptual learning was due to the learner making a detailed representation of particular talkers, and that variability that was taken as external to the speaker (i.e., speaking with a pen in one's mouth would produce variance in the speech sounds that are not typical of the speaker) was excluded from this representation of the speaker. Upon further study, Kraljic and Samuel (2011) proposed that the normal and deviant productions heard from a given speaker result in the construction of distinct phonological representations. That is, rather than there being a single model of a speaker, there may be multiple representations of a person's speech corresponding to the different types of speech episodes (e.g., pen-in-mouth vs. no pen) that are encountered. Kraljic and Samuel (2011) see an affinity between their approach and other work showing that perceptual representations have an episodic character (e.g., Goldinger, 1996; 1998).

The preceding paragraphs have suggested learning effects in the perception and comprehension of language. Learning effects have also been demonstrated in language production. These studies employ tasks to show that listeners can learn new phonotactic constraints. Dell, Reed, Adams, and Meyer (2000) asked participants to produce a string of nonsense syllables, for which a novel rule structure defined which phonemes could appear in the onset and coda positions. Participants readily learned these new phonotactic constraints. With a bit more difficulty, speakers can learn second-order phonotactic constraints (e.g., /k/ can only appear as on onset when /i/ is the vowel) under the same sort of training conditions (Warker & Dell, 2006). Thus, it appears that individuals are capable of adapting their perception and production of speech sounds on multiple layers of representation.

The following picture emerges when we consider perceptual learning in the speech domain. Learning happens rapidly. A relatively small amount of exposure is all that is required for listeners to adapt to the distinctive features presented by a new speaker. The fact that perceptual representations can shift so quickly underscores the dynamic nature of the speech perception system and highlights the more general claim that linguistic representations are in a constant state of flux. Indeed, Tuller, Case, Ding and Kelso (1994) demonstrated that categorization of ambiguous speech sounds of the sort used in the perceptual learning studies discussed here is affected by the trial-to-trial structure of the experiment. Categorization of speech sounds is affected not only by training across the course of an experiment, but also by the events that have occurred on a shorter time scale, such as the last trial or two in the study. This sort of micro-level adaptation has been taken as the hallmark of a self-organizing dynamic system, and such adaptation has been seen in other domains, including a range of binary decision tasks (such as responding to yes/no questions) and speech production (e.g., Gilden, 2001; van Orden et al., 2003; Kello et al., 2008). Thus, the patterns that are observed in perceptual learning experiments involving speech accord with more general principles about how the human cognitive system organizes its behavior within a given context.

Perceptual learning happens quickly, and it also occurs in a contextually-sensitive manner. Listeners' boundaries between speech sounds (such as /s/ and /sh/) can be shifted after exposure to a speaker who produces deviant examples of those sounds. The new boundaries between speech sounds continue to affect perception of speech from that initial speaker even when the training and test phases of the experiment are separated by exposure to a speaker who produces more normative examples of the speech sounds in question. This speed and flexibility of learning, as well as the fact that the learning can be done in a contextually-specific manner (e.g., the learning is specific to the perception of a particular person's speech) adheres to the more general principles that have emerged from the memory literature over the past several decades. For example, Crowder (1993) discusses how specificity in representations is a foundational principle of memory performance. Models such as Hintzman's (1986) MINERVA provide a ready explanation for how perceptual learning of speech sounds for individual speakers could be maintained independently of speech sounds from other speakers. The basic idea is that aspects of a speaker's voice will serve as a memory cue that will resonate more strongly with prior experiences with that same speaker than it will resonate with experience with other speakers. Thus, the rapid recovery of speaker identity from minimal speech input (see Creel & Tumlin, 2011) biases the speech perception process such that it will draw most strongly on previous experience with that speaker when interpreting the current input.

Finally, Kraljic and Samuel (2007) and Idemaru and Holt (2011) argue that learning about speech sounds is dimension-based, meaning that listeners will be most sensitive to the aspects of a speech sound that provide the most useful information for distinguishing that sound from others and for distinguishing one speaker from another. This sort of nuance in learning appears to be widespread in tasks involving statistical learning. In a typical statistical learning task, participants are given input that is structured by statistical regularities. For example, participants might be presented with a sequence of shapes in which the likelihood of one shape following another is governed by pre-determined statistical patterns, such as "A is followed by B 60% of the time, and followed by C 40% of the time." Participants are later tested for their success in extracting the relevant regularities. Turk-Browne et al. (2005) demonstrate that the outcome of the statistical learning process is determined in part by the dimensions of the input set that participants attend to (see also Whittlesea & Brooks, 1988). It therefore appears that in many domains in which learning the probabilistic structure of the environment is important (including the domain of speech perception; Idemaru & Holt, 2011), learning which features of the environment to attend to is a key aspect of the learning process. To conclude this section of the paper, phonological representations undoubtedly remain adaptable to ongoing experience, and the nature of these adaptations fits with observations about learning and memory from a wide range of experimental paradigms.

It is important to note that many of the features that we have identified as characteristic of perceptual learning parallel the features we have identified as characteristic of syntactic adaptations. In both cases, the adaptations occur quickly, are long lasting, are at least somewhat context specific, and seem to follow general principles of learning and memory. The similarities in perceptual learning, syntactic adaptation, and studies of learning and memory help to make the case that language is learned and processed using general-purpose cognitive mechanisms (and not language-specific processing mechanisms).

4 What Kind of Learning System?

We now turn to consider the nature of the learning system that is implicated in phonological and syntactic adaptations. There is a clear affinity between the effects that are discussed in this chapter and effects seen in other research paradigms in which participants adapt to the probabilistic structure of the input that they receive throughout the experiment. For example, participants are able to learn the rules that are used to generate letter strings such as AKTTYKST by keeping track of the probability with which certain letters are followed by other letters (e.g., Reber, 1993). Children are able to use the transitional probabilities between syllables (such as the likelihood of /be/ preceding /bi/, as in *baby)* to find words in a fluent stream of speech (e.g., Saffran, Aslin & Newport, 1996; Thiessen & Saffran, 2003). In addition, adults are able to use the statistical regularities in the location of particular objects that appear in visual displays to guide their eye movements as they search for target items on a computer screen (e.g., Jones & Kaschak, 2012). Many of these effects have been taken to be examples of implicit learning (see Perruchet & Pacton, 2006), and the phonological and syntactic adaptation effects that we have considered display many of the hallmarks of implicit learning. For example, the adaptation effects occur outside the participants' awareness (see Ferreira et al., 2008, for a demonstration of syntactic priming in anterograde amnesiacs); the effects are sensitive to the probabilistic structure of the learning input; the effects persist over long stretches of time (see Allen & Reber, 1980, for demonstrations of very long-term persistence of implicit learning), and the persistence of these effects over longer periods of time seems to depend (at least in some cases) on the match between the initial conditions of learning and the later test tasks (see Kolers, 1976, for a demonstration of this within a procedural learning paradigm).

It is sensible that adaptations to linguistic representations should be driven by the systems responsible for implicit learning. Given the real-time speed with which language is produced and comprehended and the lack of awareness that most of us have about the linguistic choices that we make at any given moment, it seems unlikely that explicit or conscious processes would be an ideal candidate to explain how the participants in these experiments are adapting their behavior to the input that they receive.

There is an appeal to connectionist models when considering linguistic adaptation effects, as these approaches demonstrate very nicely how encoding linguistic knowledge directly within processing mechanisms allows for a general degree of stability in the representations (over millions of utterances produced and comprehended, stable patterns will emerge in the model's behavior) while also allowing for the possibility of continued change (since the learning mechanism of the model is continually fine-tuning the representations based on ongoing experience; Chang, Dell & Bock, 2006). Although implicit learning (perhaps as implemented in a connectionist model) is likely to be a part of the story in explaining linguistic adaptations, it is clear that we have a ways to go before we have a complete picture of how linguistic adaptations work. For example, although we are often largely unaware of our patterns of language use, there are situations where we are conscious of the choices that we are making. Furthermore, there is reason to believe that explicit memory process may contribute to adaptations such as structural priming under certain conditions (e.g., Hartsuiker et al., 2008). It may therefore be important to consider the role of more conscious and explicit processes in a broader range of linguistic adaptations. Indeed, there is reason to believe that "implicit" learning processes may be more active and attention-driven (i.e., subject to influence by conscious and explicit processes) than originally believed (e.g., Perruchet & Vinter, 2002; Turk-Browne et al., 2005). Finally, it seems clear that although participants' behavior can be altered (sometimes quite strongly) within these experiments, their linguistic systems are not completely unhinged. An important step in developing models of linguistic adaptations will be to find ways to model the at times strong linguistic adaptation effects as a local, contextual event within the structure of a broader and more stable model of linguistic performance (as opposed to simply modeling the effects on one particular study).

Another factor that needs to be considered when thinking about a theoretical account of phonological and syntactic adaptations is that language use is inherently social (Clark, 1996). There are many examples of adaptations of linguistic behavior being driven by social factors. Giles, Coupland, and Coupland (1991; Ireland et al., 2011) discuss how interlocutors often align their linguistic behavior as a means of signaling affiliation. Indeed, observations of linguistic alignment are part of a larger body of evidence suggesting that alignment between individuals helps to build social bonds (Chartrand & Bargh, 1999). Labov (2001) discusses how adaptations between speakers in a community (and, broader patterns of language change) are affected by social factors such as race and gender. For example, Labov's (2001) study of sound change in Philadelphia suggests that sound changes are driven by female speakers. The more advanced forms of the sound change are therefore marked as characteristic of "female" speech, and this causes male speakers to move away from these more advanced forms. Coyle and Kaschak (2012) demonstrated that the likelihood of a male conversant matching the syntactic structures of a female conversant was affected by the timing of the interaction within the female's menstrual cycle: During periods of higher fertility, structural matching decreased.

The adaptation of linguistic behavior to linguistic surroundings may be somewhat mechanical in the studies reviewed in this chapter, but it is just as clear that this kind of adaptation can be deployed (even unconsciously) to serve a range of social functions (e.g., Ireland & Pennebaker, 2010). It should be noted that although linguistic adaptations and alignment generally occur on an unconscious level, we do not wish to claim that adjustments of one's linguistic behavior is always unconscious. There are clearly cases in which a speaker may consciously change the way they talk to adjust to their conversational partner (e.g., a person speaks differently to a young child than to their boss). Developing a full understanding of the processes through which the linguistic system changes over time will require not only specifying the implicit and explicit memory processes that operate when linguistic stimuli are processed, but also considering the ways that representations of explicit and implicit social motivations interface with the processing of language.

5 Concluding Remarks

We began this chapter by asking why languages are shaped the way they are. From a functionalist perspective, the answer to this question is that general cognitive processes of perception, learning, and memory put constraints on the ways that language can be learned, processed, and changed. When played out over thousands of generations, these constraints have fine-tuned the languages of the world so that they employ just a small fraction of the possible design features that could be used (Christiansen & Chater, 2008). The functionalist view takes the perspective that the handling of language within the cognitive system is not unique or special; language is handled just as other domains of knowledge are handled, and is subject to the same general principles of learning, memory, and processing as is everything else.

Throughout this chapter, we have attempted to demonstrate the value of the functionalist perspective by reviewing empirical demonstrations of phonological and syntactic adaptation effects. We have argued that phonological and syntactic adaptations are cases of implicit learning within the cognitive systems responsible for processing language and that phonological and syntactic adaptations follow the principles of implicit and procedural learning demonstrated in other domains. That is, there is nothing unique about the effects that occur within the linguistic domain. An important future direction in developing this literature will be to understand how what we learn about linguistic adaptations on the psycholinguistic level (as seen in the studies here) can be used to understand how languages change across time and communities. This effort will no doubt require integrating psycholinguistic, social psychological, and sociolinguistic approaches (see Pickering & Garrod, 2004, for a discussion). The current spate of studies looking at the evolution of communication systems within the lab (e.g., Fay et al., 2010; Kirby et al., 2008) provide an interesting template for how this may be done. For example, Kirby et al. (2008) discuss studies in which transmission of language across generations is mimicked by employing chains of learners where the output of one participant's learning within an experimental task is then used as the training input for the next learner in the chain. Pressing along this line, we will be in a better position to understand one of the basic tenets of Christiansen and Chater's (2008) approach, namely that it is the properties of human cognition, not an innate universal grammar, that have played a key role in shaping languages to be the way that they are.

References

Allen, R., & Reber, A. S. 1980. Very long-term memory for tacit knowledge. *Cognition, 8,* 175–185.

Bates, E., & MacWhinney, B. 1989. Functionalism and the Competition Model. In B. MacWhinney & E. Bates (Eds.), *The crosslinguistic study of sentence processing* (pp. 3–73). New York: Cambridge University Press.

Bernolet, S., & Hartsuiker, R. J. 2010. Does verb bias modulate syntactic priming? *Cognition, 114,* 455–461.

Bock, J. K. 1986. Syntactic persistence in language production. *Cognitive Psychology, 18,* 355–387.

Boyd, J. K., & Goldberg, A. E. 2011. Young children fail to fully generalize a novel argument structure construction when exposed to the same input as older learners. *Journal of Child Language.*

Boyd, J. K., Gottschalk, E., & Goldberg, A. E. 2009. Linking rule acquisition in novel phrase constructions. *Language Learning, 93,* 418–429.

Bradlow, A. R. and Bent, T. 2003. Listener adaptation to foreign accented English. In M. J. Sole, D. Re casens, & J. Romero (Eds.), *Proceedings of the XVth International Congress of Phonetic Sciences,* Barcelona, Spain, Pp. 2881–2884.

Casenhiser, D., & Goldberg, A. E. 2005. Fast mapping of a phrasal form and meaning. *Developmental Science, 8,* 500–508.

Chang, F., Dell, G. S., & Bock, K. 2006. Becoming syntactic. *Psychological Review, 113,* 234–272.

Chartrand T.L.,& Bargh J.A. 1999. The chameleon effect: The perception-behavior link and social interaction. *Journal of Personality and Social Psychology, 76,* 893–910.

Chomsky, N. 1959. A review of B. F. Skinner's *Verbal Behavior. Language, 35,* 26–58.

Chomsky, N. 1965. *Aspects of the theory of syntax.* MIT Press.

Chomsky, N. 1981. *Lectures on government and binding: The Pisa lectures.* New York: Mouton de Gruyter.

Christiansen, M.H. & Chater, N. 2008. Language as shaped by the brain. Behavioral & Brain Sciences, 31, 489–558.

Church, B. A., & Schacter, D. L. 1994. Perceptual specificity of auditory priming: Implicit memory for voice intonation and fundamental frequency. *Journal of Experimental Psychology: Learning, Memory, and Cognition, 20,* 521–533.

Clark, H. H. 1996. *Using language.* Cambridge University Press.

Coyle, J. M., & Kaschak, M. P. 2008. Patterns of experience with verbs affect long-term cumulative structural priming. *Psychonomic Bulletin and Review, 15,* 967–970.

Coyle, J. M., & Kaschak, M. P. 2012. Female fertility affects men's linguistic choices. *PLoS One.*

Creel, S. C., & Tumlin, M. A. 2011. On-line acoustic and semantic interpretation of talker information. *Journal of Memory and Language.*

Crowder, R. G. 1993. Systems and principles in memory theory: Another critique of pure memory. In A. F. Collins, S. E. Gathercole, M. A. Conway, & P. E. Morris (Eds.) *Theories of Memory* (p. 139–161). Hillsdle, NJ: Lawrence Erlbaum Associates.

Dell, G. S., Reed, K. D., Adams, D. R., & Meyer, A. S. 2000. Speech errors, phonotactic constraints, and implicit learning: A study of the role of experience in language production. *Journal of Experimental Psychology: Learning, Memory, and Cognition, 26,* 1355–1367.

Farmer, T., Fine, A.B. & Jaeger, T.F. 2011. Implicit Context-Specific Learning Leads to Rapid Shifts in Syntatic Expectations. *33rd Annual Meeting of the Cognitive Science Society.* Boston, MA.

Fay, N., Garrod, S., Roberts, L., & Swooda, N. 2010. The interactive evolution of human communication systems. *Cogntive Science, 34,* 351–386.

Ferreira, F. 2003. The misinterpretation of non-canonical sentences. *Cognitive Psychology, 47,* 164–203.

Ferreira, V. S., Bock, K., Wilson, M. P., & Cohen, N. J. 2008. Memory for syntax despite amnesia. *Psychological Science, 19,* 940–946.

Geiselman, R. E., & Bellezza, F. S. 1976. Long-term memory for speaker's voice and source location. *Memory and Cognition, 4,* 483–489.

Geiselman, R. E., & Bellezza, F. S. 1977. Incidental retention of speaker's voice. *Memory and Cognition, 5,* 658–665.

Gilden, D. L. 2001. Cognitive emissions of 1/f noise. *Psychological Review, 108,* 33–56.

Giles H., Coupland N.,& Coupland, J. 1991. Accommodation theory: Communication, context, and consequence. In: H. Giles, J .Coupland, & N. Coupland,(Eds), *Contexts of Accommodation: Developments in Applied Psycholinguistics.* Cambridge: Cambridge University Press.

Goldberg, A. E. 1995. *Constructions: A construction grammar approach to argument structure.* Chicago: University of Chicago Press.

Goldinger, S.D. 1996. Words and voices: Episodic traces in spoken word identification and recognition memory. *Journal of Experimental Psychology: Learing, Memory, and Cognition, 22,* 1166–1183.

Goldinger, S.D. 1998. Echoes of echoes? An episodic theory of lexical access. *Psychological Review, 105,* 251–279.

Hartsuiker, R. J., Bernolet, S., Schoonbaert, S., Speybroeck, S., & Vanderelst, D. 2008. Syntactic priming persists while the lexical boost decays: Evidence from written and spoken dialogue. *Journal of Memory and Language, 58,* 214–238.

Hartsuiker, R. J., & Kolk, H. H. J. 1998. Syntactic persistence in Dutch. *Language and Speech, 41,* 143–184.

Hartsuiker, R. J., & Westenberg, C. 2000. Word order priming in written and spoken sentence production. *Cognition, 75,* B27-B39.

Haviland, S. E., & Clark, H. H. 1974. What's new? Acquiring new information as a process in comprehension. *Journal of Verbal Learning and Verbal Behavior, 13,* 512–521.

Hintzman, D. L. 1986. "Schema abstraction" in a multiple-trace memory model. *Psycholoical Review, 93,* 411–428.

Hudson Kam, C. L., & Newport, E. L. 2009. Getting it right by getting it wrong: When learners change languages. *Cognitive Psychology, 59,* 30–66.

Idemaru, K., & Holt, L. L. 2011. Word recognition reflects dimension-based statistical learning. *Journal of Experimental Psychology: Human Perception and Performance.*

Ireland, M. E., & Pennebaker, J. W. 2010. Language style matching in writing: Synchrony in essays, correspondence, and poetry. *Journal of Personality and Social Psychology, 99,* 549–571.

Ireland, M. E., Slatcher, R. B., Eastwick, P. W., Scissors, L. E., Finkel, E. J., & Pennebaker, J. W. 2011. Language style matching predicts relationship initiation and stability. *Psychological Science, 22*, 39–44.

Jaeger, T. F., & Snider, N. 2008. Implicit learning and syntactic persistence: Surprisal and cumulativity. In B. C. Love, K. McRae & V. M. Sloutsky (Eds). *Proceedings of the 30th Annual Conference of the Cognitive Science Society.* Washington, DC: Cognitive Science Society.

Jones, J. L., & Kaschak, M. P. in press. Global statistical learning in a visual search task. *Journal of Experimental Psychology: Human Perception and Performance.*

Jurafsky, D. 1996. A probabilistic model of lexical and syntactic access and disambiguation. *Cognitive Science, 20*, 137–194.

Kaschak, M. P. 2007. Long-term structural priming affects subsequent patterns of language production. *Memory and Cognition, 35*, 925–937.

Kaschak, M. P. 2006. What this construction needs is generalized. *Memory and Cognition, 34*, 368–379.

Kaschak, M. P., & Glenberg, A. M. 2004. This construction needs learned. *Journal of Experimental Psychology: General, 133*, 450–467.

Kaschak, M. P., Kutta, T. J., & Coyle, J. M. in press. Long and short term cumulative structural priming effects. *Language and Cognitive Processes*

Kaschak, M. P., Kutta, T. J., & Jones, J. L. 2011. Structural priming as implicit learning: Cumulative priming effects and individual differences. *Psychonomic Bulletin and Review, 18*, 1133–1139.

Kaschak, M. P., Kutta, T. J., & Schatschneider, C. 2011. Long-term cumulative structural priming persists for (at least) a week. *Memory and Cognition, 39*, 381–388.

Kaschak, M. P., Loney, R. A., & Borreggine, K. L. 2006. Recent experience affects the strength of structural priming. *Cognition, 99*, B73-B82.

Kello, C. T., Anderson, G. G., Holden, J. G., & Van Orden, G. C. 2008. The pervasiveness of 1/f scaling in speech reflects the metastable basis of cognition. *Cognitive Science, 32*, 1217–1231.

Kirby, S., Cornish, H., & Smith, K. 2008. Cumulative cultural evolution in the laboratory: An experimental approach to the origins of structure in human language. *Proceedings of the National Academy of Sciences, 105*, 10681–10686.

Kolers, P. A. 1976. Reading a year later. *Journal of Experimental Psychology: Human Learning and Memory, 2*, 554–565.

Kraljic, T., Brennan, S. E., & Samuel, A. G. 2008. First impressions and last resorts: How listeners adjust to speaker variability. *Psychological Science, 19*, 332–338.

Kraljic, T., & Samuel, A. G. 2005. Perceptual learning for speech: Is there a return to normal? *Cognitive Psychology, 51*, 141–178.

Kraljic, T., & Samuel, A. G. 2006. Generalization in perceptual learning for speech. *Psychonomic Bulletin and Review, 13*, 262–268.

Kraljic, T., & Samuel, A. G. 2007. Perceptual adjustments to multiple speakers. *Journal of Memory and Language, 56*, 1–15.

Kraljic, T., & Samuel, A. G. 2011. Perceptual learning evidence for contextually-specific representations. *Cognition.*

Kuhl, P. K. 1991. Human adults and human infants show a "perceptual magnet effect" for prototypes of speech categories, monkeys do not. *Perception and Psychophysics, 50*, 93–107.

Labov, William. 1994. *Principles of linguistic change: internal factors*. Cambridge, MA: Blackwell.

Labov, W. 2001. *Principles of linguistic change: social factors*. Cambridge, MA: Blackwell.

Liberman, A. M., Cooper, F. S., Shankweiler, D. P., & Studdert-Kennedy, M. 1967. Perception of the speech code. *Psychological Review, 74*, 431–461.

Lightfoot, D. W. 1991. *How to set parameters: arguments from language change*. MIT Press.

Lightfoot, D. W. 1999. *The development of language: Acquisition, change, and evolution*. Blackwell: Oxford.

Luka, B. J., & Choi, H. 2012. Dynamic grammar in adults: Incidental learning of natural syntactic structures extends over 48 hours. *Journal of Memory and Language, 66*, 345–360.

Luka, B.J., & Barsalou, L.W. 2005. Structural facilitation: Mere exposure effects for grammatical acceptability as evidence for syntactic priming in comprehension. *Journal of Memory and Language. 52*, 436–459.

MacDonald, M. C., *Pearlmutter*, N. J., & *Seidenberg*, M. S. 1994. The lexical nature of syntactic ambiguity resolution. *Psychological Review, 101*, 676–703.

Maye. J., Aslin, R.N. & Tanenhaus, M.K. 2008. The Weckud Wetch of the Wast: Lexical adaptation to a novel accent. *Cognitive Science, 32*, 3, 543–562.

Newport, E. L. 1990. Maturational constraints on language learning. *Cognitive Scieince, 14*, 11–28.

Norris, D., McQueen, J. M., & Cutler, A. 2003. Perceptual learning in speech. *Cognitive Psychology, 47*, 204–238.

Nygaard, L. C., & Pisoni, D. B. 1998. Talker-specific learning in speech perception. *Perception & Psychophysics, 60*, 355–376.

Perruchet, P., & Pacton, S. 2006. Implicit learning and statistical learning: One phenomenon, two approaches. *Trends in Cognitive Sciences, 10*, 233–238.

Perruchet, P., & Vinter, A. 2002. The self-organizing consciousness. *Behavioral and Brain Sciences, 25*, 297–388.

Pickering, M. J., & Branigan, H. P. 1998. The representation of verbs: Evidence from syntactic priming in language production. *Journal of Memory and Language, 39*, 633–651.

Pickering, M. J., & Ferreira, V. S. 2008. Structural priming: A critical review, *Psychological Bulletin, 134*, 427–459.

Pickering, M. J., & Garrod, S. 2004. Toward a mechanistic psychology of dialogue. *Behavioral and Brain Sciences, 27*, 169–226.

Pinker, S. 1989. *Learnability and Cognition: The acquisition of Argument Structure*. Cambridge, Mass.: MIT Press.

Pinker, S. 1994. *The language instinct*. New York: Harper Collins.

Pinker, S. & Bloom, P. 1990. Natural language and natural selection. *Behavioral and Brain Sciences, 13*, 707 – 784.

Read, D., & Craik, F. I. M. 1995. Earwitness identification: Some influences on voice recognition. *Journal of Experimental Psychology: Applied, 1*, 6 – 18.

Reber, A. S. 1993. *Implicit learning and tacit knowledge: An essay on the cognitive unconscious*. Oxford University Press.

Reitter, D., Keller, F., & Moore, J. D. 2011. A computational cognitive model of syntactic priming. *Cognitive Science, 35*, 587–637.

Saffran, J. R., Aslin, R. N., & Newport, E. L. 1996. Statistical learning by 8-month-old infants. *Science, 274*, 1926–1928.

Saffran, J. R., & Thiessen, E. D. 2003. Pattern induction by infant language learners. *Developmental Psychology, 39*, 484–494.

Seidenberg, M. S., MacDonald, M. C., & Saffran, J. R. 2002. Does grammar start where statistics stop? *Science, 298*, 553–554.

Skinner, B. F. 1957. *Verbal behavior.* Appleton-Century-Crofts.

Sumner, M., & Samuel, A. G. 2009. The effect of experience on the perception and representation of dialect variants. *Journal of Memory and Language, 60*, 487–501.

Tanenhaus, M. K., Spivey-Knowlton, M. J., Eberhard, K. M., & Sedivy, J. C. 1995. Integration of visual and linguistic information in spoken language comprehension. *Science, 268*, 1632–1634.

Taylor, J. R. 1998. Syntactic constructions as prototype categories. In M. Tomasello (Ed.) *The New Psychology of Language.*

Thiessen, E.D., & Saffran, J.R. 2003. When cues collide: Use of statistical and stress cues to word boundaries by 7- and 9-month-old infants. *Developmental Psychology, 39*, 706–716.

Trude, A. M., & Brown-Schmidt, S. 2011. Talker-specific perceptual adaptation during online speech perception. *Language and Cognitive Processes.*

Tuller, B., Case, P., Ding, M., & Kelso, J. A. S. 1994. The nonlinear dynamics of speech categorization, *Journal of Experimental Psychology: Human Perception and Performance 20*, 1–16.

Turk-Browne, N. B., Jungé, J. A., & Scholl, B. J. 2005. The automaticity of visual statistical learning. *Journal of Experimental Psychology: General, 134*, 552–564.

Van Berkum, J. J. A., Van den Brink, D., Tesink, C. M., Kos, M., & Hagoort, P. 2008. The neural integration of speaker and message. *Journal of Cognitive Neuroscience, 20*, 580–591.

Van Orden, G. C., Holden, J. G., & Turvey, M. T. 2003. Self-organization of cognitive performance. *Journal of Experimental Psychology: General, 132*, 331–350.

Warker, J. A., & Dell, G. S. 2006. Speech errors reflect newly learned phonotactic constraints. *Journal of Experimental Psychology: Learning, Memory, and Cognition, 32*, 387–398.

Wells, J. B., Christiansen, M. H., Race, D. S., Acheson, D. J., & MacDonald, M. C. 2009. Experience and sentence comprehension: Statistical learning and relative clause comprehension. *Cognitive Psychology, 58*, 250–271.

Whittlesea, B. W. A., & Brooks, L. R. 1988. Critical influence of particular experiences in the perception of letters, words, and phrases. *Memory and Cognition, 16*, 387–399.

Zajonc, R. B. 1968. Attitudinal effects of mere exposure. *Journal of Personality and Social Psychology, 9*, 1–27.

Bernd Heine, Gunther Kaltenböck, Tania Kuteva and Haiping Long
An Outline of Discourse Grammar

1 Introduction

The main claim made in this chapter is that certain linguistic phenomena that in previous functional approaches to language were either ignored or treated as marginal play an important role in linguistc interaction and the organization of texts. To this end, an elementary distinction between two domains of speech processing is proposed, referred to as Sentence Grammar (SG) and Thetical Grammar (TG), and it is argued that these domains form the major parts of Discourse Grammar. In the sense of the term used here, Discourse Grammar thus differs from, and must not be confused with the model of Functional Discourse Grammar (Hengeveld and Mackenzie 2008), which does not make such a distinction.

We assume that SG is organized in terms of propositional concepts and clauses, and that the nucleus of the clause is the verb with its argument structure, optionally extended by peripheral participants (or adjuncts). Its main building blocks are constituent types such as phrases, words, and morphemes plus the syntactic and morphological machinery to relate these constituents to one another. TG, on the other hand, subsumes linguistic elements that are generally seen as being outside the confines of SG. They include what is traditionally referred to as "parenthetical" constructions and various extra-clausal units such as vocatives, imperatives, formulae of social exchange, and interjections.

In the course of the last decades there has been a growing awareness of issues relating to TG, resulting in a substantial body of publications (see especially Dehé and Kavalova 2007 for some summarizing accounts). An outline of TG is proposed in Kaltenböck et al. (2011), and the way in which the two domains interact in shaping discourse is proposed in Heine and Kaltenböck (forthc.). The present chapter aims at outlining the major contours of Discourse Grammar, which is taken to comprise both the domain of traditional SG and that of TG. However, since SG is well documented whereas TG is a relatively new field of analysis our main concern here will be with the latter.

The chapter differs from other works of mainstream functional linguistics in assuming a binary distinction in grammar and discourse organization and one may wonder what justification there is for this assumption. As we will see in Section 3, this distinction is based on the definition in (3); we will deal with this and related issues in more detail in Section 4.7.

The chapter is organized as follows. Section 2 gives a brief characterization of what we understand by "Discourse Grammar". Section 3 illustrates the main differences between the two domains, while Section 4 presents an inventory of the main functional categories of TG. Whereas SG has been described in detail in many different theoretical frameworks, TG is a relatively new notion (see Kaltenböck et al. 2011), and subsequent sections are devoted to central issues associated with this notion. Section 5 focuses on the communicative functions of TG in a given situation of discourse, and in Section 6 our concern is with cooptation, a central mechanism linking the two domains. Section 7 is concerned with various classifications within the domain of TG, in Section 8 we will relate the framework proposed to previous lines of research, and the final Section 9 draws attention to a number of problems that could not be solved in the chapter.

Exemplification is generally restricted to English. This is done on the one hand for practical purposes; on the other hand it reflects the Eurocentric scope of the chapter. While there exists a thorough data base on Discourse Grammar and theticals for languages such as English, German, Dutch, some Romance and Slavic languages, or for Japanese and Korean, there is so far little coherent information on such phenomena in most other languages of the world. The extent to which the observations made in this paper apply to languages other than English, especially to non-European languages, is a problem that is beyond the scope of the present treatment and requires much further research.

2 Discourse Grammar

The linguistic analysis of discourse has to do most of all (a) with the intentions of speakers and hearers[1] and the purposes that linguistic discourse is meant to serve, (b) with text planning, and (c) with the linguistic resources used for structuring texts. Discourse Grammar, as we understand it, has a narrow scope: It is composed of all the linguistic resources that are available for designing texts, irrespective of whether these are spoken, written, or signed texts. Thus, it concerns first and above (c), while (a) and (b) are only indirectly accessible to it. Note that our concern is exclusively with verbal communication; an adequate theory of human communication would include non-verbal communication, which is beyond the scope of the present framework.

What all linguistic resources of Discourse Grammar have in common, irrespective of whether they concern SG or TG, is that they consist of form-meaning units that are used for designing linearized texts.

---

[1] Throughout the paper we are using "speaker" and "hearer" as cover terms for speaker/writer/signer and hearer/reader/signee, respectively.

Discourse phenomena have many facets and they have been the subject of many different approaches. With reference to the distinction between discourse analysis and conversation analysis as proposed by Levinson (1983: 286), our concern is exclusively with the former, and we will be restricted to one particular manifestation of discourse phenomena, namely to those that are amenable to, or can be reduced to objects of linguistic study. To this end, we will rely on conventional tools of linguistic analysis for understanding and describing discourse phenomena. Discourse analysis is necessarily the analysis of language in use, and as such it has to do with the purposes or functions that linguistic forms are designed for (Brown and Yule 1983: 1).

In accordance with other works written in the functionalist tradition, tracking the communicative use of grammar via the distribution of grammar in text (Givón 1995: 305) is a central tool of the methodology employed here. Like in Conversation Analysis (CA), our concern is centrally with linguistic discourse (see e.g. Schegloff 1968; 1998; Schegloff and Sacks 1973; Sacks, Schegloff and Jefferson 1974; Schegloff, Jefferson and Sacks 1977, *inter alia*). But whereas CA takes social interaction as the primary focus of study, DG is concerned with orthodox linguistic taxonomy: Rather than with interactional structure, it has the description of both language use and linguistic structure as its primary goal. Theticals frequently, though by no means always, take the form of what in CA are called turn constructional units (Sacks, Schegloff and Jefferson 1974), and like the latter, theticals can be sentential, phrasal, or lexical. But there is no one-to-one correspondence between the two: Turn constructional units may consist in much the same way of SG and of TG units.

In terms of the grammatical framework proposed by Thompson (2002: 141–2), DG, in the sense of the term used here, can be said to consist of reusable fragments or combinations thereof, or of collocations of frequent schematic, and fully functional and combinable fragments. These fragments, or information units as we say here, are not all of the same kind.[2] First, they belong to, or may be used in at least two different domains of DG (Section 3) and, second, they are divided into a range of categories, to be discussed in Section 4.

---

2 We propose to use the term information unit as a cover term for any pairing of form-meaning units that can be separated from the remainder of an utterance by means of semantic, syntactic, and/or prosodic criteria – ideally by all three of these criteria. An information unit can be a word, but it can consist as well of a complex collocation of words. The term "information unit" thus is similar to, but is not the same as that of a discourse act in the tradition of Functional Discourse Grammar, defined as "the smallest identifiable unit of communicative behaviour" (Hengeveld and Mackenzie 2008: 308).

DG has two complementary aspects. On the one hand it is an *activity*, a real-time interactional tool – it is language in use and concerns the way people utilize the linguistic tools that are available to them in a given situation to design utterances. On the other hand it is a knowledge store or a *conventionalized object* consisting of a set of conventional linguistic units (Langacker 2010: 88), that is, of more or less fixed or schematic information units that are stored for reuse in a more or less frozen or reified form (Du Bois 1985: 362).

We may illustrate the distinction with the constructed examples in (1). As we will see in more detail below, the two information units printed in bold are both part of TG – they are theticals (see our definition in (3)), traditionally referred to as parentheticals. But they differ from one another in that the one in (1a) is fully compositional and has the appearance of a spontaneously designed information unit, being suggestive of discourse organization as a creative activity. The unit *you know* in (1b), by contrast, a comment clause or discourse marker (Brinton 2008) or reusable fragment (Thompson 2002: 141–2), is part of the conventionalized inventory of stored elements of DG.

(1) a. *Winterbottom, **I am quite sure you know that,** is a fink.*

 b. *Winterbottom **you know** is a fink.*

In our analysis of DG we thus rely both on what people do and what they know. Accordingly, we will be concerned on the one hand with products of language use, that is, spoken, written, and signed texts. On the other hand, we will also use information on the knowledge that people have about the inventory of linguistic constructions available to them, and we will use the former to reconstruct the latter.

3 The two main domains of DG

As observed in the preceding section, the linguistic resources of Discourse Grammar are form-meaning units and its organizing principle is linearization. That DG consists of at least two different conceptual domains has been argued in more detail in Kaltenböck et al. (2011). The main distinguishing features of these domains can be illustrated with the examples in (2), taken from the *Comprehensive grammar of English* by Quirk et al. (1985: 1306–7).

(2) a. *They considered Miss Hartley a very good teacher.*

b. *They considered Miss Hartley,* ***a very good teacher.***

The utterances in (2) consist of information units of Sentence Grammar (SG) on the one hand and of Thetical Grammar (TG) on the other. The unit printed in bold is called a thetical, that is, it belongs to the domain of TG, while all other units belong to SG.[3] This classification is based on the definition in (3) (for a justification of this definition, see Kaltenböck et al. 2011: 853–7). Note that (3) is a prototypical definition rather than one based on discrete categorization: The more of the properties a given information unit exhibits, the better a member of the domain of theticals that unit is.

(3) Properties of theticals

a. They are syntactically independent from their environment.

b. They tend to be set off prosodically from the rest of the utterance.

c. Their meaning is non-restrictive.

d. They tend to be positionally mobile.

e. Their internal structure is built on principles of SG but can be elliptic.[4]

That the examples in (2) are in accordance with (3) is suggested by the following observations.[5] First, the information unit *a very good teacher* is an object complement of the sentence in (2a), that is, it is licenced by the syntax of the sentence. In (2b), by contrast, it is – in accordance with (3a) – syntactically independent from the rest of the utterance: Being neither an argument nor an adjunct, it is technically known as a non-restrictive appositive. Second, it is also prosodically independent from the rest of the sentence. Thus, the information unit *a very good teacher* is part of the prosody of the sentence in (2a) while in (2b) it is separated from the preceding clause by a tone unit boundary in spoken English and by a comma in written English (Quirk et al. 1985: 1307). And third, there is also a dif-

---

3 The unit in bold is classified as an apposition (cf. Quirk et al. 1985: 1306–7), which in the framework of Kaltenböck et al. (2011) is one type of conceptual theticals.

4 The term "elliptic" (or "ellipsis") is used here exclusively to describe the relation between an SG expression and a thetical that differs from the former only in the fact that it has the appearance of a reduced form. We are aware of the problems associated with this term (see e.g. Barton 1990; 1998; Mackenzie 1998; Hengeveld and Mackenzie 2008).

5 We are ignoring here property (3d) since it does not clearly apply to the present example.

ference in meaning. Whereas the meaning of *a very good teacher* in (2a) is determined by its syntactic function as a complement of the sentence, in (2b) it is fairly
independent from the sentence meaning: It can be understood e.g. as an elaboration on one participant of the utterance. Following Huddleston and Pullum (2002:
1352) we propose to call the meaning of *a very good teacher* in (2a) restrictive and
that in (2b) non-restrictive (see Section 5).[6] In other words, by characterizing theticals as linguistic expressions with non-restrictive meaning we draw attention to
the fact that (i) they are fairly independent from the sentence meaning, and (ii)
that the sentence meaning is largely independent from them.

Many utterances, such as (2a), are exclusively SG units; others, such as (2b),
contain both, while still others consist entirely of theticals. As we will argue in
more detail in Section 4 (see also Figure 1), theticals do not require an SG utterance as a host.[7] The utterance in (4) illustrates this: It consists of a sequence of
five theticals without there being any SG host. These theticals consist of an interjection (*oh*), a vocative (*Clare*), an imperative (*turn it up*), a question tag (*will you*),
and a formula of social exchange (*please*).[8] Thetical-only utterances are perhaps
particularly common in "routine procedures" (Clark 1996: 296–8), e.g. in role
relations such as customer-ticketseller, surgeon-nurse, or mother-child.

(4) ***Oh, Clare, turn it up will you please?***   (Biber et al. 1999: 220, 221)

That the information units of (4) are all theticals is suggested by the fact that
they are in accordance with the definition in (3): They are syntactically independent from their environment, that is, they cannot normally be embedded, they
are likely to be prosodically distinct and semantically non-restrictive in the sense
that their meaning is largely independent from the rest of the utterance of which
they are a part.

To conclude, information units of the two domains can be separated on the
basis of semantic, prosodic, and semantic properties. Nevertheless, they are not
entirely independent of one another. First, as noted also by Newmeyer (2012:
11), there is not always an absolute one-to-one relationship between syntactic

---

6 Huddleston and Pullum (2002: 1352) use the term "non-restrictive" to characterize supplements, which largely correspond to our notion of theticals: "By virtue of not being integrated
into the syntactic structure, supplements are necessarily semantically non-restrictive."
7 Instead of "host", the terms anchor or frame are used by a number of authors. Note that in
grammaticalization theory "host" refers to the stable or invariable part of a combination (Himmelmann 2004), and in morphology, the term applies to the word to which a clitic is attached
(see Huddleston and Pullum 2002: 1351).
8 "Question tags" were referred to as "tag questions" in Kaltenböck et al. (2011). In this chapter
we follow Axelsson (2011) in using the former term.

structure and some other component. Accordingly, the match stipulated in (3) between different components of grammar may not be complete in some cases. And second, there are various forms of interference between them (see Kalten-böck et al. 2011, Section 3.2 for discussion). For example, the thetical *a very good teacher* in (2b) is linked to the complement of the preceding clause via reference identity and co-referencing. Thus, in spite of the fact that TG and SG are distinct domains that can be set apart on the basis of formal properties, the two neverthe-less tend to interact in jointly structuring discourse. Figure 1 illustrates this multi-domain structure of Discourse Grammar together with typical categories of TG to be discussed in Section 4.

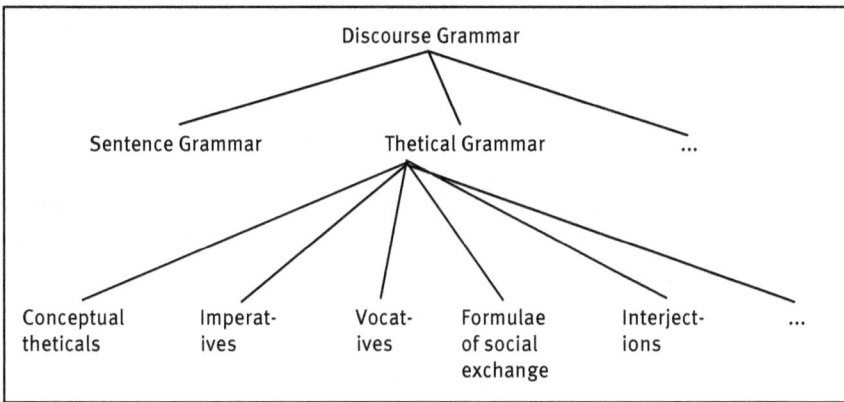

Figure 1: A skeleton of Discourse Grammar

The term thetical must not be confused with that of "thetic" statement of Kuroda (1972), Sasse (1987; 2006) and Lambrecht (1994; see Kaltenböck et al. 2011, Fn. 6);[9] rather, it is similar to what has been referred to in the past as parentheti-cal, parenthetic adjunct (Corum 1975), disjunct (Espinal 1991), interpolation, extra-clausal constituent (Dik 1997), insert, juxtaposed element (Peterson 1999: 237), syntactic non-clausal unit (Biber et al. 1999: 1082, 1099), supplement (Hud-dleston & Pullum 2002), or epistemic adverbial phrase (Thompson and Mulac 1991; Thompson 2002: 143), etc. The reasons for replacing the term parenthetical with the reduced form thetical are, first, that not all instances of this category are

---

9 Following Wehr (2000), we assume that the use of the term, at least as proposed e.g. by Sasse (1987; 2002), is redundant since "thetic statements" are more appropriately to be analyzed in terms of information structure: They represent a construction type that lacks a sentence topic.

in fact parenthetical in the sense that they are interpolated in or require a host utterance and, second, because most of the authors alluded to above are concerned only with some subset of theticals, that is, they do not take into account the whole range of categories distinguished here.[10]

It would seem that the distinction between the two domains of DG is on the one hand suggestive of differences in reasoning processes and text planning. This has been pointed out in some form or other already by earlier writers. For example, Havers (1931) argued that there are in particular two kinds of reasoning processes influencing language structure, namely on the one hand *successive thinking* (which is opposed to simultaneous thinking) and on the other hand *associative thinking*, which is concerned with loosely organized ideas and impressions. Whereas the former is reflected most clearly in SG, the latter is manifested in imaginations and impressions that are ordered loosely without being limited by sequencing rules, and associative thinking is responsible for parenthesis, that is, essentially for TG phenomena (see Schneider 2007b: 26, 39).

On the other hand, this distinction appears to be associated with contrasting principles of internal linguistic organization. Whereas SG consists of largely compositional sentence structures, many TG units are fixed holophrases (Mackenzie 1998; Hengeveld and Mackenzie 2008: 3–4), that is, non-compositional, formulaic information units, as illustrated in Table 2 of Section 4.7.3. To be sure, theticals are almost invariably coopted from SG units and, hence, can have the fully compositional format of their SG models (see Section 6); thus, the *and*-thetical in the following example has the format of a complex sentence. But such compositional units are almost entirely restricted to instantaneous theticals formed spontaneously (see 4.2).

(5) *Mr Heath's government **and I'm not complaining because I'd advocated this at a previous time** introduced the threshold system ...*

(DCPSE: DL-E02, #114; Kavalova 2007: 148)

---

10 An alternative term for "thetical" would have been "extra-clausal constituent" (ECC) as proposed by Dik (1997: 379; see Section 8 below), which is largely synonymous to our notion of thetical. The reason for not adopting "EEC" is that this term implies that the clause or, more generally, SG enjoys a privileged status vis-a-vis TG, or that the latter should be understood and/ or described with reference to the former. Neither assumption is really justified on the basis of the present framework.

4 The categories of TG

The categories so far identified are listed in Figure 1, they include conceptual theticals, imperatives, vocatives, formulae of social exchange (FSEs), and interjections. These categories are distinguished on the one hand on the basis of their respective discourse functions and on the other hand with reference to their status as theticals, according to which they are set off syntactically, prosodically, and semantically from categories of SG (see (3) above). Like our definition of theticals, thus, that of these categories is prototypical rather than based on necessary and sufficient criteria; as we will see below (4.7), the boundaries between categories are fluid rather than discrete.

4.1 Introduction

In this section we present a short sketch of the different categories of TG. Discussion is restricted to a brief characterization of each category. In doing so, we will deal with the questions in (6), which are central to the framework proposed in this chapter.

(6) Questions

    a. Is there justification for assigning SG and TG to the same domain, namely Discourse Grammar?

    b. Are theticals different enough from SG units to be excluded from the domain of SG?

    c. Are theticals similar enough to one another to justify their analysis as a domain of their own?

    d. Is the inventory of categories distinguished exhaustive?

    e. What is the nature of the boundaries of categories: Are they discrete or gradient?

    f. How to identify theticals in isolation?

We will return to these questions in the final subsection 4.7.

4.2 Conceptual theticals

Most works that have been devoted to issues of TG are largely or entirely restricted to the analysis of conceptual theticals.[11] And since they have also been discussed in detail in Kaltenböck et al. (2011), we are restricted here to a general characterization of them.

Conceptual theticals are invariably derived from sentences, phrases, words or other chunks of SG via a cognitive operation called cooptation (Kaltenböck et al. 2011: 874–5); we will return to this operation in Section 6. They exhibit a wide range of different structures and meanings and have been classified in a number of ways (Espinal 1991: 726–7; Peterson 1999; Dehé and Kavalova 2007b: 1–4; Kaltenböck 2007: 27–31; de Vries 2007: 204; Brinton 2008: 9–10). For example, conceptual theticals either take the form of full clauses that can function as utterances of their own, like *I'll just turn it off* in (7a), or they may be structurally incomplete or "elliptic", lacking e.g. a predicate, as *didn't we* is in (7b). Or they can be short, consisting of a single word, like *what* in (7c), or long and internally complex, as (7d) illustrates. We will return to the typology of theticals in Section 7.

(7) a. *So what we can do in fact **I'll just turn it off** <,> is to use that signal to train people's ability to perceive voicing.*   (ICE-GB: s2a-056–87)

b. *In fact we had a horror **didn't we** on the way t to Holland.*
      (ICE-GB: s1a-021–036)

c. *I mean I suppose he's **what** in his Early forties now* (DCPSE: DL-B23–0610)

d. *It's been a mixture of extreme pleasure **I've had hundreds of letters from all sorts of people who have enjoyed the book** and considerable irritation because of being constantly interviewed.*
      (ICE-GB; Dehé and Kavalova 2007b: 3)

---

11 Such works include but are not restricted to the following: Urmson 1952; Rutherford 1970; Kac 1972; Bayer 1973; Ross 1973; Emonds 1973; 1976; 1979; Corum 1975; Reinhart 1983; Quirk et al. 1985: 853; Safir 1986; Pittner 1995; Peterson 1999; Biber et al. 1999: 1067; Haegeman 1991; Espinal 1991; Thompson and Mulac 1991a; Peterson 1999; Dik 1997, chapter 17; Aijmer 1997; Rouchota 1998: 105; Biber et al. 1999: 1082; Ifantidou-Trouki 1993; Wichmann 2001; Kärkkäinen 2003; Shaer 2003; Shaer and Frey 2004; Grenoble 2004; Schelfhout et al. 2004; Fortmann 2006; 2007; Stowell 2005; Tucker 2005; Blakemore 2005; 2006: 1673; Dehé and Kavalova 2006; Kaltenböck 2007; 2008; 2010; 2011; Mazeland 2007; Schneider 2007b; Brinton 2008: 7–14; Dehé 2009a; 2009b; as well as the contributions in Dehé and Kavalova 2007a; Dehé and Wichmann 2010a; 2010b.

One subtype of theticals consists of discourse markers (or discourse particles, or pragmatic markers). As the rich literature on these units suggests (e.g. Schiffrin 1987; Jucker and Ziv 1998; Schourup 1999; Brinton 1996; 2008; Fischer 2000; 2006; Aijmer 2002; Dér 2008; Lewis 2011; Vandenbergen and Willems 2011), discourse markers are typically short, even if there are also multi-word units (e.g., *as it were, if you will, in other words*). What they all have in common is that their primary function is to serve the organization of texts and that they are largely or entirely invariable, that is, they typically do not allow internal modification. The boundary between formulaic theticals and other kinds of theticals, however, is fluid (see Heine in print).

As demonstrated in Kaltenböck et al. (2011), conceptual theticals behave in all respects in accordance with the definition in (3): They are syntactically independent from the rest of the utterance and are likely to be set off prosodically. Their meaning is non-restrictive in that omitting the theticals in (7) would not change the semantics of their host sentence. All theticals in (7) are built on principles of SG but some, such as (7b), differ from corresponding SG clauses in having the appearance of elliptic clauses.

4.3 Formulae of social exchange (FSEs)

FSEs constitute the primary linguistic means for establishing or maintaining mutually beneficial relations among speech participants, used e.g. to express politeness and respect (Wichmann 2004: 524). English *please* or *kindly*, for example, are commonly used to tone down the abruptness of a command, e.g.,

(8) a. *You will* please *leave the room.*

   b. Kindly *don't make a noise.* (Quirk et al. 1985: 570–1)

They are typically formulaic theticals (see Table 2, Section 4.7.3), that is, short, frozen chunks used in stereotyped communication as conventional speech act realisations (cf. Tucker 2005: 699). Nevertheless, they can be modified within limits, e.g., *Thanks!* vs. *Thanks very much!* (Wray and Perkins 2000; Wray 2002; 2009; Tucker 2005: 684), and their structure extends from fixed, unanalyzable information units to free syntactic combinations. A number of them take the form of what Pawley (1992: 23) calls semantic formulae, that is, familiar groupings of ideas expressed by a short stretch of discourse but not necessarily by the same words. For example, *Pleased to meet you* and *Delighted to make your acquaintance* are instances of one and the same semantic formula of social exchange.

FSEs are used for a range of social functions, most of all for greetings (*Good morning*) and farewell sayings (*Goodbye*), thanks (e.g. *thank you, thanks, cheers*), empathy (e.g. *bad luck, good shot)*, apologies (e.g. *sorry*), polite requests (*please*), etc. The English FSE that has presumably received most scholarly attention is *please* (e.g., Stubbs 1983; Wichmann 2004: 1522).

FSEs conform in every respect to our definition in (3): They are syntactically and prosodically independent information units (typically with rather fixed intonation contours), and they can form utterances of their own. And even if their meaning relates to the surrounding discourse, it is non-restrictive, that is, semantically independent from the rest of an utterance. Being built on principles of SG, some FSEs are reduced forms historically derived via ellipsis from more elaborated, clausal expressions (Biber et al. 1999: 1047; Wichmann 2004). For example, *please* is a reduced form of *if you please, if it please you*, and/or *be pleased to*, while *Goodbye* is an eroded form of *God be with you!* (see e.g. Hengeveld and Mackenzie 2008: 78; Traugott forthc.).

Like vocatives and interjections, the preferred position is utterance-initial in English, but some FSEs, such as *please, sorry*, or *thanks* are floating theticals, that is, they are positionally highly variable (see Section 7). Others are constrained in their placement by the particular function they serve in discourse; greetings, for example, are likely to be placed initially and farewell formulae last in an utterance. The following utterance consists of two FSEs interrupted by a vocative (*Cindy*):

(9) ***Good morning, Cindy, how are you?***

Use of FSEs is optional in English, but in many registers and genres of discourse, e.g. in letter writing (*Dear Sir, Yours faithfully*, etc.), it is indispensible.
The boundaries separating FSEs from interjections (see 4.6) are largely unclear, the two are best described as overlapping categories (see 4.7).

4.4 Vocatives

Vocatives, also called address forms or address terms, serve "to call the attention of an addressee in order to establish or maintain a relationship between this addressee and some proposition" (Lambrecht 1996: 267). But they may have other functions in addition, depending on the context and/or the intonation used (Aikhenvald 2010: 7).[12] They are pragmatically accessible in the text-exter-

---

12 For a discussion of features associated with vocatives, see Lambrecht (1996: 267ff.).

nal world (Lambrecht 1996: 268ff.) or, as we say here, they serve speaker-hearer interaction, which is one of the main components of the situation of discourse (Section 5).

That vocatives should not be regarded as just one of the "cases" of a language, such as Latin, but rather as an entity *sui generis* has been argued by a range of linguists since the 19th century (see Floricic 2012 for a detailed survey of previous work). For August Schleicher (1862: 162), for example, the vocative was neither a case nor an element of a sentence but rather a word which has assumed the form of an interjection – "a gesture translated into sound."

Having been treated as minor clauses or a sentence type that can form an utterance of its own (e.g., *Mary!*, *Waiter!*, *Dr Newman!*) (Hockett 1958: 200–1; Halliday 1985: 63), they typically consist of proper names, possibly accompanied by titles, functions, or references to the relation between the speaker and the hearer (Dik 1997: 385), but they may as well be pronominal forms (*You, Somebody, Everyone*; Fraser 1990: 391),[13] as in (10).

(10) *"Look,* you," *he said, finally turning to the chief inspector, "what do you think you're doing?"* (Barnes, *A Midsummer Killing*, BNC; Brinton 2008: 185)

A number of languages, such as Latin, Old Church Slavonic, Modern Bulgarian, many Omotic languages of Ethiopia, Yupik Eskimo of Siberia, or the Amazonian languages Tariana and Tocano (Aikhenvald 2010: 111), have a special grammatical form dedicated to vocative expressions, namely a vocative case inflection or clitic. Our concern here, however, is not with vocative as a morphological category but rather as a discourse category, as in (11) (McCawley 1988; Espinal 1991: 727, Nosek 1973: 101, Ziv 1985: 191; Lambrecht 1996: 267ff.; Kaltenböck 2007: 31).

(11) *Today's topic,* ladies and gentlemen, *is astrophysics.* (Kaltenböck 2007: 31)

That vocatives, like interjections, "are outside the formal structure of the sentence" (Onions 1971: 231), encoding "an entire parallel message" (Fraser 1990: 391), has been pointed out in many works, and some authors specifically treat them as parentheticals, that is, as a part of TG (e.g., Peterson 1999: 231–2; Kaltenböck 2007: 31).

In fact, vocatives conform to all the criteria in (3) that we proposed for theticals: They are syntactically independent from their environment, and they are set off prosodically from the rest of the utterance, signaled in (12) by the use of

---

13 A classification of types of English vocatives is found in Fraser (1990: 891–2). Note that Fraser also includes some theticals that are not vocatives in the sense of the term used here.

commas. And their meaning is non-restrictive: Thus, the semantics of (12) would not be dramatically affected by the omission of the vocative unit. And their internal structure is built on principles of SG but can be elliptic: Vocatives are frequently coopted from referential nouns or noun phrases, but compared to corresponding noun phrases of SG they may lack morphological material.[14] For example, English nouns require the use of articles in many contexts. But when coopted as vocatives, they occur without articles, as (11) shows.

That vocatives are not arguments of any kind is indicated by their not participating in VP ellipsis, as in the following dialog:

(12) A: *Didn't you claim,* **John,** *that Bill would pass?*

    B: *I didn't.*
    (= *I didn't claim that Bill would pass.* ≠ **I didn't claim, John, that Bill would*
    pass.)   (McCawley 1988: 763; Burton-Roberts 2005)

Like other thetical categories, vocatives tend to be marked off in some way. In some languages they are particularly short and unmarked. For example, in some Bantu languages, such as Runyankore of western Uganda, the initial vowel of a noun is omitted in the vocative, i.e. when someone is addressed directly (Morris and Kirwan 1957: 150). And in the Yurok language of Northwestern California, there are vocative forms for kin terms that are less marked than nouns are in other functions, e.g., *kok!* 'Mother!' vs. *kokos* 'mother', or *pic* 'Grandfather!' vs. *picowos* 'grandfather' (Robins 1958: 23), or Fox *iʃkwe* 'woman!' vs. *iʃkwɛ:wa* 'woman' (Bloomfield 1962 [1933]: 177).

Of all thetical categories, vocatives are perhaps positionally the most variable: Not only can they be inserted in most slots of an utterance but they frequently occur also as independent utterances (e.g., *Waiter!*). And of all thetical categories, they occur most frequently in collocation with other categories such as FSEs (e.g., *Happy Birthday, my dear father!*) or imperatives (*Anne <,> listen*; ICE-GB: s1a-019–097; *Have some gravy Rob*; ICE-GB: s1a-012–085; *Keep talking you idiot*; ICE-GB: s1a-041–057).

To conclude, vocatives appear to be an uncontroversial category of TG, being in accordance with our definition of theticals. Rather than contributing to the semantics of a sentence, their function concerns the situation of discourse, more specifically speaker-hearer interaction.

---

14 Rather than lacking material, however, some languages use extra morphological material for vocatives, such as vocative case forms (see above).

4.5 Imperatives

Imperatives are a universal category in the sense that they can be expected to exist in some form or other in any language, even if there are a few languages that lack a dedicated imperative construction. They have been characterized as being morphologically unusual (Zanuttini and Portner 2003: 42), as having "an extragrammatical, extrasyntactical form" (Watkins 1963: 44),[15] and as being "a law unto themselves" Aikhenvald (2010: 7, 399). They have also been described as being "defective" or as belonging to the "sentences of some minor type" (Hockett 1958: 200–1), or as not necessarily following phonotactic rules of the grammar of a language (Floricic and Molinu 2008). To account for the illocutionary and syntactic features of imperative constructions, a specific imperative operator or feature has been proposed (e.g., Rivero and Terzi 1995; Han 1998).

That imperatives are distinguished conceptually and structurally is suggested e.g. by the fact that they may be suppletive, that is, have a verb form not found in a corresponding SG unit. It would seem that roughly 20 % of all languages have at least one suppletive imperative verb (Veselinova 2006: 135–47; see also Aikhenvald 2010: 322–3).

With reference to the situation of discourse (Section 5), imperatives relate unambiguously to only one component, namely speaker-hearer interaction: The speaker claims some form of obedience from the hearer, and the speaker assumes that the action expressed by the imperative can be controlled by the hearer.[16] Imperatives constitute crosslinguistically the paradigm form for eliciting action (Givón 2001: 31).

Imperatives behave in most respects like other thetical categories (see (3) above):[17]

(a) They are syntactically independent from their environment, that is, they cannot normally be embedded in other clauses (Sadock and Zwicky 1985; Whaley 1997: 237; Aikhenvald 2010: 112), exceptions being rare (e.g., Dixon 2010b: 171).[18]

---

15 Concerning the term "extragrammatical", see Hjelmslev (1928: 240).

16 In quite a few languages, some verbs lacking a controlling agent can acquire one in imperatives (Aikhenvald 2010: 324).

17 An anonymous reviewer of this chapter doubts whether imperatives in fact belong to TG. While imperatives differ in fact in a number of their features from other thetical categories, we consider the reasons given below to be sufficient to justify their inclusion (see also Floricic and Molinu 2012). But more research is needed on this issue.

18 A few languages from the Papuan area, such as Hua and Yagaria, have been reported to have imperatives that occur in dependent clauses (Aikhenvald 2010: 109, 399; see also Takahashi 2005; 2008).

(b) They form separate prosodic units, typically having their own intonation contour and being set off from their environment by small pauses; in writing, they tend to be marked off by punctuation marks – as Aikhenvald (2010: 399) concludes in her worldwide survey of imperative constructions, "imperatives sound different from other types of clauses".
(c) That imperatives have non-restrictive meaning is largely derivative of (a): Since they cannot normally be embedded in other clauses, their meaning is essentially independent of the surrounding information units.
(d) Their internal structure is built on principles of SG but can be elliptic. Ellipsis concerns information unit whose meaning is recoverable from the situation of discourse (Section 5). It tends to affect on the one hand subject marking: In the majority of the world's languages, canonical (singular) imperatives differ from corresponding SG verb forms in lacking an overt subject marker (whose reference is implied but not expressed). On the other hand, it also tends to affect morphological distinctions of tense, aspect, and modality in a number of languages.

Imperatives can be viewed as forming a continuum, both crosslinguistically and, frequently, also language internally. At one end of the continuum there are full-fledged verbal structures, marked for person, number, case, tense, aspect, modality, etc. At the other end there can be a morphologically extremely reduced structure consisting of the bare verb stem that lacks all these morphological markings, being what Aikhenvald (2010: 4) calls a canonical imperative.[19]

To conclude, that imperatives form one of the categories of TG is suggested most of all by the following observations: They conform to our definition of theticals in (3), and they serve a paradigm function of TG, namely speaker-hearer interaction (see Section 5).

4.6 Interjections

Interjections have been portrayed as being "indefinable" (see Cuenca 2000), and what counts as an interjection is a question that is answered somewhat differently by each of the authors concerned. While there are a number of fairly uncontrover-

---

[19] Canonical imperatives are positive (singular) imperatives, that is, information units having an (implicit) second person singular subject referent as a hearer (or reader or signee) and expressing commands or requests directed at the hearer. There is some evidence to suggest that canonical imperatives constitute the most prototypical form of the category. In many languages across the world it is the shortest and the simplest verb form (Aikhenvald (2010: 18; see below).

sial instances of interjections, such as English *oops, ouch,* or *wow,* the boundary area is extremely fuzzy. Obviously, this problem is constantly present throughout this section. We will say that an interjection is an invariable and syntactically independent linguistic form that typically indexes a change in the emotional or cognitive state of the speaker. We are aware that this characterization takes care of many but certainly not of all properties of interjections (cf. Quirk et al. 1985: 853; Fraser 1990: 391; Ameka 1992: 867; Rhodes 1992: 222; Wharton 2003; Norrick 2009: 876).

That interjections are not "paralinguistic" or other appendages to SG but rather form an independent category of Discourse Grammar is suggested in particular by the following. First, like SG units they are form-meaning units, and they cover a range of meanings that are different from but complement those of SG units. Second, they may play a role similar to that of other categories of DG in organizing texts. For example, while they are typically non-referential and cannot normally be addressed in discourse, these are not features that are entirely ruled out. Thus, in the following example, the secondary interjection *oh Lord* is referred to and commented on in the subsequent turn of line 5 (see also Norrick 2009: 878–9):[20]

(13) English (LSWEC-AC 145201; Norrick 2009: 879)

1	Freda:	*was Chris married in ninety three.*
2	Bud:	**oh Lord.**
3	Carol:	((laugh))
4	((?)):	*yes.*
5	Carol:	**oh Lord is right.**
6		*that was the year of all the weddings.*

And third, at least some interjections can undergo grammaticalization like SG units. For example, English secondary interjections such as *hell, fuck* or *shit* can be placed before *yeah* and *no,* respectively, and in this context lose their status and function as independent units, being grammaticalized to intensifiers (Norrick 2009: 880). Thus, in the following example, *fuck* and *yeah* are in a

---

20 Primary interjections (e.g. English *ah, hm, huh, mhm, mm, oh, ooh, oops, ouch, uh, um, wow*) cannot be used in any other sense than as interjections. Secondary interjections by contrast (e.g. *boy, damn, fuck, hell, hey, okay, shit*) have an independent semantic value but can be used as utterances by themselves to express a mental attitude or state (Ameka 1992) and many have their roots in religion, sex, and scatology (Norrick 2009: 868).

modifier – head relation in that *fuck* has lost its interjective meaning in favor of an intensifying function (desemanticization), and *fuck* has also undergone decategorialization in that, in its grammaticalized form as an intensifier, it is no longer free to move around in an utterance.

(14) 1 AW> *Flying Man was a good horse.*

   2 BH> **fuck yeah** *it placed third in the derby in his year.*
          and fourth in the Great Northern Derby.

(WSC DPC032; Norrick 2009: 880)

That interjections are not part of orthodox syntax but pattern with some other thetical categories has been pointed out independently by a number of authors (e.g., Petola 1983: 107–108; Ziv 1985: 190; Dik 1997: 384; Peterson 1999: 231–2; Huddleston and Pullum 2002: 1360–1361; Kaltenböck 2007: 31; de Vries 2007: 204). In fact, they conform on the whole to our definition of theticals in (3): They are syntactically independent from their environment, they are set off prosodically from the rest of the utterance, and their meaning is non-restrictive. Even if that meaning may relate to that of surrounding text material, it is essentially independent from the latter. There is, however, one criterion (3e) that is to some extent at variance with the definition: At least primary interjections (such as *oops, ouch,* or *wow*) are not transparently built on principles of SG and, hence, cannot be said to be "elliptic". Secondary interjections on the other hand are mostly derived from SG units and tend to be "elliptic", cf. English *blimey*, which goes back to *God blind me*.

While most interjections index a change in the emotional or cognitive state of the speaker, this is only one of their functions, namely that of expressive interjections, such as *aw!, damn!,* or *yuck!*. Phatic interjections, by contrast, express the mental state of the speaker towards the on-going discourse, e.g., *mhm, yeah,* while conative interjections are used to get the hearer's attention or demand the hearer's response, e.g., *pst!* or *sh!* (cf. Ameka 1992; Bloomfield 1962 [1933]: 121; Ekman et al. 1972; Jackendoff 2002: 240; Dixon 2010b: 27). These types thus concern three of the main components of the situation of discourse (Section 5), namely text organization (phatic interjections), speaker attitudes (expressive interjections), and speaker-hearer interaction (conative interjections).

Interjections are positionally mobile, but they are less so than some other thetical categories. Their preferred position, not only in English, is the beginning of an utterance, preceding all other categories of DG. Thus, when combined with other theticals that also occur utterance-initially, interjections tend to precede, like in the following constructred example, where the interjection (*hey*) precedes both an FSE (*good morning*) and a vocative (*Annie!*).

(15) ***Hey, good morning, Annie!***

Due to lack of space we are ignoring here other features typically associated with interjections, such as the fact that some of them show phonetic features that do not occur elsewhere in the grammar or the lexicon (see e.g. Bloomfield 1962 [1933]: 121; Ameka 1992; Dixon 2010a: 283).

To conclude, interjections form a well-established category within TG: First, like other theticals, they are syntactically and prosodically independent, and they have non-restrictive meaning. Second, at least one type of interjections (secondary interjections) is built on principles of SG but may be elliptic compared to corresponding SG units. Third, they express paradigm functions of TG, namely primarily speaker attitudes and secondarily speaker-hearer interaction (cf. Section 5). And fourth, most of them are short and formulaic in structure.

Where the boundary separating interjections from other thetical categories is to be located is a question that is answered differently by each of the authors who have dealt with this category. In the present paper we include not only exclamatives (e.g., *Isn't he the cutest thing!*, *What a nice guy he is!*; Zanuttini and Portner 2003), but also pause fillers and hesitation markers (*uh, um;* O'Connell and Kowal 2003; Hayashi and Yoon 2006; 2010) within an overall category of interjections – being aware that both are more or less marginal members of the category: Exclamatives differ from paradigm exemplars of interjections in having some "recoverable propositional content" (Michaelis and Lambrecht 1996: 378). And pause fillers and hesitation markers do not typically index a change in the emotional or cognitive state of the speaker (see above) and have received various classifications, including that of discourse markers (Croucher 2004).

4.7 Conclusions

We are now in a position to return to the questions raised in the introductory Section 4.1 and will deal with each of them in turn.

4.7.1 Is there justification for assigning SG and TG to the same domain, namely Discourse Grammar?

There are a number of arguments that can be adduced to answer this question in the affirmative. First, both domains coexist and jointly contribute to forming utterances, and the two have largely complementary functions: Whereas SG takes care of the meaning of sentences and their parts, TG is concerned with relating utterances to the situation of discourse.

Second, there is some relationship of dependence between the two: Many conceptual theticals, such as question tags or dislocations, would be incomplete without there being an SG utterance that provides a host. At the same time, the meaning of an SG utterance can be incomplete or lack significant information content without the presence of a thetical. For example, an utterance such as (16) would receive a somewhat different interpretation depending on whether there is no reporting clause, as in (16a), or there is one, as in (16b): Presence vs. absence of the thetical *Judy whispered* makes it clear whether the state of affairs asserted in the utterance applies to the speaker or to some other referent:

(16) a. *By the way, I am pregnant.*

   b. *By the way,* **Judy whispered,** *I am pregnant.*

Third, the two domains are linked via cooptation, in that most theticals are derived from SG units (see Section 6). And finally, there are various ways in which the two domains interfere with one another. One kind of interference concerns crossreference, involving various forms of anaphoric relationship. Another kind of interference is the result of regular cooccurrence: Linguistic discourse commonly consists of combinations of SG units and theticals within one and the same utterance. Some of these combinations occur frequently, and the result can be that the information units concerned assimilate to one another prosodically, syntactically and/or semantically.

4.7.2 Are theticals different enough from SG units to justify their analysis as not belonging to the same domain as SG?

Observing that there are instances of usage that are governed by pragmatic rules, Morris ([1938] 1971: 48) suggested that "interjections such as *Oh!*, commands such as *Come here!*, ... expressions such as *Good Morning!* and various rhetorical and poetical devices, occur only under certain definite conditions in the users of the language." That theticals, such as interjections, imperatives, formulae of social exchange (FSEs), etc. are different from SG units is supported by the fact that all categories conform overall to our definition of theticals in (3) while SG units do not. But the problem is whether SG and TG are really as neatly separable from one another as we argued in the preceding sections, considering that in most previous linguistic works, TG phenomena were treated as a part or appendage of SG, or as not being a part of any kind.

There would be at least one reason for answering this question in the negative. As we will see below, SG and TG phenomena are in fact not clearly separated from each other in a number of cases for a reason alluded to above: When two linguistic information units cooccur regularly, there likely will be interference, in that the two tend to adapt to one another. Interference affects all parts of language structure, from prosody to syntax and information structure, and it can affect any kind of linguistic material. It therefore comes as no surprise that it may also be at work when a thetical regularly combines with a unit of SG.

One might argue that the presence of interference suggests that SG and TG belong to the same domain. But interference is not restricted to linguistic material; rather, it can also be observed in the interaction between linguistic material and the context, that is, the extra-linguistic situation of discourse. Take the following constructed example. Mr and Mrs Carlton are on a walk in the neighborhood and at some point she makes the utterance in (17a). Mr Carlton has no problem establishing the referential identity of *she* in (17a) since the only conceivable referent is a small girl sitting in front of them on the lawn. Thus, the personal pronoun establishes a link between the situation of discourse and a linguistic utterance, in much the same way as it does in (17b), where an SG unit coocurs with a thetical such as a question tag.

(17) a. *Isn't she cute?*

    b. *That's a cute girl,* ***isn't she?***

In a similar fashion, the context can be responsible for "elliptic" behavior. Suppose that at a different point of the walk Mrs Carlton would ask the question in (18a): While not a full-fledged sentence, Mr Carlton would presumably infer on account of the relevant situation of discourse that (18a) is equivalent to (18b).

(18) a. *This way?*

    b. *Shall we go this way?*

To conclude, from the fact that SG and TG may interact structurally, e.g. in the form of coreference or "ellipsis", it does not necessarily follow that the two form one linguistic domain since such mechanisms can also be at work between linguistic and extra-linguistic phenomena.

Consider the following examples illustrating three different categories of theticals: What does the conceptual thetical *confidentially* in (19a) have in common with the vocative *Paul* in (19b) or the interjection *Damn* in (19c)? Is it justified to allocate all three to the same domain, namely TG?

(19) a. **Confidentially,** *I didn't expect this.*

b. **Paul,** *I didn't expect this.*

c. **Damn,** *I didn't expect this.*

We argue that it is in fact justified to treat TG as one domain rather than as consisting of a number of independent domains, for the following reasons. The first, and also the main reason, concerns our definition in (3): Theticals are distinguished from SG units both syntactically and prosodically, but also on account of their positional mobility. Thus, the theticals in (19) are likely to be set off from the following clause both syntactically and prosodically, and instead of being placed initially, they can also appear utterance-finally.

Second, their function is not determined by the utterance in which they occur but rather by the situation of discourse (Section 5). Thus, the meaning of the theticals in (19) relates primarily to the interaction between speaker and hearer in (19a) and (19b), and to the attitudes of the speaker in (19c), rather than modifying the meaning of the following clause. Although SG is not independent from the situational context either, it is concerned with the construction of propositional content rather than being a more immediate response to the situation of discourse.

Third, rather than being organized in terms of propositional sentence structures, a substantial number of theticals is formulaic, taking the form of what Mackenzie (1998: 283) and Hengeveld and Mackenzie (2008: 3–4) call holophrases of the fixed type, that is, of unanalyzable information units (see 4.7.3 below).[21]

And the final reason is the following: While a number of theticals show interference with and/or are hosted by SG units, not all of them really do, as we saw above.

4.7.3 Are theticals similar enough to one another to justify their analysis as a domain of their own?

For example, how to account for the fact that highly contrasting theticals such as interjections and comment clauses belong to the same domain?[22] Note that interjections (e.g., *ouch, wow*) can, and frequently do form independent utterances, whereas comment clauses (*I think, you know*) are not independent: They require

---

21 Concerning the way in which clause-like theticals may develop into short, unanalyzable holophrases, see Schwyzer (1939: 40–1).
22 We are grateful to Walter Bisang (p.c.) for having drawn our attention to this issue.

a host and have the appearance of elliptic information units. If such units really belong to the same domain, how to account for all the differences?

An answer to this question has several parts. The first is the following: Such disparate kinds of units can be observed in much the same way in SG. For example, what do adverbs (e.g., *tomorrow*) have in common with articles (*the, a*)? The former can occur as independent utterances (e.g., *When will you come? – Tomorrow.*) whereas the latter require a host, that is, a head noun. And while the former are positionally fairly free, the latter are restricted to the position preceding a noun. In short, much the same degrees of contrast can be observed in both TG and SG units.

The second part of an answer also has parallels in SG: In much the same way as SG units, TG units can be affected by processes such as grammaticalization (see Section 4.6). Accordingly, comparing different units of one and the same domain makes only sense if the units do not differ with reference to such processes.

In sum, this question as well can be answered with reference to our definition of theticals in (3): They all, including interjections and comment clauses, conform overall to the definition.

The first important piece of evidence concerns the functions of theticals. Whereas SG is determined by the structure of sentences and their conceptual-propositional content, TG is determined by the situation of discourse, most of all by the nature of speaker attitudes and speaker-hearer interaction. Table 1 lists the paradigm functions associated with each of the categories; we will return to this issue in the next section.

Table 1: The main functions of thetical categories.

Category	Component of the situation of discourse
Conceptual theticals	Text organization
FSEs	Speaker-hearer interaction
Vocatives	Speaker-hearer interaction
Imperatives	Speaker-hearer interaction
Interjections	Speaker attitudes

Another piece of evidence concerns the internal structure of theticals. While some, in particular conceptual theticals and imperatives, can have a highly complex internal structure, all categories of TG are characterized by a predominance of short, unanalyzable chunks that are formulaic and take the form of fixed holophrases, i.e. units that have no propositional organization or other internal structure (see 4.7.2), being supported in their interpretation by the situation of discourse. This preference for short and formulaic units allows for quick retrieval and therefore sits well with the typical discourse function of theticals, which is that of a spontaneous response to the situation of discourse (Section 5). Table 2 lists a few examples of such chunks.

Table 2: Some formulaic theticals of English.

Category	Examples
Conceptual theticals	*as it were, for example, if at all, if you will*
FSEs	*Good morning, hello, please, Thank you*
Vocatives	*Sir!, Waiter!*
Imperatives	*Come on!, Piss off!*
Interjections	*boy, damn, fuck, hell*

Second, there is comparative evidence that TG constitutes a cognitively and communicatively motivated domain, as is suggested by typological observations on genetically and areally unrelated languages. A few examples may suffice to illustrate this point. In the Eastern Nilotic language Bari of Southern Sudan, a grammatical category called *sutɛsi* ('interjections') is distinguished (Spagnolo 1933: 216–22). This category includes the whole range of thetical categories: Interjections proper include expressions for emotive concepts such as surprise, pain, wonder, or indignation, FSEs contain the formulaic expressions for social interaction, such as greetings, replies, well-wishings, etc., and it also includes vocatives and some conceptual theticals. The *sutɛsi* category consists of fairly short, frequently "elliptic" units that form, or can form utterances of their own, being set off from the rest of an utterance.

In the Atlantic language Kisi of Guinea, Sierra Leone, and Liberia there is also a category of interjections that includes FSEs (*ìdìíyó* 'good-bye', *báléká* 'thank you'), interjections proper ("exclamations", e.g., *èèè* disappointment, *kpóù* surprise or astonishment), and formulaic conceptual theticals such as question tags (*nɛ́ɛ́*) (Childs 1995: 145–7). Similarly, in Zulu and other Nguni Bantu languages of South Africa there is a functional category of interjectives, "which conveys a complete concept without the implication of any subject" (Doke [1927] 1988: 279). It includes FSEs (e.g., *nxephepha* 'excuse me!, I beg your pardon!'), interjections (*wewu* 'ah! of wonder'), vocatives (*bafana* 'boys!'), and imperatives (*Woza lapa!* 'Come here!').

A final example of a domain that comes close to our notion of thetical categories is that of "discourse adverbs" in Korean (Sohn 1999: 212), which occur outside the boundary of a sentence and are conditioned by discourse contexts or speech situations: "They usually occur alone, or precede a sentence, as in a yes/no response, a term of address, or an interjection". Discourse adverbs include four types of thetical categories, namely FSEs, vocatives, interjections, and conceptual theticals, even if they are not confined to these.

Third, it is also preferred patterns of collocation that may be indicative of a closer relationship between thetical categories as against information units outside TG. For example, FSEs such as greetings tend to collocate with vocatives (*Good morning, Lucy!*) in English and many other languages, and in some Romance languages, vocatives tend to be preceded by interjections, with the effect that the two may merge into one unanalyzable information unit (Floricic 2011).[23] Another common collocation pattern combines imperatives with vocatives.[24]

And finally there is also some evidence based on the placement of theticals. In a number of languages it is some specific position within the utterance that provides the preferred slot for the placement of thetical categories. In the Arawá language Jarawara of Southern Amazonia this appears to be the clause-initial position (Dixon 2004: 388–93): Most clause-initial elements of Jarawara have properties of theticals or, conversely, all thetical categories have at least some members placed in this slot. Examples are FSEs like *hima!* 'come on, let's go!', vocatives[25] (*Safato!* 'Safato!', male name), interjections (*ai* 'hey', expression of surprise, when impressed), or the discourse particle *faja* 'then', which indicates e.g. a new pivot in the discourse.

4.7.4 Is the inventory of categories distinguished exhaustive?

Another major problem concerns the overall architecture of Discourse Grammar. In the catalog of thetical categories distinguished in Figure 1, the reader may miss a number of types of information units that for some reason or other show characteristics of thetical categories but were not considered here due to insufficient empirical support, in particular questions and ideophones.

Crosslinguistically, questions tend to be syntactically independent and prosodically distinct, and their meaning typically relates to speaker-hearer interaction, that is, to the situation of discourse – in short, they conform in

---

23 In Sardinian, for example, the full form of a first name in a vocative can be truncated and preceded by the interjection ô [ɔ], e.g. ˈpeːdru (full form of name) vs. ɔ ˈbɛ (vocative), ˈpɛpːe (full form) vs. ɔˈβɛ (vocative) (Floricic 2011: 114).

24 Note, for example, that the final *-o* of the Rumanian imperative form *Vino!* 'come!' is presumably a relic of a vocative ending (Franck Floricic, p.c.)

25 Vocatives, such as names or kin labels, do not only occur at the very beginning but also at the very end of a clause (Dixon 2004: 388).

central aspects to our definition in (3).[26] Conceivably therefore, future research might establish that both polar and word questions qualify as a distinct category of TG.

And much the same applies to ideophones, that is, vivid expressions accompanying actions in the narrative, representing sounds, size, movement, smell, or color (e.g., *bang!, blob!*). While showing some similarities to interjections, ideophones need to be looked at in their own light rather than being conflated with interjections (Voeltz and Kilian-Hatz 2001), and their place in Discourse Grammar still needs to be determined (cf. Dixon 2010b: 30). A noteworthy characteristic that ideophones share with interjections is that both tend to show phonetic features that do not occur elsewhere in grammar or the lexicon.

4.7.5 What is the nature of the boundaries of categories: Are they discrete or gradient?

In many works within the paradigm of functionalism, especially but not only in grammaticalization theory, it is assumed that linguistic categories are generally discontinuous and gradient rather than discrete. The categories of TG sketched above are in fact far from being discrete units separated from each other by clear-cut boundaries. There are various semantic, syntactic and morphological overlaps, with the effect that boundaries are notoriously fuzzy, and some information units can be related to more than one category.

For example, a thetical such as an opening to a letter (*Dear Sir*) has features of both an FSE and a vocative, hesitation markers such as *uh* and *um*, which we loosely classified as interjections, have for equally good reasons been treated as discourse markers like *you know* and *like* (Croucher 2004), particles such as *yes, yeah, no,* or *hi* are frequently assigned to the category of interjections (Peterson 1999: 231; Kockelman 2003) but can also be said to do service as formulaic expressions of social exchange, and much the same applies to expressions like *Congratulations!*.

4.7.6 How to identify theticals in isolation?

One central issue concerns theticals used in isolation, that is, occurring without an SG host: How can stand-alone theticals be distinguished from ordinary SG

---

26 It goes without saying that this applies only to direct questions, not e.g. to indirect questions.

units? That the information unit *it's true* in (20) is a thetical in (20a) through (20d) is uncontroversial on account of our definition in (3). But what about the status of *it's true* in (20e), which can be interpreted either as a thetical in isolation or an utterance of SG? This question cannot be answered at the present stage of research but needs much further work on the prosody and the discourse status of the information units concerned.

(20)a. *John,* ***it's true,*** *went to Paris on Sunday.*

b. *John went,* ***it's true,*** *to Paris on Sunday.*

c. *John went to Paris,* ***it's true,*** *on Sunday.*

d. *John went to Paris on Sunday,* ***it's true.***

e. *It's true.*   (Knowles 1980: 382)

There is, however, evidence to the effect that theticals can form utterances of their own, without requiring a host. For example, restrictive relative clauses are generally classified as units of SG, while non-restrictive (or appositive) relative clauses are constructional theticals (Kaltenböck et al. 2011: 852–3, Table 1; cf. Emonds 1976; 1979; Fabb 1990; Stowell 2005). When used in isolation, only non-restrictive relative clauses can be used (Burton-Roberts 1999: 37). Thus, when a relative clause is added by another speaker, as in the following example, it must be construed as a non-restrictive and never as a restrictive relative clause:

(21) A: *My publications will include the article in* Scientific American.

B: ***Which you've not even begun to write yet.***   (Burton-Roberts 1999: 37)

Nevertheless, identifying theticals used in isolation frequently turns out to be hard, if not impossible. In accordance with our definition in (3) we will say that the more of the properties listed there apply, the more likely it is that a given information unit qualifies as an instance of a thetical – in other words, when used as stand-alones, theticals are best analyzed in terms of a cline of theticality rather than as a discrete category.

5 Non-restrictive meaning and the situation of discourse

Each of the two domains of Discourse Grammar has its own principles for processing information. SG is confined essentially to the propositional meaning of sentences and their constituents, and in this sense it is restrictive. As we saw in (3), one of the defining properties of theticals is non-restrictive meaning. Whereas restrictive meaning is grounded in the semantic structure of a sentence or its constituents, non-restrictive meaning concerns reasoning processes and inferential mechanisms that are, as we argue, not grounded in a sentence but rather in the situation of discourse (see Section 3). To be sure, any act of linguistic communication requires a situation of discourse, but in the case of SG its impact is minimal, being restricted to a few factors such as spatial, temporal and personal deixis. Such restrictions do not appear to exist when TG is involved.

Drawing on the situation of discourse enables the speaker to introduce a universe of "metadiscourse". This allows the hearer on the one hand to recover the speaker's intentions "by explicitly establishing preferred interpretations of propositional meanings"; on the other hand it alerts the hearer to the speaker's perspective, thereby establishing a mutually beneficial speaker-hearer relationship (cf. Hyland 1998: 442–3; see also Dér 2010: 23–4). The situation of discourse consists of a network of linkages between the components listed in (22) (Kaltenböck et al. 2011: 861). Note that the activation of these components is by no means mutually exclusive; rather, in a given discourse act one (or more) of them may be foregrounded while the others are backgrounded. The factors that determine the mechanism of foregrounding are still ill-understood and need much further research.

(22) Components determining the situation of discourse
 Text organization
 Source of information
 Attitudes of the speaker
 Speaker-hearer interaction
 Discourse setting
 World knowledge

In accordance with this distinction, SG units differ from theticals in their semantic-pragmatic scope potential: Whereas the former have scope over the sentence or some constituent of it, theticals have scope over the situation of discourse. Accordingly, the meaning of theticals has been described with reference to notions such as "discourse", "metatextual", or "meaning beyond the sentence" (relating to the component of text organization), "subjectification" (relating to attitudes of the speaker) and/or "intersubjectification" (speaker-hearer interaction) (e.g., Traugott and Dasher 2002; Brinton 2008; cf. also Mithun 2008).[27]

Consider the example in (23). In (23a), the adverb *frankly* is a part of an SG unit, it modifies the meaning of the verb form *spoke*. In (23b), by contrast, *frankly* is a conceptual thetical: It is set off syntactically and prosodically from the rest of the utterance, and unlike *frankly* in (23a) it is positionally mobile. And its meaning is also not the same as that of *frankly* in (23a): It does not serve to modify the meaning of the verb or the clause. Rather, it appears to evoke a different conceptual world – one that concerns speaker-hearer interaction, in that the speaker proposes a particular kind of social relationship between the interlocutors concerned.[28]

(23) a. *She spoke frankly about herself now and then.*

b. ***Frankly**, Kris didn't want to know.*   (Biber et al. 1999: 132)

Most of the components in (22) have significant correlates in certain constructional theticals. For example, appositives are likely to foreground the component of text organization (24a), reporting clauses that of source of information (24b), comment clauses that of attitudes of the speaker (24c), and question tags that of speaker-hearer interaction (24d) (cf. Kaltenböck et al. 2011: 852–3).

(24) a. *The warning – **that prices should be lowered** – was inored.*

b. *In the near future, **John announced**, I will move to Paris.*

c. *Peter will get married next Sunday, **I guess**.*

d. *Peter doesn't know Arabic, **does he?***

---

27 Traugott (2010) defines subjectification as a process of change giving rise to expressions of the speaker's beliefs and stance toward what is said, while intersubjectification is a process leading to the development of markers that encode the speaker's attention to the cognitive stances and social identities of the hearer/addressee (Traugott 2003: 124).

28 In analogy to Widdowson's (2004: 26–29) trinity of positions encoded in personal pronouns one could also say that in (23a) the use of *frankly* conveys the first person (I, speaker) position in relation to the third person world (i.e. how s/he interprets reality in reference to self), while in (23b) *frankly* relates to the first person's (I, speaker's) position vis-à-vis the second person (you, hearer).

Nevertheless, the network of components is complex, and many instances of theticals involve an interaction of more than one component. We may illustrate this with a kind of conceptual thetical that has figured prominently in the early phases of research on the syntax of theticals (Rutherford 1970; Kac 1972; Lakoff 1974: 330–1). The examples in (25) consist of two clauses, C_1 and C_2. The *because*-clause C_2 in (25a) is an instance of restrictive subordination, an SG reason clause, whereas that in (25b) exhibits a non-restrictive relationship, it is a thetical; in the terminology of Kac (1972: 627), C_2 is an intradiscursory clause in (25a) but an extradiscursory clause in (25b).

(25) a. *Jenny isn't here because she's sick.*

   b. *Jenny isn't here, **because I don't see her**.* (Kac 1972: 626)

In our interpretation, the distinction is not only one of syntax but also of meaning: (25a) describes a causally coherent relation between the meaning content of C_1 and C_2. In (25b), by contrast, it is independent of the sentence meaning: It is based on a reasoning process that is located outside the sentence semantics but rather foregrounds two of the components distinguished in (22), namely world knowledge ('not being visible' implies 'not being present') and source of information, more specifically a recurrent experience according to which the information in C_2 provides the source of evidence entitling the speaker to conclude C_1.

Which of the components is foregrounded can be influenced by the particular situation of discourse that is invoked. We may illustrate this with the English interjection *hey*. As we observed in Section 4.6, the most salient function of interjections concerns the emotional or cognitive state of the speaker, that is, it relates to the component of speaker attitudes. But there is also a significant portion of interjections that serve speaker-hearer interaction, *hey* being one of them. For example, with the interjection *hey* in line 3 of (26), Anna seeks to obtain Jenn's attention (Norrick 2009: 881). The interjection here serves as a summonsing or attention-getting device – in other words, the component foregrounded is speaker-hearer interaction.

(26) 1. Ann: *oh are you going to drink that out of the bottle?*

   2. Catherine: *I always drink them out of the bottle.*

   3. Anna: ***hey** Jenn there's a diet coke out if you want one.*

   4. Jennifer: *um, yeah I'll have a diet coke.*
      (LSWEC-AC 122001; Norrick 2009: 881)

But depending on the particular situation of discourse, *hey* may as well foreground other components. Thus, in line 2 of example (27), *hey* serves "to switch and refocus the topic of conversation" (Norrick 2009: 881), that is, it appears to be primarily a marker of text organization.

(27) 1. Cooper: *can I have a bite of that cookie?*

 2. Sara: ***hey** they're low calorie.*

 3. *you can have the whole cookie.*

 4. Cooper: *thank you.*

(LSWEC-AC 115301; Norrick 2009: 881)

Non-restrictive meaning has been described as being metacommunicative, metadiscursive, or metatextual in nature (Bayer 1973; Petola 1983: 103; Ortner 1983; Thim-Mabrey 1988; Traugott 1995: 6; Brandt 1996; Grenoble 2004: 1953), or as having a framing function (Auer 1996; 1997; see also Günthner and Imo 2003). It provides the speaker with a tool for placing the utterance in a wider context, for elaborating on his or her cognitive or emotive state, for guiding the hearer in achieving the intended interpretation of an utterance, or for creating text coherence.

6 Cooptation

Cooptation is an operation whereby a chunk of SG, such as clause, a phrase, a word, or any other unit is deployed for use as a thetical (Kaltenböck et al. 2011: 874–5). Its functions are in particular (a) to overcome constraints imposed by linearization in structuring texts, (b) to package together larger segments of discourse, (c) to place a text in a wider perspective, e.g. by providing explanations, comments, and supplementary information, (d) to describe the inner state of the speaker, and (e) to involve the hearer in the discourse.

The result is a shift in semantic-pragmatic scope from syntax to a larger discourse setting, namely the situation of discourse (Kaltenböck et al. 2011; see also Mithun 2008 on (functional) extension).[29] When coopted from SG to TG, the unit concerned is freed from its constraints as a syntactic constituent: Its meaning is no longer defined with reference to its syntactic function but is redefined by

---

29 Mithun (2008: 108) discusses extention with reference to patterns of grammatical dependency that can be extended from the sentence into larger discourse and pragmatic domains.

its new "environment", viz. the situation of discourse. This entails a number of syntactic and semantic changes. First, the unit is no longer restricted to requirements of its erstwhile syntactic function: Obligatory constituents may no longer be required since their function can be inferred from the situation of discourse. Second, the unit is now responsive to that "environment", relating to components such as text organization, speaker-hearer interaction, and speaker attitudes (see Section 5). And third, this entails that its meaning is more complex since the situation of discourse involves a number of different variables.

Take the following example. In (28a), the unit *briefly* is an adverb, a constituent of SG determining the meaning of the predicate. In (28b), the very item *briefly* is not an SG unit; it fulfills the criteria that we proposed for a thetical in (3), serving the organization of the text.

(28) a. *They talked briefly about my case.*

b. ***Briefly,** there is nothing more I can do about it.*

(Quirk et al. 1985: 615)

Cooptation is a fully productive operation whereby a unit of SG, such as *briefly* in (28a), is used to serve within the domain of TG: *briefly* is no longer a prosodic or syntactic part of the clause, and its meaning is also no longer restricted by rules of SG but rather is shaped by the situation of discourse, as sketched in Section 5.

The exact nature of cooptation as a cognitive operation is still largely unclear and must be the subject of a separate analysis. But on the basis of the evidence available it would seem that it can be characterized as in (29).

(29) Features characterizing cooptation

a. It is an instantaneous operation whereby a unit of SG is used to serve as a thetical.[30]

b. The result is an information unit that is syntactically and prosodically autonomous, that is, one that corresponds to the definition of theticals in (3).

c. The meaning of the coopted unit is shaped by its function in discourse. This may entail e.g. a drastic widening of scope, where widening is not restricted to the text concerned but relates to the entire situation of dis-

---

[30] The reason for not referring to this process as "change" is because cooptation is in principle a unique, instantaneous operation. It is only when this operation is performed frequently that it may lead to grammatical change and, in some cases, to grammaticalization.

course. As Tom Givón (p.c.) suggests, theticals may be structurally placed into an anchor utterance, but functionally they are in an "anchor discourse", their functional scope/range/import is a much wider chunk of discourse. Accordingly, Traugott and Dasher (2002: 40) conclude that widening may lead from "scope within proposition" to "scope over discourse".

d. Having been coopted for use as a thetical, the unit is freed from the syntactic and semantic constraints of SG, it may have the appearance of an elliptic piece compared to the corresponding structure of SG.

e. But even when coopted as an elliptic piece, the unit can inherit valency features, although such features may no longer relate to surrounding text pieces but rather to the situation of discourse in general.

Among the questions that we are not able to answer there is most of all the following: Are theticals conceptualized and designed within SG and subsequently coopted in TG, or do speakers conceive them in the domain of TG and subsequently draw on appropriate expressions in SG? A partial answer is provided by the presence of formulaic theticals, such as interjections (*oh, wow*, etc.) or FSEs (*Goodbye, How are you?*). Such units have no corresponding SG counterpart and hence must be deployed directly into discourse without involving SG. Whether or to what extent the same applies to other kinds of theticals is an issue that needs much further research.

7 Types of theticals

Theticals differ in a number of ways from one another as has been pointed out in a number of works (see especially Espinal 1991: 726–7; Peterson 1999; Dehé and Kavalova 2007b: 1–4; Kaltenböck 2007: 27–31; Brinton 2008: 9–10; Kaltenböck et al. 2011); the reader is referred to these works for more details.

The most fundamental classification concerns that of thetical categories, as it was outlined in Figure 1; we have discussed the categories identified so far in some detail in Section 4.

In the present section we are restricted to a small range of additional distinctions that are particularly relevant for an understanding of the nature of the domain. These distinctions concern (i) the relative degree of fixation of theticals, (ii) their meaning, and (iii) their placement.

The first typological criterion concerns what we loosely refer to as the degree of fixation of a thetical. The following types are distinguished by Kaltenböck et al.

(2011: 870–2). Note that these types are not discrete entities being separated from one another by clear-cut boundaries; rather, the transitions between the three are fluid and continuous.

(a) Instantaneous theticals: They are fully compositional, can be formed freely any time and anywhere, and quite a few of them are uttered only once and never again.

(b) Constructional theticals: They are recurrent patterns or constructions of theticals, being compositional but having some schematic structure and function. For a catalog of English constructional theticals, see Kaltenböck et al. (2011: 852–3, Table 1).

(c) Formulaic theticals:[31] These are non-compositional information units, that is, their shape is essentially invariable. They are usually short chunks, morphosyntactically unanalyzable, and tend to be positionally flexible. For a list of formulaic theticals, see Table 2 (Section 4.7.3).

The second distinction relates to text meaning. We have described the meaning of theticals as non-restrictive, that is, as independent from that of their host utterance. Nevertheless, many theticals are not entirely independent from their SG environment. The examples below show that theticals differ greatly in the way and the extent to which they contribute to the information content of an utterance. There are on the one hand theticals such as in (30) which can be described as being in some sense "text-irrelevant". Their meaning concerns the discourse setting (see (22)) but does not relate directly to the sentence meaning. (31a), by contrast, contributes more directly to the content of their host utterance. This semantic distinction tends to have morphosyntactic correlates. For example, the latter, but not the former, can be linked to the preceding discourse by means of *and*, cf. (31b).[32] Thus, it would be possible to arrange theticals along a cline extending from least to most "text-relevant" information units.

(30)*And what we found <,> was uhm <,>* **could you turn the slide projector off please** *uhm very substantial mortality difference within the population.*
(ICE-GB: s2a-047–110)

---

31 A formulaic sequence is "a sequence, continuous or discontinuous, of words or other elements, which is, or appears to be, prefabricated: that is, stored and retrieved whole from memory at the time of use, rather than being subject to generation or analysis by the language grammar" Wray (2002: 9; see also Wray 2009).

32 By adding *and*, the thetical in (31b) turns into a constructional *and*-clause (see Kavalova 2007; Kaltenböck et al. 2011, Table 1).

(31) a. *What I've done here **I hope you don't entirely disapprove** is try and limit the time taken on this item by putting it in writing.* (ICE-GB: s1b-075–180)

b. *What I've done here, **and I hope you don't entirely disapprove**, is try and limit the time taken on this item by putting it in writing.*

Another criterion of classification is provided by their placement. Placement of theticals is generally characterized as being mobile (Brinton 2008: 18; Wichmann 2001: 179). Still, there are constraints on placement, most of all relating to their discourse-specific functions (see Emonds 1973: 338, Peterson 1999: 237–40, Grenoble 2004: 1966–7, or Brinton 2008: 8 for a discussion of English comment clauses), and certain theticals are restricted to specific positions of an utterance.

Kavalova (2007: 149–52) proposes to distinguish between anchored and floating *and*-clauses. Whereas the former occur "to the right of an anchor located in the host", the latter "are not related to a particular element of the host", and their position is not strictly fixed. We adopt this distinction to highlight two major types of theticals but will refer to the former as fixed theticals, reserving the term "anchored thetical" for theticals having a semantic-pragmatic anchor.[33] Fixed theticals occur next to their host, while floating theticals do not show such a constraint. The two types are best described as forming focal points on a continuum that extends from entirely fixed position to complete freedom of placement.

Fixed theticals serve to elaborate on some referential information unit of the host utterance, such as to modify, qualify, edit, elaborate on, or revise that anchor unit. In accordance with their function, these theticals exhibit two major constraints in their placement: (a) They follow the host unit, and (b) the two are as a rule placed next to each other.[34] Theticals differ in whether they obey only (a) or both constraints. The following constructional theticals are paradigm instances of fixed theticals: Appositions, non-restrictive relative clauses, and right-dislocations.

Note, however, that these constraints are not without exceptions. For example, instead of placing the apposition *a die-hard conservative* in (32a) after its host noun phrase it may precede in appropriate contexts, cf. (32b).

---

[33] Whereas Kaltenböck et al. (2011, Fn. 3) do not distinguish between a "host" and an "anchor", using the latter as a general term, we now propose to reserve the term "host" for linear placement and "anchor" for semantic-pragmatic linking, or scope relations, of thetical elements (cf. also Heine and Kaltenböck 2012).

[34] The adjacency constraint of (b) captures what Kavalova (2007: 149) calls proximity loyalty.

(32) a. *Her father,* ***a die-hard conservative,*** *refused to even consider the proposal.*

    b. ***A die-hard conservative,*** *her father refused to even consider the proposal.*
                          (Huddleston and Pullum 2002: 1358)

Floating theticals can be placed virtually anywhere in an utterance, as the comment clause *it is true* in (20) has shown. Paradigm examples of floating theticals are vocatives and some formulae of social exchange but not others. Within the category of conceptual theticals they include most of all comment clauses and reporting clauses.

8 Earlier accounts

That language structure, or language knowledge, is not a monolithic entity that can felicitously be reduced to syntax has been argued in a number of different frameworks. Taking issue with what he calls the "syntactocentric" view of generative theory, Jackendoff (2002; 2011) maintains that there is need to distinguish four levels or domains of language structure, namely phonological, syntactic, semantic/conceptual, and spatial structure. The distinction between two domains proposed here is of a different kind: Rather than representing distinctions in the levels or components of language structure, it is based on the assumption that there are two different, and competing modes of structuring discourse (Heine and Kaltenböck forthc.).

While early works drawing attention to this distinction can be traced back to the 19th century (e.g. Wackernagel 1897; see Schneider 2007b: 38–9), TG and its contribution to structuring spoken and written texts is a young field of study. There are a number of historical overviews, e.g. Espinal (1991: 736–41), Grenoble (2004), Blakemore (2006), Dehé and Kavalova (2007b), Kaltenböck (2007), Brinton (2008: 7–14), and Kaltenböck et al. (2011: 876–8), but the most detailed account is found in Schneider (2007b: 37–63). What is common to essentially all of mainstream linguistics is that TG, or specific parts of it, are treated at best as an appendix of SG.

It is most of all two characteristics of theticals that were highlighted in earlier linguistic reference works. On the one hand it was the internal structure that attracted the interest of researchers, more narrowly the "reduced" form of many theticals (cf. our definitional property (3e)). A classic example can be found in the work of Bloomfield (1962 [1933]: 176). He proposed a basic distinction between full sentences, or the "favorite sentence-form", and minor sentences. The former consist of an "actor-action phrase" (*John ran away*) or a command, i.e., an imperative (*Come! Be good!*). Minor sentences, by contrast, are almost entirely restricted to theticals. They were conceived by Bloomfield somehow as a negative category, in that they include sentences that do not have a favorite sentence-form. Exclamatory minor sentences "occur under a violent stimulus"; they include interjections (*Ouch, damn it!*), vocatives (*Sir, Ma'am! John! You with the glasses!*), and some FSEs (*Hello! Please!*).

The distinction proposed by Bloomfield reflects to some extent our distinction between two domains of Discourse Grammar: His class of full sentences largely corresponds to our concept of SG, even if there is one notable exception, namely imperatives. His minor sentences on the other hand are essentially a class of thetical categories, being largely coextensive with TG. His completive minor sentences belong with few exceptions to the category of conceptual theticals, while his exclamatory minor clauses include most other thetical categories except imperatives.

Presumably influenced by Bloomfield's earlier work, Hockett (1958) proposed what can be considered to be an outline of our notion of Discourse Grammar. His class of "sentences of the favorite type" has essentially the same kind of membership as our category of SG. And his class of "sentences of some minor type" shows the characteristics of thetical categories: They are syntactically and prosodically independent, and many have the elliptic features of theticals. Note that Hockett diverges from Bloomfield in excluding imperatives from the "sentences of the favorite type".

The massive congruence between Bloomfield's and Hockett's classification on the one hand and our distinction of two domains is noteworthy since the criteria used by these earlier authors differ from those adopted in the present work: Whereas both Bloomfield and Hockett focus on the internal structure of information units, i.e., on differences in sentence structure, our emphasis is on external relationship, in particular on how information units are related syntactically and prosodically to other material of discourse.

On the other hand it was the external structure of theticals, and more specifically their peculiar syntax (cf. (3a)), that aroused the interest of general linguists: Theticals are not arguments of any kind of the utterance in which they occur, they do not normally form constituents with units of SG (see e.g. Peterson 1999: 241ff.), and they differ from adjuncts in being syntactically unintegrated or detached from the host clause or any other SG structure (e.g., Fortmann 2006; Howe 2008; Quirk et al. 1985: 853; Biber et al. 1999: 1067).

Being aware of the peculiar syntactic behavior and the challenge that they pose for existing syntactic models, students of generative grammar attempted to account for this behavior with reference to existing templates of semantic (Jackendoff 1972) or – more commonly – of syntactic analysis (e.g., Ross 1970; 1973;

Rutherford 1970; Kac 1972; Emonds 1973; 1976; 1979; Lakoff 1974; McCawley 1982); see also Rizzi (1997) and Cinque (1999) for more recent positions within this paradigm. But, some have also volunteered a contrasting interpretation. For example, being aware that non-restrictive (or appositive) relative clauses and other thetical structures cannot be taken care of appropriately in terms of the tree diagram structure postulated for orthodox sentence syntax, Emonds (1979) proposed an extended tree structure.

All this work produced a wealth of insights on theticals. Nevertheless, the positions maintained in this work were questioned by syntacticians of subsequent generations who argued that theticals cannot clearly be reconciled with established tree-structure types of syntactic representation (Haegeman 1991; Espinal 1991: 740; Peterson 1999; Huddleston and Pullum 2002: 1353–4; Burton-Roberts 1999; 2005; Shaer 2003; Shaer and Frey 2004; Averintseva-Klisch 2008). There are a number of different views, especially on the question of where exactly theticals are to be located in syntax. For most of these authors, theticals are not constituents of any structure but are integrated into the host utterance in some kind of "post-syntactic procedure", e.g., via a discourse-governed process of linearization (Dehé and Kavalova 2006), or at the pragmatic level of utterance interpretation (Espinal 1991; Haegeman 1991; Burton-Roberts 1999; Averintseva-Klisch 2008: 236).

Another line of research within the generative paradigm concerns the contrast between sentential and non-sentential ("incomplete") utterances, where a basic distinction between a syntactic and a pragmatic module was proposed (see especially Barton 1990; 1998). While this distinction shares a number of features with our distinction between SG and TG, the linguistic phenomena examined by the authors concerned are not exactly the same and so is the theoretical perspective underlying this work.

What may be called an embryonic sketch of TG also surfaces in the English grammar of Huddleston and Pullum (2002: 1350–62). With the notion of supplementation they describe a wide range of phenomena that conform to our definition of theticals. Supplements are, first, syntactically independent and mobile, they are elusive to an analysis in terms of coordination or subordination, or of parataxis and hypotaxis. Second, they are marked as such by the prosody, being intonationally separate from the rest of the sentence, normally set off in writing by commas, dashes, parentheses, or colons. Third, they are semantically non-restrictive and unintegrated (2002: 1353). And finally, supplements are not restricted to conceptual theticals but also include at least one other thetical category, namely interjections.

While TG phenomena and their place in a theory of language have found quite some attention in formal-generative theories for almost half a century now, the interest that they found in functionalist lines of research was more modest. A notable exception can be seen in Dik's work on *extra-clausal constituents* (ECCs). ECCs as proposed by Dik (1997: 379–407) are to quite some extent in accordance with our definition in (3). Dik proposed the features (33a), (33b), and (33c) below to be "recurrent properties of ECCs which, though not providing a watertight definition, nevertheless help us in identifying them". Furthermore, he adds the observations summarized in (33d) through (33g) in order to characterize ECCs.

(33) Recurrent properties of ECCs   (Dik 1997: 380–1)

    a. They either occur on their own, or are typically marked off
       from the clause proper by breaks or pause-like inflections in their prosodic
       contour.

    b. They are never essential to the internal structure of the
       clause with which they are associated: Even if they are omitted, the clause
       continues to form an integral whole.

    c. They are not sensitive to the grammatical rules of the
       (host) clause although they may be related to the clause by rules of coreference, parallelism, and antithesis.

    d. They are especially common in the spoken register.

    e. They are typical of linguistic expressions in ongoing discourse.

    f. They are rather loosely associated with the clause, and
       cannot easily be described in terms of clause-internal rules and principles.

    g. They can only be understood in terms of pragmatic rules
       and principles.

And with reference to their placement, Dik (1997: 383) distinguished between (i) absolute or free-standing ECCS, (ii) preclausal ECCs, (iii) clause-internal or parenthetical ECCs, and (iv) postclausal ECCs. Furthermore, he proposed four main functions of ECCs, namely the ones listed in Table 3 (Dik 1997: 384ff.). Further seminal observations made by Dik concern the pragmatic functions, the organization of discourse (Dik 1997: 386ff.), and the interaction between SG ("clause-internal grammatical phenomena") and TG (EECs) (Dik 1997: 380).

Table 3: The main functions of extra-clausal constituents (ECCs; Dik 1997: 384)

Function	Examples
Interaction management	Greetings, leave-takings: *Hello! Hi!*
	Summonses: *Hey there.*
	Addresses: *John!, O Lord!*
	Minimal responses: *yes, no, mm, mhm*
Attitude specification	*Ouch!, Damn it!, Hurray!*
Discourse organization	*well, by the way, okay, anyway*
Discourse execution	Responses: *yes, no, perhaps, I hope not, it is, she certainly is; well*
	Tags: *isn't it?, will you?*

In other functionalist accounts, specific groupings of thetical categories are singled out, such as the disjuncts and conjuncts of Quirk et al. (1985: 631–47, 612–31), the expressives of Langacker (2008: 475), or the interpersonal level of representation in Functional Discourse Grammar (Hengeveld and Mackenzie 2008: 4). But in most of these accounts, no general concept of TG is recognized. The interest in such works is confined essentially to conceptual-propositional, or "thematic" forms of language structure, much in accordance with the following quotation by Halliday: "Some [independent clauses], like *John!* and *good night!*, are MINOR clauses; they have no thematic structure and so will be left out of account" (Halliday 1985: 44).

9 Conclusions

Work carried out in the functionalist tradition over the last decades has shown that linguistic discourse is composed of a wide range of meaningful elements. These elements are not all of the same kind, and many different frameworks and taxonomies have been proposed to account for them. The present chapter proposes a distinction that has received little attention in previous work.

Speakers are constantly confronted with a general problem in communication, namely how to handle the dichotomy between the linearity of verbal communication and the immediate communicative and cognitive needs arising from the discourse situation. Sentence Grammar (SG) is somehow ideally suited for presenting conceptual-propositional information in a linear format, relying on mechanisms such as clause structure, phrase structure, coordination, subordination, etc. Thetical Grammar (TG) by contrast has the entire situation of discourse in its scope: the speaker, the hearer, their relation to one another, to the text, and to the situation in which discourse takes place (see Section 5; Kaltenböck et al. 2011).

Throughout the chapter we avoided discussing an issue that has figured in a number of works on theticals, namely the differential role played by the medium of language use. Theticals are widely assumed to be a characteristic of speech and, in fact, a number of them are felt to be unusual when found in writing (see e.g. Dik 1997: 380–1). It would seem, however, that theticals are much more common in written texts than is widely assumed (see e.g. the quantitative data volunteered by Biber et al. 1999); more research is needed on this issue.

The chapter could achieve hardly more than providing a skeleton of Discourse Grammar, highlighting its main parts and ignoring others; the reader is referred to the works cited in the course of the chapter for more detailed analyses. Work on the framework sketched is still in its beginnings and there remain a number of issues that are in need of further research and will be the subject of separate publications.

One issue concerns "ellipsis". A thetical can be self-contained, that is, be entirely in accordance with the rules of SG, but it may as well be at variance with requirements of SG. Many theticals are "elliptic" in ways corresponding information units of SG are not, and our definition of theticals in (3e) stipulates that theticals are on the one hand built on principles of SG but on the other hand may be elliptic. Also referred to as deletion, omission, reduction, or truncation (Knowles 1980: 397), ellipsis has been described in terms of operations such as equi-deletion, gapping, etc. (see e.g. Shopen 1973). Ellipsis of text pieces whose meaning can be retrieved from the context can be observed anywhere in language use and language structure. But which material exactly can or cannot be ellipsed, and why is it ellipsed? While there are few generalizations on the former question (Kaltenböck et al. 2011: 867–70), the latter question cannot be answered without reference to an appropriate theory of discourse organization. Such a theory is beyond the scope of the present chapter, which is restricted to defining an outline of some formal properties of Discourse Grammar.

Another issue that has not received the attention it deserves concerns the information value of theticals. A common thread across the relevant literature is that the use of theticals is optional or "non-essential" and that they can be dropped without affecting the meaning or grammatical acceptability of utterances (cf. Dik 1997: 380–1; Fortmann 2006; Schneider 2007a; 2007b). Theticals constitute one of the main communicative tools for planning texts, but it is so far largely unclear how their use relates to the intents of interlocutors.

Third, we were not able to do justice to the analysis of the external "syntax" of theticals. In principle, each instance of a thetical has its specific constraints on where it can appear in an utterance, and many of them can be placed virtually anywhere while others are highly restricted in their placement (see Section 7). Placement does not appear to be a matter of strict syntactic rules or norms but rather of planning preferences, and rather than by syntactic conventions, these preferences appear to be shaped by reasoning processes anchored in the situation of discourse. Obviously, without a more profound knowledge of the latter, crucial questions on the nature of Discourse Grammar must remain unanswered (see Heine and Kaltenböck 2012 for details).

Fourth, preliminary observations suggest that TG plays an important role in first language acquisition. Young children use their first words to make requests for actions and objects, to comment on what is happening, and to accept or reject adult proposals, and according to Clark (2003: 82), the first words uttered by English-speaking children by age 1;5 include what appear to be formulae of social exchange (*hi, bye*), vocatives (*daddy, mommy*), and interjections (*ouch, baa baa*). As they grow older, children start combining clauses, and in their first steps to form complement clauses by means of verbs such as *guess, bet, mean, know,* or *think,* children acquire these verbs first in "parenthetical use." It is only at a later stage that structures of clause complementation evolve (Diessel and Tomasello 2000; Clark 2003: 255–6; Diessel 2005: 175–6). It is largely unclear, however, how the two domains of Discourse Grammar interact in shaping the process of language acquisition.

Finally, there remains the question of whether, or to what extent, there are neurological correlates to the distinction between the two domains. That the two sides of the human cortex perform different functions is an old assumption in systems of neuroscience, and one of these differences concerns speech or language processing. While both hemispheres are needed in normal communicative settings, it seems to be fairly uncontroversial that the left hemisphere is "language-dominant," playing an essential role in processing speech phenomena, not only with spoken but also with signed sentence input (Sakai et al. 2005). But some observations suggest that the distinction between the two domains of Discourse Grammar might correlate to some extent with the lateralization of the human brain: Whereas Sentence Grammar phenomena are primarily activated and processed in the left cerebral hemisphere, activation of the right hemisphere appears to be centrally involved when categories of Thetical Grammar are concerned (see Heine et al. forthc. for more details). Whether these observations can be substantiated by means of experimental testing, however, is an issue for future research.

Abbreviations

DG = Discourse Grammar; FSE = formula of social exchange; ICE-GB = International Corpus of English, British component; SG = Sentence Grammar; TG = Thetical Grammar.

Acknowledgements

We wish to express our gratitude to a number of colleagues who have been of help in writing this paper, providing many critical comments, in addition to Carmen Jany, Shannon T. Bischoff and an anonymous reviewer, these are in particular Sasha Aikhenvald, Felix Ameka, Jim Bennett, Walter Bisang, Laurel Brinton, Ulrike Claudi, Nicole Dehé, Bob Dixon, Wolfgang Dressler, Jack DuBois, Franck Floricic, Tom Givón, Martin Haspelmath, Sylvie Hancil, Jack Hawkins, Evelien Keizer, Christa König, Arne Lohmann, Andrej Malchukov, Aliyah Morgenstern, Britta Mondorf, Maarten Mous, Gábor Nagy, Heiko Narrog, Fritz Newmeyer, Klaus-Uwe Panther, John Joseph Perry, Seongha Rhee, Lotte Sommerer, Kyung-An Song, Barbara Soukup, Danjie Su, Marilena Thanassoula, Linda Thornburg, Elizabeth Traugott, Arie Verhagen, Barbara Wehr, Henry Widdowson, Björn Wiemer, as well as to the participants of the International Conference on *Final Particles*, held in Rouen on 27–28 May 2010, to the participants of the conference *Beyond Dichotomies*, held in Budapest on 25–26 October, 2010, to the participants of the conference on *Competing Motivations*, held in Leipzig on 23–25 November 2010, and of the conference on *Complexité syntaxique et variété typologique*, held in Paris, 12–14 October 2011, to our colleagues at Leiden University, at Paris 3 (Sorbonne), the University of Mainz, Beijing Language and Culture University, and Beijing Capital Normal University for critical comments. Finally, the first-named author is also grateful to Matthias Brenzinger and the University of Cape Town, as well as to the Korean Ministry of Education, Science and Technology for generously having sponsored the research leading to this paper within its World Class University Program. The third author would like to thank the Alexander von Humboldt Research Foundation as well as UCL, University of London, and SOAS, University of London, for the generous financial support and the stimulating scientific atmosphere.

References

Aijmer, Karin. 1972. *Some Aspects of Psychological Predicates in English*. Stockholm: Almqvist and Wiksell.

Aijmer, Karin. 1997. "I think" – an English modal particle. In T. Swan and O. Jansen Westvik (eds.), *Modality in Germanic Languages. Historical and Comparative Perspectives*. Berlin, New York: Mouton de Gruyter. Pp. 1–47.

Aijmer, Karin. 2002. *English Discourse Particles: Evidence from a Corpus*. Amsterdam, Philadelphia: John Benjamins.

Aikhenvald, Alexandra Y. 2010. *Imperatives and Commands*. (Oxford Studies in Linguistic Theory.) Oxford: Oxford University Press.

Ameka, Felix. 1992. Interjections: The universal yet neglected part of speech. *Journal of Pragmatics* 18: 101–18.

Auer, Peter. 1996. The pre-front field position in spoken German and its relevance as grammaticalization position. *Pragmatics* 6: 295–322.

Auer, Peter. 1997. Formen und Funktionen der Vor-Vorfeldbesetzung im gesprochenen Deutsch. In Schlobinski, Peter (ed.), *Syntax des gesprochenen Deutsch*. Opladen: Westdeutscher Verlag. Pp. 55–92.

Averintseva-Klisch, Maria. 2008. To the right of the clause: Right dislocation vs. afterthought. In Fabricius-Hansen, Cathrine and Wiebke Ramm (ed.), *'Subordination' versus 'Coordination' in Sentence and Text: A Cross-Linguistic Perspective*. (Studies in Language Companion Series, 98.) Amsterdam, Philadelphia: Benjamins. Pp. 217–39.

Axelsson, Karin. 2011. A cross-linguistic study of grammatically-dependent question tags: Data and theoretical implications. *Studies in Language* 35, 4: 793–851.

Barton, Ellen. 1990. *Nonsentential Constituents: A Theory of Grammatical Structure and Pragmatic Interpretation*. Amsterdam, Philadelphia: John Benjamins.

Barton, Ellen. 1998. The grammar of telegraphic structures: sentential and nonsentential derivation. *Journal of English linguistics* 26: 37–67.

Bayer, Klaus. 1973. Verteilung und Funktion der sogenannten Parenthese in Texten. *Deutsche Sprache* 1: 64–115.

Biber, Douglas, S. Johansson, G. Leech, S. Conrad and E. Finegan. 1999. *Longman Grammar of Spoken and Written English*. London: Longman.

Blakemore, Diane. 1987. *Semantic Constraints on Relevance*. Oxford: Blackwell.

Blakemore, Diane. 2005. *And*-parentheticals. *Journal of Pragmatics* 37: 1165–81.

Blakemore, Diane. 2006. Divisions of labour: The analysis of parentheticals. *Lingua* 116: 1670–87.

Bloomfield, Leonard. 1962. [1933] *Language*. London: George Allen & Unwin.

Brandt, Margareta. 1996. Subordination und Parenthese als Mittel der Informationsstrukturierung in Texten. In Motsch, Wolfgang (ed.), *Ebenen der Textstruktur: Sprachliche und kommunikative Prinzipien*. Tübingen: Niemeyer. Pp. 211–40.

Brinton, Laurel J. 1996. *Pragmatic Markers in English: Grammaticalization and Discourse Functions*. (Topics in English Linguistics, 19.) Berlin and New York: Mouton de Gruyter.

Brinton, Laurel J. 2008. *The Comment Clause in English: Syntactic Origins and Pragmatic Development*. (Studies in English Language.) Cambridge: Cambridge University Press.

Burton-Roberts, Noel. 1999. Language, linear precedence and parentheticals. In Collins, Peter and David Lee (eds.), *The Clause in English*. Amsterdam, Philadelphia: Benjamins. Pp. 33–52.

Burton-Roberts, Noel. 2005. Parentheticals. *Encyclopedia of Language and Linguistics*. 2nd edition, volume 9. Amsterdam: Elsevier. Pp. 179–82.

Bybee, Joan. 2003. Mechanisms of change in grammaticization: The role of frequency. In Joseph, Brian D., Janda, Richard D. (eds.), *The Handbook of Historical Linguistics* (Blackwell Handbooks in Linguistics.). Oxford, Malden, MA: Blackwell. Pp. 602–23.

Bybee, Joan. 2007. *Frequency of Use and the Organization of Language*. Oxford: Oxford University Press.

Childs, G. Tucker. 1995. *A Grammar of Kisi, a Southern Atlantic Language*. (Mouton Grammar Library, 16.) Berlin, New York: Mouton de Gruyter.

Cinque, Guglielmo. 1999. *Adverbs and Functional Heads*. New York: Oxford University Press.

Clark, Eve V. 2003. *First Language Acquisition*. Cambridge: Cambridge University Press.

Clark, Herbert H. 1996. *Using Language*. Cambridge: Cambridge University Press. Corum, Claudia 1975. A pragmatic analysis of parenthetic adjuncts. *Chicago Linguistic Society* 11: 133–41.

Croucher, Stephen M. 2004. *Like, you know, what I'm saying*: A study of discourse marker frequency in extemporaneous and impromptu speaking. http://www.nationalforensics. org/journal/vol22no2-3.pdf.

Cuenca, Josep M. 2000. Defining the indefinable? Interjections. *Syntaxis* 3: 29–44.

de Vries, Mark. 2007. Invisible constituents? Parentheses as B-merged adverbial phrases. In Dehé, Nicole and Yordanka Kavalova (eds.), *Parentheticals*. (Linguistics Today, 106.) Amsterdam, Philadelphia: Benjamins. Pp. 203–34.

Dehé, Nicole. 2009a. Parentheticals. In Cummings, Louise (ed.), *The Pragmatics Encyclopedia*. London, New York: Routledge. Pp. 307–8.

Dehé, Nicole. 2009b. Clausal parentheticals, intonational phrasing, and prosodic theory. *Journal of Linguistics* 45, 3: 569–615.

Dehé, Nicole and Yordanka Kavalova. 2006. The syntax, pragmatics, and prosody of parenthetical *what. English Language and Linguistics* 10: 289–320.

Dehé, Nicole and Yordanka Kavalova (eds.), *Parentheticals*. (Linguistics Today, 106.) Amsterdam, Philadelphia: Benjamins.

Dehé, Nicole and Yordanka Kavalova. 2007b. Introduction. In Dehé, Nicole and Yordanka Kavalova 2007, *Parentheticals*. (Linguistics Today, 106.) Amsterdam, Philadelphia: Benjamins. Pp. 1–22.

Dehé, Nicole and Anne Wichmann. 2010a. Sentence-initial *I think (that)* and *I believe (that)*: Prosodic evidence for use as main clause, comment clause and discourse marker. *Studies in Language* 34, 1: 36–74.

Dehé, Nicole and Anne Wichmann. 2010b. The multifunctionality of epistemic parentheticals in discourse: Prosodic cues to the semantic-pragmatic boundary. *Functions of Language* 17, 1: 1–28.

Dér, Csilla Ilona. 2010. On the status of discourse markers. *Acta Linguistica Hungarica* 57, 1: 3–28.

Diessel, Holger. 2005. *The Acquisition of Complex Sentences*. (Cambridge Studies in Linguistics, 105.) Cambridge: Cambridge University Press.

Diessel, Holger and Michael Tomasello. 2000. Why complement clauses do not include a *that*-complementizer in early child language. *Berkeley Linguistics Society* 25: 86–97.

Dik, Simon C. 1997. *The Theory of Functional Grammar, Part 2: Complex and Derived Constructions*. (Functional Grammar Series, 21.) Berlin, New York: Mouton de Gruyter.

Dixon, R.M.W. 2004. *The Jarawara Language of Southern Amazonia*. Oxford: Oxford University Press.

Dixon, R.M.W. 2010a. *Basic Linguistic Theory. Volume 1: Methodology*. Oxford: Oxford University Press.

Dixon, R.M.W. 2010b. *Basic Linguistic Theory. Volume 2: Grammatical Topics*. Oxford: Oxford University Press.

Doke, Clement M. 1988. [1927] *Textbook of Zulu Grammar*. Sixth edition. Cape Town: Maskew Miller Longman.

Du Bois, John. 1985. Competing motivations. In Haiman, John (ed.), *Iconicity in Syntax*. (Typological Studies in Language, 6.) Amsterdam: Benjamins. Pp. 343–66.

Ekman, Paul, Wallace V. Friesen, and Phoebe Ellsworth. 1972. *Emotion in the Human Face: Guidelines for Research and an Integration of Findings*. New York: Pergamon.

Emonds, Joseph. 1973. Parenthetical clauses. In Corum, C. et al. 1973. *You take the high node and I'll take the low node*. Chicago: Linguistic Society. Pp. 333–47.

Emonds, Joseph. 1976. *A Transformational Approach to English Syntax*, Academic Press, New York.

Emonds, Joseph. 1979. Appositive relatives have no properties. *Linguistic Inquiry* 10, 2: 211–43.

Espinal, M. 1991. The representation of disjunct constituents. *Language* 67: 726–62.

Fabb, N. 1990. The difference between English restrictive and non-restrictive relative clauses. *Journal of Linguistics* 26: 57–78.

Fischer, Kerstin. 2000. *From Cognitive Semantics to Lexical Pragmatics. The functional Polysemy of Discourse Particles*. Berlin/New York: Mouton de Gruyter.

Fischer, Kerstin (ed.). 2006. *Approaches to discourse particles,* [Studies in Pragmatics 1]. Bingley, UK: Emerald Group Publishing.

Floricic, Franck. 2011. Le vocatif et la périphérie du système des cas: entre archaïsmes et innovations. *Mémoires de la Société Linguistique de Paris* (Nouvelle Série) 19: 103–34.

Floricic, Franck and Lucia Molinu. 2012. Romance monosyllabic imperatives and markedness. Typescript.

Fortmann, Christian. 2006. The complement of *verba dicendi* parentheticals. In Miriam Butt and Tracy Holloway King (eds.), *Proceedings of the LFG06 Conference, Universität Konstanz, 2006*. Konstanz: CSLI Publications.

Fortmann, Christian. 2007. The complement of reduced parentheticals. In Dehé, Nicole and Yordanka Kavalova (eds.), *Parentheticals*. (Linguistics Today, 106.) Amsterdam, Philadelphia: Benjamins. Pp. 89–119.

Fraser, Bruce. 1990. An approach to discourse markers. *Journal of Pragmatics* 14, 3: 383–98.

Givón, T. 1995. *Functionalism and Grammar*. Amsterdam, Philadelphia: Benjamins.

Givón, T. 2001. *Syntax: An Introduction*. Volume 1. Amsterdam, Philadelphia: Benjamins.

Grenoble, Lenore. 2004. Parentheticals in Russian. *Journal of Pragmatics* 36, 11: 1953–74.

Günthner, Susanne and Wolfgang Imo. 2003. Die Reanalyse von Matrixsätzen als Diskursmarker: *ich mein*-Konstruktionen im gesprochenen Deutsch. *InLiSt* (Interaction and Linguistic Structures) 37: 1–31.

Haegeman, Liliane. 1991. Parenthetical adverbials: The radical orphanage approach. In Chiba, S., A. Shuki, A. Ogawa, Y. Fuiwara, N. Yamada, O. Koma, and T. Yagi (eds.), *Aspects of Modern Linguistics: Papers Presented to Masatomo Ukaji on his 60th Birthday*. Tokyo: Kaitakushi. Pp. 232–54.

Halliday, Michael A.K. 1985. *An Introduction to Functional Grammar.* London, New York, Melbourne, Auckland: Arnold.

Han, Chung-Hye. 1998. *The Structure and Interpretation of Imperatives: Mood and Force in Universal Grammar.* Ph.D. Dissertation, University of Pennsylvania, Philadelphia.

Havers, Wilhelm. 1931. *Handbuch der erklärenden Syntax. Ein Versuch zur Erforschung der Bedingungen und Triebkräfte in Syntax und Stylistik.* Heidelberg: Carl Winter.

Hayashi, Makoto and Kyung-Eun Yoon. 2006. A cross-linguistic exploration of demonstratives in interaction: With particular reference to the context of word-formulation trouble. *Studies in Language* 30: 485–540.

Hayashi, Makoto and Kyung-Eun Yoon. 2010. A cross-linguistic exploration of demonstratives in interaction: With particular reference to the context of word-formulation trouble. In Amiridze, Nino, Boyd H. Davis, and Margaret Maclagan (eds.), *Fillers, Pauses and Placeholders.* (Typological Studies in Language, 93.) Amsterdam, Philadelphia: Benjamins. Pp. 33–65.

Heine, Bernd. in print. On discourse markers: Grammaticalization, pragmaticalization, or something else? *Linguistics* in print.

Heine, Bernd and Gunther Kaltenböck. 2012. On the placement of conceptual theticals. Typescript.

Heine, Bernd and Gunther Kaltenböck. forthc. Sentence Grammar vs. Thetical Grammar: Two competing domains? To appear in Edith Moravcsik and Andrej Malchukov (eds.), *Competing Motivations.* Oxford: University Press.

Heine, Bernd, Gunther Kaltenböck and Tania Kuteva. forthc. On the origin of grammar. In Lefebvre, Claire, Bernard Comrie and Henri Cohen (eds.) (forthc.), *Current Perspectives on the Origins of Language.* Cambridge: Cambridge University Press.

Hengeveld, Kees and J. Lachlan Mackenzie. 2008. *Functional Discourse Grammar: A Typologically-Based Theory of Language Structure.* Oxford: Oxford University Press.

Hjelmslev, Louis. 1928. *Principes de grammar générale.* Copenhagen: Munksgaard.

Himmelmann, Nikolaus P. 2004. Lexicalization and grammaticization: Opposite or orthogonal? In Walter Bisang, Nikolaus P. Himmelmann, and Björn Wiemer (eds.), *What Makes Grammaticalization – A Look from its Fringes and its Components.* Berlin: Mouton de Gruyter. 19–40.

Hockett, Charles F. 1958. *A Course in Modern Linguistics.* New York: MacMillan.

Howe, Chad. 2008. Parentheticals. A review of Dehé and Kavalova 2007. LIGUIST List 19.1761, June 2, 2008.

Huddleston, R. and G. K. Pullum. 2002. *The Cambridge Grammar of the English Language.* Cambridge: Cambridge University Press.

Hyland, Ken. 1998. Persuasion and context: The pragmatics of academic metadiscourse. *Journal of Pragmatics* 30: 437–55.

Ifantidou-Trouki, Elly. 1993. Sentential adverbs and relevance. *Lingua* 90, 1–2: 69–90.

Jackendoff, Ray. 1972. *Semantic Interpretation in Generative Grammar.* Cambridge, Ma.: MIT Press.

Jackendoff, Ray. 2002. *Foundations of Language: Brain, Meaning, Grammar, Evolution.* Oxford: Oxford University Press.

Jackendoff, Ray. 2011. The Parallel Architecture and its place in cognitive science. In Heine, Bernd and Heiko Narrog (eds.), *The Oxford Handbook of Linguistic Analysis.* Oxford: Oxford University Press. Pp. 583–605.

Jucker, Andreas H. and Yael Ziv (eds.). 1998. *Discourse Markers: Description and Theory*. Amsterdam, Philadelphia: Benjamins.

Kac, Michael B. 1972. Clauses of saying and the interpretation of *because*. *Language* 48, 3: 626–32.

Kaltenböck, Gunther. 2007. Spoken parenthetical clauses in English. In Dehé, Nicole and Yordanka Kavalova (eds.), *Parentheticals*. (Linguistics Today, 106.) Amsterdam, Philadelphia: Benjamins. Pp. 25–52.

Kaltenböck, Gunther. 2008. Prosody and function of English comment clauses. *Folia Linguistica* 42, 1: 83–134.

Kaltenböck, Gunther. 2010. Pragmatic functions of parenthetical *I think*. In Kaltenböck, Gunther, Gudrun Mihatsch and Stefan Schneider (eds.), *New Approaches to Hedging*. Emerald Publishers. Pp. 243–72.

Kaltenböck, Gunther. 2011. Linguistic structure and use: explaining diverging evidence. The case of clause-initial *I think*. In Schönefeld, Doris (ed.), *Converging evidence: methodological and theoretical issues for linguistic research*. Amsterdam: Benjamins. Pp. 81–112.

Kaltenböck, Gunther, Bernd Heine, and Tania Kuteva. 2011. On thetical grammar. *Studies in Language* 35, 4: 848–93.

Kärkkäinen, Elise. 2003. *Epistemic Stance in English Conversation: A Description of its Interactional Functions, with a Focus on* I think. Amsterdam, Philadelphia: Benjamins.

Kavalova, Yordanka. 2007. *And*-parenthetical clauses. In Dehé, Nicole and Yordanka Kavalova (eds.), *Parentheticals*. (Linguistics Today, 106.) Amsterdam, Philadelphia: Benjamins. Pp. 145–72.

Knowles, John. 1980. The tag as a parenthetical. *Studies in Language* 4, 3: 379–409.

Kockelman, Paul. 2003. The meanings of interjections in Q'eqchi' Maya: From emotive reaction to social and discursive action. *Current Anthropology* 44: 467–90.

Kuroda, S.-Y. 1972. The categorical and the thetic judgment. Evidence from Japanese syntax. *Foundations of Language* 9: 153–85.

Lakoff, George. 1974. Syntactic amalgams. *Chicago Linguistic Society* 10: 321–44.

Lambrecht, Knud. 1994. *Information Structure and Sentence Form*. Cambridge University Press.

Lambrecht, Knud. 1996. On the formal and functional relationship between topics and vocatives: evidence from French. In Goldberg, Adele E. (ed.), *Conceptual Structure, Discourse and Language*. (CSLI Pulications.) Stanford: Center for the Study of Languge and Information. Pp. 267–288.

Langacker, Ronald W. 2008. *Cognitive Grammar: A Basic Introduction*. Oxford: Oxford University Press.

Levinson, Stephen C. 1983. *Pragmatics*. Cambridge: Cambridge University Press.

Lewis, Diana M. 2011. A discourse-constructional approach to the emergence of discourse markers in English. *Linguistics* 49, 2: 415–43.

McCawley, James D. 1982. Parentheticals and discontinuous constituent structure. *Linguistic Inquiry* 13: 91–106.

McCawley, James D. 1988. *The Syntactic Phenomena of English*. Two volumes. Chicago: The University of Chicago Press.

Mackenzie, J. Lachlan. 1998. The basis of syntax in the holophrase. In Hannay, Mike and A. Machtelt Bolkestein (eds.), *Functional Grammar and Verbal Interaction*.

Mackenzie, J. Lachlan. Amsterdam, Philadelphia: Benjamins. Pp. 267–95.

Mazeland, Harrie. 2007. Parenthetical sequences. *Journal of Pragmatics* 39: 1816–69.

Michaelis, Laura A. and Knud Lambrecht. 1996. The exclamative sentence type in English. In Goldberg, Adele E. (ed.), *Conceptual Structure, Discourse and Language.* (CSLI Pulications.) Stanford: Center for the Study of Languge and Information. Pp. 375–89.

Mithun, Marianne. 2008. The extension of dependency beyond the sentence. *Language* 84, 1: 69–119.

Morris, C. W. 1971. [1938] *Writings on the General Theory of Signs.* The Hague: Mouton.

Morris, H. F. and B. E. R. Kirwan. 1957. *A Runyankore Grammar.* Nairobi, Kampala and Dar-es-Salaam: Eagle Press.

Newmeyer, Frederick J. 2012. Parentheticals, 'fragments', and the grammar of comple-mentation. Paper presented at the conference on *Les verbes parenthtétiques: hypotaxe, parataxe or parenthèse?* Université Paris Ouest Nanterre, 24–26 May2012.

Norrick, Neal R. 2009. Interjections as pragmatic markers. *Journal of Pragmatics* 41: 866–91.

Nosek, J. 1973. Parenthesis in modern colloquial English. *Prague Studies in English* 15: 99–116.

Onions, C. T. 1971. *Modern English Syntax.* London: Routledge and Kegan Paul.

Ortner, Hanspeter. 1983. Syntaktisch hervorgehobene Konnektoren im Deutschen. *Deutsche Sprache* 11: 97–121.

O'Connell, Daniel C. and Sabine Kowal. 2005. *Uh* and *um* revisited: Are they interjections for signaling delay? *Journal of Psycholinguistic Research* 34: 555–76.

Pawley, Andrew. 1992. Formulaic speech. In Bright, William H. (ed.) 1992. *Oxford International Encyclopedia of Linguistics.* Volume 2. New York, Oxford: Oxford University Press. Pp. 22–5.

Peterson, Peter. 1999. On the boundaries of syntax: non-syntagmatic relations. In Peter Collins and David Lee (eds.), *The Clause in English: In Honour of Rodney Huddleston.* Amsterdam, Philadelphia: John Benjamins. Pp. 229–250.

Petola, Niilo. 1983. Comment clauses in present-day English. In Kajanto, Iiro et al. (eds.), *Studies in Classical and Modern Philology.* Helsinki: Suomalainen, Tiedeakatemia. Pp. 101–13.

Pittner, Karin. 1995. Zur Syntax von Parenthesen. *Linguistische Berichte* 156: 85–108.

Quirk, Randolph, Sidney Greenbaum, Geoffrey Leech, and Jan Svartvik. 1985. *A Comprehensive Grammar of the English Language.* London, New York: Longman.

Reinhart, Tanya. 1983. Point of view in language – the use of parentheticals. In Gisa Rauh (ed.), *Essays on Deixis.* Tübingen: Narr. Pp. 169–194.

Rhodes, Richard A. 1992. Interjections. In Bright, William H. (ed.) (ed.), *Oxford International Encyclopedia of Linguistics.* New York, Oxford: Oxford University Press. P. 222.

Rivero, María Luisa and Arhonto Terzi. 1995. Imperatives, V-movement and logical mood. *Journal of Linguistics* 31: 301–32.

Rizzi, Luigi. 1997. The fine structure of the left periphery. In Haegeman, L (ed.), *Elements of Grammar,* pages 281–337. Kluwer, Amsterdam: Kluwer.

Robins, R. H. 1958. *The Yurok Language: Grammar, Texts, Lexicon.* (University of California Publications in Linguistics, 15.) Berkeley and Los Angeles : University of California Press.

Ross, John Robert. 1970. On declarative sentences. In Jacobs, Roderick A. and Peter S. Rosenbaum (eds.), *Reading in English Transfomational Grammar.* Waltham, MA: Ginn. Pp. 222–77.

Ross, John Robert. 1973. Slifting. In Maurice Gross, Morris Halle, Marcel-Paul Schützenberger (eds.), *The Formal Analysis of Natural Languages: Proceedings of the First International Conference.* The Hague, Paris: Mouton. Pp. 133–69.

Rouchota, Villy. 1998. Procedural meaning and parenthetical discourse markers. In Jucker, Andreas H. and Yael Ziv (eds.), *Discourse Markers: Descriptions and Theory*. Amsterdam, Philadelphia: Benjamins. Pp. 97–126.

Rutherford, William W. 1970. Some observations concerning subordinate clauses in English. *Language* 46, 1: 97–115.

Sacks, Harvey, Emanuel A. Schegloff, and Gail Jefferson. 1974. A simplest systematics for the organization of turn-taking for conversation. *Language* 50, 1: 696–735.

Sadock, Jerold M. and Arnold M. Zwicky. 1985. Speech act distinctions in syntax. In Shopen, Timothy (ed.), *Language Typology and Syntactic Description: Clause Structure*. Cambridge: Cambridge University Press. Pp. 155–96.

Safir, K. 1986. Relative clauses in a theory of binding and levels. *Linguistic Inquiry* 17, 4: 663–89.

Sakai, Kuniyoshi L., Tatsuno, Yoshinori, Suzuki, Kei, Kimura, Harumi, and Ichida, Yasuhiro. 2005. Sign and speech: amodal commonality in left hemisphere dominance for comprehension of sentences. *Brain* 128, 6: 1407–17.

Sasse, Hans-Jürgen. 1987. The thetic/categorical distinction revisited. *Linguistics* 25: 511–580.

Sasse, Hans-Jürgen. 2006. Theticity. In G. Bernini and M. L. Schwartz (eds.), *Pragmatic Organization of Discourse in the Languages of Europe*. Berlin and New York: Mouton de Gruyter, 255–308.

Schegloff, Emanuel A. 1968. Sequencing in conversational openings. *American Anthropologist* 70: 1075–95.

Schegloff, Emanuel A. 1998. Reflections on studying prosody in talk-in-interaction. *Language and Speech* 41: 235–63.

Schegloff, Emanuel A., Jefferson, Gail and Sacks, Harvey. 1977. The Preference for Self-Correction in the Organization of Repair in Conversation. *Language* 53, 2: 361–82.

Schegloff, Emanuel A. and Harvey Sacks. 1973. Opening up closings. *Semiotica* 8: 289–327.

Schelfhout, Carla, Peter-Arno Coppen, and Nelleke Oostdijk. 2004. Finite comment clauses in Dutch: A corpus-based approach. *Journal of Linguistics* 16: 331–49.

Schiffrin, Deborah. 1987. *Discourse Markers*. (Studies in Interactional Sociolinguistics, 5.) Cambridge: Cambridge University Press.

Schleicher, August. 1865. *Die Unterscheidung von Nomen und Verbum in der lautliche Form*. Leipzig: Hirzel.

Schneider, Stefan. 2007a. Reduced parenthetical clauses in Romance languages. In Dehé, Nicole and Yordanka Kavalova (eds.), *Parentheticals*. (Linguistics Today, 106.) Amsterdam, Philadelphia: Benjamins. Pp. 237–58.

Schneider, Stefan. 2007b. *Reduced Parenthetical Clauses as Mitigators, A Corpus Study of Spoken French, Italian and Spanish*. Amsterdam, Philadelphia: Benjamins.

Schourup, Lawrence Clifford. 1999. Discourse markers. *Lingua* 107: 227–65.

Schwyzer, Eduard. 1939. *Die Parenthese im engern und weitern Sinne*. (*Abhandlungen der Preußischen Akademie der Wissenschaften, Jahrgang 1939 Philosophisch-historische Klasse, 6*.) Berlin: Verlag der Akademie der Wissenschaften.

Shaer, Benjamin. 2003. An ‚orphan' analysis of long and short adjunct movement in English. In Garding, G. and M. Tsujimira (eds.), *WCCFL 22 Proceedings*. Sommerville, MA: Cascadilla Press. Pp. 450–63.

Shaer, Benjamin and Werner Frey. 2004. 'Integrated' and 'non-integrated' left-peripheral elements in German and English. *ZAS Papers in Linguistics* 35, 2: 465–502.

Shopen, Timothy. 1973. Ellipsis as grammatical indeterminacy. *Foundations of Language* 10: 65–77.

Spagnolo, L.M. 1933. *Bari Grammar*. Verona: Missioni Africane.

Stowell, Tim. 2005. Appositive and parenthetical relative clauses. In Hans Broekhuis, Norbert Corver, Jan Koster, Riny Huybregts and Ursula Kleinhenz (eds.), *Organizing Grammar: Linguistic Studies in Honor of Henk van Riemsdijk*, Berlin, New York: Mouton de Gruyter. Pp. 608–17.

Stubbs, Michael. 1983. *Discourse Analysis: The Sociolinguistic Analysis of Natural Language and Culture*. Oxford: Blackwell.

Takahashi, Hidemitsu. 2005. Imperatives in subordinate clauses. *Annual Report on Cultural Science* 117: 45–87.

Takahashi, Hidemitsu. 2008. Imperatives in concessive clauses: compatibility between construtions. http://www.constructionsonline.de/articles/1280/Imperatives_in_ concessive_clauses.pdf

Thim-Mabrey, Christiane. 1988. Satzadverbialia und andere Ausdrücke im Vorvorfeld. *Deutsche Sprache* 16: 25–67.

Thompson, Sandra A. 2002. ‚Object complements‘ and conversation: Towards a realistic account. *Studies in Language* 26, 1: 125–64.

Thompson, Sandra A. and Anthony Mulac. 1991. A quantitative perspective on the Prgrammati-cization of epitemic parentheticals in English. In Traugott, Elizabeth C. and Bernd Heine (eds.), *Approaches to grammaticaltion*. Volume 1. (Typological Studies in Language, 19, 1.) Amsterdam, Philadelphia: Benjamins. Pp. 313–29.

Traugott, Elizabeth C. 1995. The role of discourse markers in a theory of grammaticalization. Paper presented at the 12th Internationa Conference on Historical Linguistics, Manchester, England, August 1995.

Traugott, Elizabeth C. 2003. Constructions in grammaticalization. In Joseph, Brian D. & Richard D. Janda (eds.), *The Handbook of Historical Linguistics*. Oxford: Blackwell. Pp. 624–47.

Traugott, Elizabeth C. 2010. Revisiting subjectification and intersubjectification. In Kristin Davidse, Lieven Vandelanotte, & Hubert Cuyckens (eds.), *Subjectification, Intersubjecti-fication and Grammaticalization*. Berlin: de Gruyter Mouton, 29–70.

Traugott, Elizabeth C. forthc. Intersubjectification and clause periphery. In Brems, Lieselotte, Lobke Ghesquière, and Freek Van de Velde (eds.), *English Text Construction* 5 (special issue).

Traugott, Elizabeth C. and Richard B. Dasher. 2002. *Regularity in semantic change*. Cambridge Studies in Linguistics, 96.) Cambridge: Cambridge University Press.

Tucker, Gordon. 2005. Extending the lexicogrammar: Towards a more comprehensive account of extraclausal, partially clausal and non-clausal expressions in spoken discourse. *Language Sciences* 27, 6: 679–709.

Urmson, J. O. 1952. Parenthetical verbs. *Mind* 61: 480–96.

Vandenbergen, Anne-Marie Simon and Dominique Willems. 2011. Crosslinguistic data as evidence in the grammaticalization debate: The case of discourse markers. *Linguistics* 49, 2: 333–64.

Veselinova, Ljuba N. 2006. *Suppletion in Verb Paradigms: Bits and Pieces of the Puzzle*. (Typological Studies in Language, 67.) Amsterdam, Philadelphia: Benjamins.

Wackernagel, Jacob. 1897. Vermischte Beiträge zur griechischen Sprachkunde. In *Programm zur Rektoratsfeier der Universität Basel*. Basel: Universität Basel. Pp. 3–62.

Voeltz, F. K. Erhard and Christa Kilian-Hatz (eds.). 2001. *Ideophones*. (Typological Studies in Language, 44). Amsterdam, Philadelphia: Benjamins.

Watkins, Calvert. 1963. Preliminaries to a historical and comparative analysis of the syntax of the Old Irish verb. *Celtica* 6: 1–49.

Wehr, Barbara. 2000. Zur Beschreibung der Syntax des *français parlé* (mit einem Exkurs zu "thetisch" und "kategorisch"). In Wehr, Barbara and Thomaßen, Helga (eds.), *Diskurs-analyse: Untersuchungen zum gesprochenen Französisch*. Frankfurt, Berlin: Peter Lang. Pp. 239–89.

Whaley, L. J. 1997. *Introduction to Typology: The Unity and Diversity of Laguage*. London: Sage.

Wharton, Tim. 2003. Interjections, language, and the 'showing/saying' continuum. *Pragmatics and Cognition* 11, 1: 39–91.

Wichmann, Anne. 2001. Spoken parentheticals. In Aijmer, K. (ed.), *A Wealth of English: Studies in Honour of Goran Kjellmer*. Gothenburg: Gothenburg University Press. Pp. 171–93.

Wichmann, Anne. 2004. The intonation of *Please*-requests: a corpus-based study. *Journal of Pragmatics* 36, 9: 1521–49.

Widdowson, H. G. 2004. *Text, Context, Pretext. Critical Issues in Discourse Analysis*. Oxford: Blackwell.

Wray, Alison. 2002. *Formulaic Language and the Lexicon*. Cambridge: Cambridge University Press.

Wray, Alison. 2009. Identifying formulaic language: Persistent challenges and newoppor-tunities. In Corrigan, Roberta, Edith A. Moravcsik, Hamid Ouali, and Kathleen M. Wheatley (eds.), *Formulaic Language. Volume 1: Distribution and Historical Change*. (Typological Studies in Language, 82.) Amsterdam, Philadelphia: Benjamins. Pp. 27–51.

Wray, Alison and Michael R. Perkins. 2000. The functions of formulaic language: An integrated model. *Language and Communication* 20: 1–28.

Zanuttini, Raffaella and Paul Portner. 2003. Exclamative clauses: At the syntax-semantics interface. *Language* 79,1: 39–81.

Ziv, Yael. 1985. "Parentheticals and Functional Grammar". In Bolkestein, A.M. et al. (eds.) *Syntax and Pragmatics in Functional Grammar*. Dordrecht: Foris, 181–199.

Lise Menn, Cecily Jill Duffield, and Bhuvana Narasimhan
Towards an Experimental Functional Linguistics: Production

1 Introduction

If an explanation of a linguistic phenomenon makes sense, why would someone want to bother with an experiment to test it? Experiments do not, strictly speaking, prove anything, so what do they add to what we already think to be true? Certainly there are no royal roads to knowledge: indeed, this paper is mostly about how hard it is to do experiments that actually add to our understanding of language production. But it's also about why language production experiments are essential to understanding how language works – along with corpus studies, comprehension experiments, thoughtful analyses of texts, and even old-fashioned contemplation of what makes two imagined ways of saying roughly the same thing appropriate in different contexts. For some linguists, the idea that experimental studies can be helpful is nothing new, but it is difficult for people who have little working contact with psycholinguists and neurolinguists to get a sense of their methods and findings, or of how their approaches can and cannot aid in the overall enterprise of functional linguistics: explaining why we use particular words and structures at particular points in text and discourse.

Much of the authors' experimental work has focused on one of the major threads of functional linguistics: explaining the order in which noun phrases are used in spoken language. Experimental studies of noun phrase order go all the way back to work on the effect of given and new information in children's production by Bates (1976) and Greenfield & Smith (1976). We will situate our discussion of noun phrase order studies, including our own work on children, people with aphasia, and normal adult populations, in the context of experimental functional production studies as a whole. We will also discuss our work in progress on another topic, subject-verb agreement, as an illustration of further issues in the study of language production.

2 Why do experiments?

There are three major reasons why we need experimental functional linguistics; we introduce the problems here, and then explain how experiments address them.

2.1 Three problems

1. *Many factors compete in the process of choosing particular structures and putting words into a particular order.* This is because of the 'linearization problem' – the problem of transforming rich, multi-valued, multi-dimensional information about our internal and external worlds into a structured but necessarily linear string of words. A particular functional school of thought can be blind to a whole realm of influences: for example, if one is focused on information structure, one may overlook emotional factors like the emotional loading involved in the use of an addressee's name when it is logically unnecessary (i.e. when there is no ambiguity about who is the addressee). Without experiments, there is no way to tease apart those competing factors – animacy, topicality, empathy, newness, solidarity, attention, etc. – or to see how they interact and compromise.

2. *The way our brains work constrains the resources we can deploy for communication. Not everything 'functional' can be fully explained in terms of interpersonal or informational needs; the way the wetware inside our skulls happens to work is also relevant.* Expecting introspection to give us an understanding of how we think is no more reasonable than expecting to discover the mechanics of vision by trying to see the insides of our own eyes. Our brains are not only complicated beyond imagining, they are also incapable of reporting on their own states. Furthermore, assuming that every choice in language production is made in order to help the listener is redolent of Dr. Pangloss's optimistic assurance that we have noses in order hold up our spectacles.

Neuroscience and psycholinguistics have given us a substantial amount of information about the way the brain happens to work, and quite a bit of that information turns out to be relevant to how we find the words and structures that we need in speaking. Our fast-fading memory for details, limited-capacity conscious attention, and some of their effects on communication are well-known to linguists, but a family of more recent and less introspectively accessible findings are just as important, namely, the short term and long-term persistence of structures we have heard and used, and the similar persistence of words and collocations. We know that these brain-based constraints exist, but we cannot investigate how and when they interact with functional motivations simply by looking at texts. Psycholinguistic experiments – on both comprehension and production – are the only way to move towards understanding how the mechanisms of our brains interact with our communicative needs.

3. *Purely text-based functional explanations of word order, choices of referring expression, and structure are inherently circular*, as recognized even by people

who have spent much of their lives working in the grammar-in-text tradition, e.g. Dickinson and Givón (2000). Text analyses alone cannot answer the question of whether "the observable discourse contexts indeed correspond to some unobservable discourse functions" (Dickinson and Givón, p. 155). No matter how brilliant and intuitively satisfying the analysis, and how carefully features of a text (written or spoken, monologue or dialogue) are enumerated and counted, the analyst is presuming on the basis of the text itself – often reasonably, but still, only presuming – that certain information is new or old, topical or focused, backgrounded or foregrounded. Experiments are the only way to climb out of the inherent circularity of text-based definitions – but that doesn't mean it is easy.

2.2 How successful experiments help to deal with these problems

2.2.1 Dealing with Problem 1: Competing factors.

Experiments can be designed to tease apart competing factors, such as animacy, topicality, empathy, newness, solidarity, and attention, and to see how they interact and compromise. For example, a number of studies have given speakers a succession of stimuli – pictures, arrangements of real objects, wordless cartoon strips, or short movie/video stories – to describe or narrate, systematically varying the animacy, visibility, mobility, expectedness, etc. of the people, animals, objects, and forces in the stories. With this method, and with all due caution, we can go behind cover variables such as 'attention' or 'salience' (Sridhar 1989, Tomlin 1995, 1997) and explore what it is that makes an entity attention-getting. We can, for example, play off, say, 'motion/force' against 'similarity to narrator', or 'size' against 'novelty-in-context', by varying one of these factors while holding all others constant. Doing this might show that different attention-getting factors have distinct effects on speakers' choices.

2.2.2 Dealing with Problem 2: Constraints imposed by how the brain works.

Experiments that are designed to hold constant or systematically vary what a speaker has recently heard or said are essential, because speakers are more likely to use more structures and words that they have recently heard: the general term for this is 'priming' (although distinctions within this category must be made; see Section 6 below and Kaschak & Gernsbacher, this volume). Experiments are needed in order to explore how priming phenomena account for speaker-driven choices and how they interact with recipient design. Likewise, well-designed experiments can help to control for other such constraints as fading memory and limited-capacity attention by controlling when stimulus items are presented and what distractor items (fillers) are presented between those stimuli.

2.2.3 Dealing with Problem 3: Purely text-based functional explanations are inherently circular.

Sorry, that seems to be a rude statement, but first let us consider why it is true and then how experiments offer a partial (but only partial) way out of that circularity. Functional explanations invoke animacy, topicality, newness, and other factors like the ones discussed in Problem 1, as explanations for choices of words and structures. But these factors are mental states; they are in people's heads, not in the texts that people hear and produce. For example, how do we *know* what the topic of a sentence or a discussion really is – what it is 'about' as far as each speaker is concerned? 'Topic' is not discoverable by asking the speakers, because their introspectively/retrospectively available orientation is not necessarily what influenced their formulation of their utterances at the moment they were producing them. And maybe there wasn't anything that could really be called a topic just at that moment, or maybe there were multiple competing referents (including events and states) that could reasonably have been regarded as 'topics'.

Or how do we know – independently of the text produced – what is 'figure' and what is 'ground', where a speaker's empathy lies, etc.? We don't. These are mental states, the speaker's construals of the world, and we have no access to them, nor can we control them.

But the matter is not hopeless. Experiments can still help us test hypotheses about the relationship between speakers' mental states and what they say, just not as directly as we would like. Remember that most (if not all) terms of scientific explanation – not just in psychology – are not things that are directly observable: consider gravity, chemical valence, or heritability. They cannot be manipulated directly as independent variables (like amount of illumination), nor can they be measured directly as dependent variables (like response time). Instead, they are *intermediate constructs*, valid (only) to the extent that they give good explanations of the relationship between the independent and dependent variables.

For example, Menn and colleagues (1998, 1999, discussed further below), following Kuno (1987), proposed that empathy with the undergoer is one reason that speakers use structures (e.g. fronting, passive) that mention the undergoer early in an utterance in English and Japanese. You cannot control whether a speaker feels empathy with a pictured undergoer, but if you vary properties of the undergoer that you think should increase empathy for most people (for example, making it more human-like) *and* you find a correlated increased use of undergoer-fronted clause structures, you have support for treating empathy as a useful term of explanation – at least until something better comes along.

We have just suggested how experiments can deal with three major problems for functional linguistics. However, designing experiments to accomplish these ends is no easy task. Experiments that are not carefully designed – for example, by not controlling for multiple (and possibly correlated) factors such as animacy and empathy, or that do not take into consideration the multiple constraints on how the brain works – are likely to fail or give spurious results. Even with careful planning, experiments that try to investigate functional motivations for linguistic behaviors can go awry. We will discuss this in more detail below, as we outline several studies. Despite these challenges, we maintain that experimental work is a necessary companion to rigorous linguistic study in a functional approach to the explanation of the structures of language and how they are deployed.

Nothing in what we are saying is intended to suggest that psycholinguistics is a viable enterprise without linguistics. But it is also becoming increasingly likely that linguistics is not fully viable without psycholinguistics: see Kaschak & Gernsbacher's chapter in this volume, which explores some general implications of long-term 'priming' phenomena for the concept of 'having a grammar' in a usage-based framework. And, by the way, one cannot argue directly from brain to language; the distance is far too great. The connection between them is language processing: psycholinguistics.

3 Why study production?

Most of the experimental work in psycholinguistics has concerned comprehension. This is no surprise; it is easier to study how people comprehend language rather than produce it, because you can present someone with a particular bit of language that you are interested in investigating, and see how they respond to it by pushing buttons, answering questions, looking at particular parts of images on a screen, or emitting brainwaves.

But if we as functional linguists believe that language is driven by the nature of human communicative interaction rather than by an innate language faculty, we need to study production too. Comprehension focuses on what listeners do with language, but listeners can choose to engage with the language presented to them, or they can choose to ignore it; they are not automatically compelled to fully process the communication being offered to them. If we wish to understand how language structure is shaped by communicative function, we need to understand the reasons that speakers choose particular output forms. While an increasing number of studies have linked comprehension processes to production processes (e.g., Staub 2009; Bock, Dell, Chang & Onishi 2007; Gennari & MacDonald 2009), production is in no way 'comprehension in reverse'. Production and comprehension involve different tasks. This is supported by studies showing different results in comprehension and production of the same linguistic structure. For example, current work by Francis & Michaelis (2012) examining extraposed relative clauses suggests that relative clause length significantly affects performance in comprehending such structures, whereas verb phrase length is more significant in producing them. Work by Tanner (2012) on subject-verb agreement suggests that clause-bounding effects that have been shown in production do not influence comprehension. So when we investigate the role of communicative function in the determination of linguistic choices, we cannot assume that results of comprehension experiments supporting a particular functional story can be extended to production. If we want to know the functionality of language, we must study the choices that the speaker, rather than the listener, makes.

4 The observer's paradox and the 'design space' of functional language production experiments

An overview of experiments in language production will help us in handling a perennial problem: the undeniable unnaturalness of experimental settings. Every science faces the observer's paradox – the fact that data collection affects the data to some extent. Minimally, even observational data collection (e.g. studying naturally-occurring internet corpora) introduces the question of whether your sample is representative (and what it is representative of). The more tightly you try to control the context in which language is produced, the further you are from the ecological real-world setting in which events normally occur. So, linguistics, like other sciences, needs to cycle its questions through as wide a range of settings as possible. Work in a maximally-controlled setting – a test tube, a Skinner box, a reaction-time experiment, a cloze (fill-in-the-blank) language task – is essential because it isolates a few variables and makes it possible to pit them against one another. Rare events can be stimulated and repeated measures can be made to check reliability – but you cannot tell whether your work will scale up to the real world, because you do not know what else might be going on in a more natural setting.

Table 1: Design space of production experiments

Production Experiments	One speaker, no listener contact	One speaker, back-channel listener	Two interacting speakers
channel control but no content control, very large number of participants			'Call Home', Switchboard, & other elicited telephone corpus studies e.g. Godfrey, Holliman, & McDaniel (1992); Duffield (2012)
one item per subject, loose control, many participants		Extended narrative elicitations, cross-linguistic: Pear stories starting with Chafe (1980); Frog story, Berman & Slobin (1994)	Map location & other tasks involving instructions across a visual barrier, e.g. McNamara, Ratcliff, McKoon (1984), Clark & Wilkes-Gibbs (1986)
several elicitation items per participant, contrasting contexts		Karmiloff-Smith (1979) (French); given/new studies, e.g. Greenfield & Smith (1976); Bates, Hamby, & Zurif (1983); English & Japanese cartoon strips, Menn, Reilly, Hayashi, Kamio, Fujita, & Sasanuma (1998), Menn, Kamio, Hayashi, Fujita, Sasanuma, & Boles (1999)	Children requested to ask specific questions of a 3rd party, Tanz (1980); aphasic speakers narrating 'I Love Lucy' episodes, Ramsberger & Rende (2002)
many items per participant, very tight control of content	Sridhar (1988, 1989) 14-language film study; Tomlin (1995, 1997) FishFilms	description of many simple pictures or object configurations e.g. Menn, Gottfried, Holland, & Garrett (2005); Narasimhan & Dimroth (2008)	Branigan, Pickering & Cleland (2000)

On the other hand, work in a minimally-controlled setting – corpus study, field observation – allows for the interplay of many more factors, some of which you would never have guessed at *a priori*; but particular events cannot be repeated on demand to check reliability, rare events may escape detection for years (or forever), and your interpretation – your claim that A causes B – can be harder to defend, because what you can observe are only correlations.

Bridging the gap between these extremes of maximal and minimal control, many intermediate experimental situations have been designed over the years. In Table 1, we give a brief guide to the 'design space' of experimental functional language production studies. This chart of production studies represents only two dimensions graphically: the number of participants/ items (these two factors being tightly and inversely correlated, given the finite resources of investigators), and the number of speakers in the elicitation setting. An implied third dimension is language variation: many of these studies are monolingual (in English or German), but some, as noted, are cross-linguistic. A fourth dimension is speaker demographic; while most of these studies involve language-normal adults, a few look at children, and others look at speakers with aphasia. While the chart is far from complete, it indicates something of the range of topics that have been investigated experimentally.

A hypothesis or a conclusion about the choice of referring expression or word order or structure that was arrived at from one part of this design space – or from text analysis or introspection or anywhere else – should hold up when it is tested in some other part. If it does not, there are three possibilities: the conclusion was flawed (probably because of additional variables that weren't taken into account), the study wasn't sensitive enough to check it properly (probably because of some unrecognized factor that has affected the participants' responses), or perhaps the original study design happened to be a special case whose results wouldn't hold up under conditions different from those that happened to be used in the original study.

5 Beyond recipient design: Strategies, choices, and brain-traps

Before going on, we need to work out the differences between (1) a listener-oriented strategy (also called recipient design), (2) a so-called speaker-driven strategy, and (3) a usage choice that is not strategic, but rather is an automatic consequence of how the speaker's brain works – even if we cannot always tell which is which in practice. This is consonant with the generally accepted position that functional explanations in linguistics deal with how speakers and listeners 'work'– what they do because of the ways their brains (and bodies) are constructed – as well as with choices they make to improve communication (cf. Ferreira and Firato 2002). Even the word 'choice' can be misleading because of its connotation of consciousness, but we, like our colleagues, intend it to mean selection among alternative forms regardless of whether that selection is strategic or is driven by automatic processes.

What is a strategy, and what is not? We use the term 'strategy' sparingly, to mean an action that is under – or can be brought under – a fair degree of conscious control. This is not yet standard practice, but we suggest that it should be, because that is the sense that a reader will normally bring to the word. One of our major points in this paper, then, is that many of the choices that speakers make are not 'strategic' in the normal sense. This does not preclude their serving a communicative function, but it means that choices of this type cannot be fully explained solely in terms of the demands of communication.

Consider a standard example in discussions of recipient design: deciding how to indicate a referent so that a listener can identify it well enough to follow the conversation. (We set aside, for the moment, any social/emotional influences on choice among possible referring terms). Suppose the referent is one of your household's several cats; the referring term might be, e.g. *she, the smallest cat, the spotted one, Tanya*, or a raised eyebrow and a nod towards the couch where the cat in question is sleeping.

Consider the following cases:

1. A normal adult speaker under typical circumstances has a choice of referring expression and can adapt it to a listener's presumed knowledge of your menagerie; we take as a working assumption, therefore, that her choice, whatever it is, is strategic and listener-oriented.
2. Suppose, instead, that the speaker is your three-year-old, who knows the names of all the cats but is focused on the one on the couch, and who just says *the kitty* even though you're in the next room and can't see which one he's talking about. The child had a choice of referring expressions, but the one he made was not as helpful to you as it could have been. Is his egocentric choice a 'strategy', designed to accomplish a communicative goal that calling the cat by name would not satisfy? It does not seem very likely, so we describe this kind of choice as being a result of 'speaker's impulse', rather than describing it as resulting from a 'speaker-oriented strategy'.
3. Now suppose the speaker is a severely aphasic adult who can only use a nonverbal gesture to refer. He has little or no choice; is his gesture still a strategy? Barely so, if at all; his stark choice is to communicate or not.

4. Suppose that the speaker is a visitor who is linguistically and cognitively normal and knows the names of your cats, but is distracted, perhaps under stress, and accidentally calls the cat by the name of his own cat. We – and often, the speaker – recognize this as an involuntary slip of the tongue. It is neither a strategy nor an impulse; instead, his brain has momentarily failed to serve his communicative needs, as if it were playing a trick on him.

5. Finally, suppose a visitor in a tip-of-the-tongue state refers to the cat as *uh-Tammy*, with a questioning look, certain that this is not the correct name but being unable to come up with any other. Is that a strategy? You've been in that state (although perhaps not with respect to the naming of cats): you don't feel like you're making a free choice, but as though you are imprisoned by your inability to discard the wrong name. You might as well be aphasic for the moment. Again, this is neither a strategy nor an impulse. Your brain is choking up on you; what you have said is again an automatic product of its (hopefully brief) malfunction.

As we discuss various patterns of speech production, sometimes we will be able to argue whether we are dealing with listener-oriented strategy, speaker's impulse, or an automatic consequence of how the speaker's brain is functioning, and sometimes we won't have enough evidence to argue one way or another. Often enough, two or all three of these possibilities pull in the same direction: what's easiest for the speaker to produce at a given moment may also be what's best for the hearer. But it is important to be able to consider which of the three might be in play at any given time, because sometimes, as we have seen, the speaker's choice is far from optimal for the hearer.

What do we mean by calling the production of a word or a phrase 'an automatic consequence of how the speaker's brain is functioning'? In Section 6 we consider how the activation of words and structures in our brain works, and how automatic spreading of that activation might cause speakers to use particular forms regardless of what might be optimal for communication. For example, the way that using a particular word may automatically activate re-using the same word or a closely-related word can account for some speaker-driven preferences in choice of word order.

6 Two things that functional linguists need to know about how the brain works: Lexical and structural priming

First, just what is priming? The basis of brain computations – at least, those that we are beginning to understand – is the activation of the neurons that are networked in our brains, resulting in thoughts, actions, and feelings, both conscious and unconscious. Priming is a change in the level of activation of a particular neural structure due to the automatic spreading of activation from a neural structure that handles related information, or to the maintenance of activation in a particular neural structure persisting long enough to affect a later action carried out by that structure.[1] The fact that activation spreads automatically in our brains produces major but unconscious influences on our choices of referring expressions, word order, and structure. Lexical priming – the spread of activation to particular words when related words have been aroused Ior the maintenance of activation on a word once it has been aroused) – and structural priming – the maintenance of activation of particular syntactic structures that have recently been used (read, heard, written, or spoken), have been studied in depth over the years in psycholinguistics laboratories like those of Kay Bock, Victor Ferreira, and many others. Priming may be helpful or cause problems; in particular, it may collude with or collide with functional factors in word choice and structural choice (e.g., helping the listener track referents or follow the speaker's emotional alignment). Therefore no experimental study of recipient design can afford to ignore priming; it can ruin your data and/or invalidate your conclusions. Importantly, priming is not just an issue for experiments: lexical and structural priming operate all the time, so they affect natural discourse as well. Some priming-induced shifts in usage are probably helpful to communication (see Pickering & Ferreira 2008: 441–442 on alignment), some are probably neutral, and some can interfere with communication.

Some lexical priming can be recognized by introspection: for example, in conversations, we often find ourselves using a recently-heard word that is semantically inexact, a profanity we have heard recently in a movie, or a new slang term

---

1 Harley 2001: 17: "if two things are similar to each other and involved in the same level of processing, they will either assist with or interfere with each other, but if they are unrelated, they will have no effect". As an example, you will find it easier to recognize a word (e.g. BREAD) if you have just seen a word that is related in meaning (e.g. BUTTER). If priming causes processing to be speeded up, we talk about facilitation; if priming causes it to be slowed down, we talk of inhibition.

that 'pops up' inadvertently when we are speaking to a listener who would not know it. Corpus studies have also provided some evidence for structural priming in spontaneous conversation (Schenkein 1980; but see Branigan, Pickering & Cleland 2000:B15 for why experimental work is necessary to rule out alternate explanations of the effects found in corpora). Structural priming is harder than lexical priming for speakers to detect by observing their own natural language, but it exists, and we next review some of the evidence for it.

Structural priming. Here is an example of structural priming that could have ruined an experiment designed at the Institute for Cognitive Science at the University of Arizona: an unwanted propagation of locative/presentational structures throughout the responses of pilot normal control participants in the study that was eventually published as Menn, Gottfried, Holland & Garrett (2005). This study looked at how normal and aphasic speakers described simple spatial relationships between 50 different pairs of common household objects, such as a picture of a carton of milk in a refrigerator or of a boot in a dishwasher; the independent variable was how expected or unexpected those relationships were. In pilot work with normal speakers, the Arizona group found that participants who start out describing the spatial relationship between a smaller and a larger object with an existential structure fronting the smaller object (*There's an axe on a bed*) are likely to persist in this pattern throughout the experiment. Regardless of changes in the spatial relationships and the weirdness of the juxtaposition of the objects, these participants tend to continue with the existential structure and 'figure-ground' order through an entire set of pictures. Conversely, speakers who happen to start out with the opposite order of mention (*There's a bed with an axe on it*) or with a simple Noun Phrase-Prepositional Phrase response (*An axe on a bed*) tend to continue using their first structure for dozens of subsequent responses (Menn 2000). Because the normal participants more-or-less kept on using whatever structure they had described the first picture with for the rest of the 49 stimulus pictures, the Arizona group had to re-design the elicitation procedure before proceeding with the main experiment, which looked at speakers with aphasia. This shows how strong structural priming can be in a situation where participants have a series of fairly similar pictures to describe and nothing intervening to distract or derail them.

In a typical experiment that is designed to investigate structural priming in production, participants are asked to read aloud or to listen to (and perhaps repeat) sentences that have a particular structure, and then to produce new sentences to describe pictured events, or to complete new sentences that have been started. They may also be asked to use particular words in the new sentences. What researchers look at is whether participants use the structure that they just heard or said in their own picture descriptions or sentence completions. If the structure persists, and cannot be attributed to the repetition of particular words, we say that structural priming has occurred. Pickering & Ferreira (2008) give a thorough and subtle review, not only of the twenty-odd years of experimental work on structural priming and its complexities (beginning with Bock 1986), but also of its probable subconscious influence on our choice of the structures we use in discourse. We strongly recommend reading their paper, but their main points, for our purposes, are as follows (all direct quotes from Pickering & Ferreira):

1. Structural priming "arises automatically, and does not depend on particular communicative intentions (Levelt & Kelter 1982)...or discourse factors...it occurs from comprehension to production, both in isolation (Potter & Lombardi, 1998) and in dialogue (Branigan, Pickering, & Cleland, 2000)". Structural priming in production is independent of the particular function words (e.g. *to, by, for*) used to signal the structural relations (Bock 1989, see also Hare & Goldberg 1999). For example, repeating a 'for'-dative sentence (benefactive construction) like *The secretary was baking a cake for her boss* primed the use of the prepositional dative with *to* in describing pictures of object-transfer events, and it did so just as much as repeating a 'to'-dative sentence like *The girl is handing the paintbrush to the man on the ladder*. Indeed, structural priming can take place across languages, without help from cognate words (Hartsuiker, Pickering, and Veltkamp 2004, Loebell and Bock 2003).

2. Structural priming is also independent of the particular verbs used to signal the structural relations, and it is very fast. Consider an eye-tracking study on German, which explores structural priming from production to comprehension (Scheepers & Crocker 2004). This study relies on the fact that when people listen to sentences while looking at pictures with multiple entities in them, they look directly at the item that they expect will be referred to *next*. The experimental procedure in the Scheepers & Crocker study goes like this: First, each participant in the study reads an undergoer-subject passive sentence aloud (production task). Then they are shown a complex set-up picture containing people and actions that are totally unrelated to those in the sentence that they have just read. In each set-up stimulus picture, there are three people and two actions. (The people in the picture are easily distinguished by their clothing, so that there are no reference problems.) As they are shown the picture, the participants also hear the first noun phrase of a new sentence that describes it (comprehension task), while their gaze is monitored. For example, the picture might show person A (say a hunter) acting on person B (say a nurse), who in turn acts on person C (a priest). What Scheepers and Crocker found was that if a participant heard 'the nurse' as the first noun phrase of a sentence about the picture in front of them, they looked at the hunter (the person acting on the nurse) rather than at the priest (the person

the nurse was acting on) even *before* they heard the verb or knew what its voice was. Apparently they did this because they had already anticipated – solely on the basis of the structure of the unrelated sentence that they had just read aloud – that the first person mentioned, the nurse, would be the Undergoer of the action and therefore that the next person mentioned would be the one who was acting on her, rather than the one that she was acting on.

3. Hearing a structure makes it easier to comprehend a following utterance that uses the same structure, as shown by an event-related potential (ERP) study that found reduced effort in dealing with ambiguous sentences whose structures matched those of priming sentences (Ledoux, Traxler, & Swaab 2007). (See why the people who taught you to write insisted that you use conjuncts with parallel structures? It may have been taught to you as an arbitrary rule of style, but structural priming from one conjunct to the next is what makes parallel structures easier to process.)

4. 'Structural' priming is not only at the level of surface structure: *provide-with* sentences (AGENT provided RECIPIENT with OBJECT) primed and were primed by double-object sentences (AGENT gave RECIPIENT OBJECT), but not by the structurally more similar prepositional dative (AGENT gave OBJECT to RECIPIENT). The order of the semantic roles themselves has an effect. However, nothing supports a direct deep-structure account of priming: when speakers produced prime sentences with animate entities as deep objects, they did not then tend to produce target sentences with animate entities as deep objects (Pickering & Ferreira 2008: 26).

5. Structural and lexical priming serve the function of promoting what Pickering and Ferreira call *alignment* between interlocutors, promoting "ease of production or fluency, perhaps because it reduces the time or resources needed to plan utterances (Pickering & Ferreira 2008: 67)."

6. "The priming effects themselves are incidental and automatic. The broad range of tasks...that exhibit priming illustrate that no special task demands need be in place for priming to be observed... no current evidence shows that any feature of structural priming is affected by nonlinguistic dual-task effort or interference, suggesting that structural priming is indeed an automatic phenomenon." (p. 70)

This concluding point is one of our major take-home lessons for functionalists: Some of the usage patterns we observe in production are not present because of any strategy adopted by the speaker either for her own benefit – to keep track of her own story, say – or in consideration of the listener. They are automatic consequences of the way the brain works – and this can be true *even when they in fact help the listener.*

Lexical-semantic priming. Lexical priming (the way one word automatically arouses others that it is linked to) has strong effects on lexical access – that is, on the ability to find a word one needs to say in production, or to understand a word one has heard or read in comprehension. In production, a primed word is easier to retrieve from the lexicon when the speaker needs to say it than a word that is not primed, other things being equal. But if too many competing words have been primed, the competition among them will impede the choice of the correct one (Belke, Meyer, and Damian 2005). Priming can be phonological or syntagmatic ('go' arouses 'to') as well as semantic, but in this paper, we will focus on lexical-semantic priming: how one word arouses other words that are semantically related to it.

To make the concept of lexical-semantic priming vivid, we look at a simple example of a context where it interferes with lexical access: errors in names for common objects in pictures when people with aphasia tried to describe them. We already discussed the unwanted effects of structural priming in the pilot data of Menn et al. 2005, the experiment in which aphasic speakers and language-normal control participants were asked to describe pictures of household objects in various sorts of ordinary and weird arrangements (plate on table, boot in dishwasher). There were many kinds of errors, including lexical errors that the aphasic participants made in referring to some of those objects (Menn & Gottfried 2007). These errors were far from random; instead, there was 'selective semantic perseveration' – that is, the names of items seen earlier in the sequence of pictures showed up as the wrong names for closely associated objects seen later in the sequence: 'sofa', 'divan', and 'settee' for footstool' (the sofa had been shown earlier in the sequence), and also 'stove' in a picture that showed only a kitchen table and chair. This is an aphasic manifestation of the more subtle lexical access problem that Belke et al. (2005) found in normal speakers who had to rapidly name pictures of items that were all in the same semantic category. And of course it is the same mental process as in the classic Freudian slip, where the name of one person on your mind replaces the name of another in a similar semantic category.

Lexical priming may provide unintended effects in your experiment as described above. But the phenomenon also provides a processing explanation for many of the relatively speaker-driven functional explanations for the order of arguments and the related choice of syntactic structure (e.g. active or passive; *load* A *on* B or *load* B *with* A locative alternation). These accounts turn on the claim that the most accessible argument is placed early in an utterance. A processing explanation for this preference is grounded in the incrementality of speech production: we begin speaking before we have a fully assembled plan for the entire utterance, and we start with the most activated (or 'accessible') expression first

(Bock 1982). Therefore, if you wanted to test whether such a claim is valid, you would be deliberately trying to vary the accessibility of the entities that you want your participants to put into their sentences. One way to do so is to 'prime' – or activate – (the label of) one of the entities.

Like empathy, accessibility is an intermediate theoretical construct. You can't directly manipulate it, because it is a cognitive status, sealed away inside your participants' skulls. To test claims about how accessibility affects order of mention of arguments, you would vary one or two of the factors that are likely to affect the accessibility of the referring expression: how recently the entities have been seen or mentioned, how frequent the referring words are, their probable emotional loading or lack thereof, or others that you can find in the literature – or perhaps a new factor that you think ought to be relevant. If your manipulation of one of these factors in fact affects the order of mention of arguments (when everything else is controlled) in the way that you predicted, you are entitled to feel more confident that you have affected the accessibility of the referring expression – at least until a competing hypothesis comes along and does an even better prediction job.

7 Experiments and their design

In the next several sub-sections, we'll discuss, as object lessons, some of our experiences in designing and re-designing studies – efforts that have met with varying degrees of success.

7.1 Experiments on Conjunct Order: Information flow vs. accessibility.

In a set of studies exploring the role of information structure in influencing language production, Narasimhan & Dimroth (2008) investigated the order in which German-speaking children and adults mention noun phrases within phrasal conjuncts (e.g. *an apple and a spoon*). Information structure involves notions such as 'topic' and 'comment', 'given' and 'new' information that have to do with how referents are represented in mental models of the situational/discourse context. The 'given-new' distinction has to do with accessibility: how available a referent is in the minds of speakers and listeners in a particular communicative context. The term 'topic' refers to what the utterance is about, whereas the term 'comment' refers to what is said about the topic (Hockett 1958; Firbas 1964; Daneš 1970; Sgall, Hajičová, & Panevová 1986).

How do the topic/comment and given/new distinctions in information structure affect a speaker's choice in word order? Linguistic research generally suggests that speakers prefer to present given information before new (Prince 1981); this preference has been so widespread that a given-new ordering preference has even been posited as a language universal (Clark & Clark, 1978).[2] But experimentally investigating the influence of these basic dimensions of information structure on word order presents some interesting challenges, especially for the language acquisition researcher. First, as we have already noted, an experimenter has no direct way to manipulate the cognitive status of a referent–whether it is functioning as 'given' or 'topical' for the person participating in one's experiment. Further, the topicality and givenness of the same referent can fluctuate within the same communicative context, often with no perceptual correlates of these changes, e.g., the same entity is 'new' at one point in time, 'given' at another point in time, and 'new' again at a later point in time, all depending on whether it has been activated in a variety of ways, e.g. by prior mention or presence in the physical context.

Second, the topicality and accessibility of a referent are generally confounded in spontaneous discourse. Although the topic is typically accessible to the speaker and listener and the comment is often inaccessible and 'new', the two distinctions are orthogonal in principle (Ertel 1977; MacWhinney & Price 1980; von Stutterheim and Klein 2002). Gundel (1988: 229) notes the interaction between these two dimensions in their influence on word order. She suggests that adults are motivated by two competing ordering preferences: the 'First Things First Principle' – 'Provide the most important information first'; and the 'Given Before New Principle' – "State what is given before what is new in relation to it". Topics are considered to be 'given' relative to comments, so when topics are new to the discourse, the two principles conspire to encourage early mention of the topic. However, these two principles can also conflict, so they must not be conflated. In cases where the topic is old (so, less informative), and the comment is considered to be more important information, the speaker must decide which principle dictates the final ordering.[3] Thus, we do not see a clear preference deter-

---

2 However, it is not the case that all languages show a given-new ordering preference. See Mithun (1987) for a discussion of Cayuga, Ngandi, & Coos, where 'new' information tends to appear earlier in utterances (within pragmatic constraints).

3 In presentational sentences (*There is a broom leaning against the cupboard*) there is no asymmetry in givenness or importance (newsworthiness) of either noun phrase in the sentence; in such cases other principles influencing word order may dominate, e.g. 'figure-before-ground'.

mined by either the topic/comment distinction or the given/new distinction. Mithun's (1987: 304–307) discussion of the 'Newsworthiness Principle' in Cayuga, Ngandi, and Coos, whereby the most newsworthy information is presented first ('newsworthy' being new information, a new topic, or a topic shift) highlights the complexity of the interaction between the topic/comment and given/new dimensions. Unfortunately in an experimental setting, separating the two dimensions may impair naturalness of communication. If one wants to study the influence of one of these variables independently of the other, it is important to design a task that preserves a natural interaction between participants to the extent that it is possible.

Third, because the form-function associations are probabilistic and highly context-dependent, studies focusing on the same phenomenon in the domain of information structure may nevertheless come up with different findings if different experimental paradigms are employed and if different constructions were investigated. These problems become especially pronounced when studying language development in children, a demographic that, by definition, is continuously in a state of transition. Thus, a survey of child language studies on the influence of information structure on word order reveals a "new-old preference" (Bates, 1976; MacWhinney 1982), an "old-new" preference (Menyuk 1969), or no significant ordering preference at all (MacWhinney & Bates 1978). Overall, there appears to be little evidence that young children have a consistent ordering preference based on information status. But the contradictory findings in child language may have to do with the influence of the different factors mentioned in the previous paragraph. For instance, several cognitive factors influence the accessibility of a word, including prior mention of referents in the discourse, and their prototypicality (Kelly, Bock, & Keil 1986) and imageability (Bock & Warren 1985). In addition to the topic-comment distinction, accessibility may also interact with other relational asymmetries: for example, agent-patient or subject-object status may also influence word order at the sentence level in children acquiring language (O'Grady 1997, chapter 4) and other speakers with limited syntax.

Because of such potential confounds at the sentential level, researchers have experimentally investigated how accessibility influences linear order at the phrasal level, viz. in conjunct noun phrases. In phrasal conjuncts, the conjoined elements share the same semantic and grammatical role and are symmetrical with respect to the topic-comment dimension. For instance, even though both *vodka* and *orange juice* in the answer to the question (in a) do not differ in semantic or grammatical roles, and are part of the 'comment' in the utterance, adults prefer the order *vodka and orange juice* (versus *orange juice and vodka*) when *vodka* is mentioned in the preceding context (Bock, 1977):

a. *A man went into a bar and ordered a screwdriver, but the bartender said he was out of vodka. What difference does it make?*

b. *A screwdriver is made of vodka and orange juice.*

Bock's procedure was adapted in order to investigate the influence of the accessibility of referents on order of mention at the phrasal level (Narasimhan & Dimroth 2008; Dimroth & Narasimhan 2009, 2012). To improve the ecological validity, they used a referential communication task involving picture-matching in order to elicit descriptions of objects in contexts that are interactive and yet controlled (Yule 1997). German-speaking adults and young children were first shown a single object (e.g. an apple) in a transparent, round container. An experimenter who could not see the container asked the question: *Was ist da drin?* "What's in there?" in response to which the participant described the contents of the container. The experimenter repeated the participant's object description and identified the picture matching the object. The participant was then shown two objects in a container, one of which consisted of the object that had been described before (e.g. an apple and a spoon), and asked again to describe its contents to help the experimenter find the matching pictures. The dependent variable was the order of noun phrases in their response (*an apple and a spoon* versus *a spoon and an apple*).

The (discourse) accessibility of referents in the study is determined by just one factor: prior mention of a referent in a specific discourse context ("old" information) versus the first introduction of a referent ("new" information). However, to be certain that the ordering preferences seen in participants' responses were due to discourse accessibility, and not to other processing factors that might contribute to accessibility (as discussed above), many variables needed to be controlled including the weight, gender, and frequency of referring expressions, the spatial relationship between referents, the animacy of the references, the kinds of determiners used in the referring expressions, the conventional order of noun phrases in certain collocations, and the fluency of the utterance (Arnold, Wasow, Losongco, and Grinstorm 2000; Clark and Chase 1972; Cooper and Ross 1975; Pinker and Birdsong 1979; Prat-Sala, Shillcock, and Sorace 2000; Wright, Hay, and Bent 2005). For instance, in order to avoid showing the participant the two objects in a fixed spatial relation to each other, the container was rotated during the presentation, so that the two objects were viewed from different spatial perspectives. Further, in order to avoid collocations where the word order is fixed (e.g. *bread and butter*), the 24 objects were grouped into 12 pairs that were unlikely to be combined in participants' everyday experience, e.g. 'egg' and 'bed' (Table 1). Object pairs were also matched on the number of syllables, grammatical gender, and frequency of use of the corresponding object labels. Filler events were included consisting of some object pairs that were both new, so that the participants could not presuppose that the 'old' referent would always be one of the paired objects in the trials where two objects are shown to the participant.

But participants were free to choose the wording of their responses, so in spite of these methodological precautions they showed variation in several respects. For instance, the overall 'weight' of each of the noun phrases in the conjuncts varied across participants (e.g. the number of syllables in *the apple* is more than in *apple*). Their responses also varied with respect to the type of conjoining word used (*and* or *with*), the determiners that co-occurred with each noun, and the fluency of the utterance as a whole. Each of these factors may influence ordering strategies, so the responses were coded for each factor and entered in a statistical analysis that allowed us to examine the role of accessibility when these other sources of variation were controlled for.

This research demonstrated that German-speaking adults prefer to mention old referents (objects seen and labeled earlier) before they mentioned newly introduced referents, supporting prior research showing similar effects in speakers of English (Arnold, Wasow, Losongco, and Grinstorm 2000; Bock 1977). But 3–5-year-old children acquiring German had the opposite ordering preference, mentioning 'new' entities first (Narasimhan & Dimroth 2008). Follow-up studies revealed that 4–5-year-old children's 'new-old' word order preference is quite stable; it even resisted a discourse manipulation that encouraged early mention of the 'old' referent by making it a discourse topic (Dimroth & Narasimhan, 2009). But by 9 years of age, German-speaking children have switched to the adult-like 'old-new' preference. The 'new-old' preference in young children that was initially observed at the sentential level in spontaneous interactions by Bates (1976) and Baker & Greenfield (1988) thus holds up in experimental studies of the same phenomenon, albeit at the phrasal level.

These findings show that younger children and adults are sensitive to the 'old' versus 'new' distinction, but we do not yet have an explanation for the developmental differences in ordering preferences. And although the researchers used the term 'preference' in describing the ordering patterns in the data, it is an open question as to whether participants' responses are motivated by a listener-oriented strategy to facilitate comprehension, a speaker-driven strategy (or 'impulse') to communicate information status distinctions, or whether they are an automatic consequence of the way the language production mechanism works in the speakers' brains. If the adults' 'old-new' preference is accounted for in terms of lexical priming effects from prior mention of the 'old' referent (an 'ease of processing' explanation, i.e. an automatic speaker-internal process), why would children, with more limited processing resources, resort to a 'more diffi-cult' strategy? Some other factors – for example, the novel items arousing atten-tion – must be involved in younger children's use of 'new-old' order. Whatever the nature of the preferences that drive the ordering patterns, it is clear that such pref-erences are not categorical, but are highly malleable. Changes in cognitive load or the type of discourse can shift word order choices in different ways. A study of English-speaking adults showed that increasing speakers' cognitive load during this task by means of a concurrent recall task *reduces* adults' 'old-new' preference (Slevc, 2007; Narasimhan, Duffield, Dimroth & Kim, 2010) – one explanation may be that the 'old-new' ordering is a hearer-oriented strategy that requires cognitive resources. Whereas embedding the conjunct order task in a 'magician' show that required a more extended narrative from 4–5-year-old German-speaking children increases their 'old-new' preference (Narasimhan & Dimroth, under revision); perhaps the story genre influences this choice.

These studies demonstrate that focused investigation of the form-function relationships in children and adults can be fruitfully investigated using psy-cholinguistic methods even in a relatively complex domain such as information structure. They provide converging evidence for prior findings from the child and adult literature. But they also allow for controlled variations of the same commu-nicative task in systematic ways that can isolate the influence of one particular variable – accessibility – and its interactions with different speaker populations, and with different processing, and discourse conditions. Clearly, there is more work waiting to be done for us to fully understand even the relatively simple matter of the order of conjoined noun phrases.

7.2 Argument order

Now consider another series of experiments in functional linguistics, dealing with a fundamental syntactic variable: the order of arguments in a simple clause. The background for this work is a classic discrepancy between language produc-tion in formal testing and language production in elicited complex narratives (conversation, complex action picture descriptions). Like L1 English-learning children around the age of 3 years, speakers with agrammatic aphasia have great difficulty sorting out the agent and the undergoer in typical passive voice, ani-macy-neutral test sentences like 'The horse was pushed by the goat' (Bever 1970; Saffran, Schwartz, & Marin 1980 a,b), in both production and comprehension. People with moderate and severe aphasias – especially agrammatic aphasia – make so-called 'reversal errors'; sometimes their choice of agent and undergoer seems random, and sometimes they systematically assign the Agent role to the first noun phrase, mapping the linear order of the noun phrases onto the English canonical order Agent-verb-Undergoer. It seemed that people with agrammatic aphasia had lost the ability to use morphological and syntactic cues to compute a mapping from thematic roles onto word order. Intricate formalist and function-alist arguments about the nature of the connection between argument structure and argument order raged – and to some extent, still rage – about why (many) people with agrammatic aphasia have this well-documented difficulty, spawn-ing an enormous literature (a representative sample: Bates, Friederici, Wulfeck, & Juarez, 1988, Bates, Wulfeck, & MacWhinney 1991, Caplan and Futter 1986, Grodzinsky 1984). There were two principal non-formalist descriptions of what the agrammatic speakers were doing instead of making normal connections between word order and thematic roles: the Bates psycholinguistics group (e.g. Bates et al. 1988, Bates, Wulfeck, and MacWhinney 1991) described it as a reliance on canonical form (considered in thematic role terms as Agent-Verb-Undergoer), and the neurolinguistics team of Saffran, Schwarz and Marin described it as reli-ance on an animacy strategy, which would randomly assign referents to thematic roles – even in the active voice – if both agent and undergoer were both animate or both inanimate.

But was the reversal problem with passive really due to a default mapping of first-noun-phrase-to-agent or of animate-to-agent? Maybe it was instead because the people with aphasia were hearing or using undergoer-first word order without being able to decode or deploy the complex morphology of passive. This question could not be answered from existing data, because all the experimental work – in both developmental and clinical settings – had been done with verbs whose subjects are agents. To test whether aphasic speak-ers in this severity range could in fact understand the relationship between position in a verb frame and thematic role if they were not also challenged by the verb morphology and the case marking, it would be necessary to get them to try to produce sentences with active-voice transitive verbs whose first noun phrase is not Agent, such as Experiencer-subject (*The nurse heard a burglar*) and Recipient-subject verb phrases (*The boy got a puppy*). It is hard to control this kind of task because scenarios involving reversible sentences with events of this type are hard to construct.

A reason to doubt all of the functionalist and formalist accounts of rever-sal errors was that they seemed to be absent in free-form elicited connected dis-course, according to the contributors to the Cross-Language Aphasia Study (CLAS I, Menn and Obler 1990, Ch. 20). In the twenty-six elicited personal and cartoon strip narratives elicited from speakers from fourteen languages who had agram-matic aphasia, sometimes animates acted on one another (e.g. a nurse shaved the narrator) and sometimes inanimates acted on or affected animates (e.g., an alarm clock wakes a man). Yet the aphasic speakers, across languages of very different typologies (Finnish, Hindi, Serbo-Croatian, Japanese, Chinese and Hebrew as well as Germanic and Romance languages), made essentially no production errors in which the Undergoer of an action was marked as the Agent or the reverse. Why was there such a difference between elicited narratives and isolated sentences? What property of connected discourse was keeping these aphasic speakers on track and able to map thematic roles onto word order – if that was really their problem?

One possibility was that in connected discourse, emotional reactions like empathy help speakers keep track of who is doing what to whom. From the early days of functional linguistics, Kuno (1987) had argued that speakers prefer to have the first noun phrase of a sentence refer to the empathic focus, defined as the person in a story whose viewpoint appears to be shared by the narrator. Ordinary stories are set up to have one protagonist; that is, if there are several characters in a story, one of them is likely to evoke more empathy than the others. So maybe speakers in single-sentence comprehension and production studies became confused about toy horses and goats – especially when the verb morphology got difficult – because they didn't give a damn about either of them, whereas in connected narrative, they would be usually talking about themselves, their families, or moderately interesting fictional characters. And of course in the real world, reversible transitive clauses – ones with fully interchangeable referents – are fairly rare; that is a separate issue.

A Japanese – American subset of the CLAS group decided to pursue the empathy idea, inspired by a cartoon narrative already in use in the standard Japanese aphasia test (Figure 1a). They created a set of mildly amusing naturalistic cartoon narratives that used all combinations of animate and inanimate Agent and Undergoer (examples in Figures 1b,c).

Our participants were people with aphasia and age-matched normal controls who were native speakers of Japanese and of English; the principal results were published in Menn, Reilly, Hayashi, Kamio, Fujita, and Sasanuma (1998) and Menn, Kamio, Hayashi, Fujita, Sasanuma, and Boles (1999). In these more controlled studies, no reversal errors were found when inanimate acted on inanimate (wind blows hat off, a ball hits a lamp) or when animate acted on animate.

However, the grammars of the two languages made a difference in rates of other kinds of errors. The inanimate-inanimate panels posed problems for some aphasic Japanese speakers, who tried to begin their responses with the affected object and then couldn't come up with the case particles and/or verb forms that the Undergoer-first order of mention requires. (Japanese subject and object case particles can be omitted colloquially, but only when they can be inferred from context.) English speakers had fewer problems with these panels, apparently because they could use active voice and still have the affected object as the subject in these stories, e.g. *The hat blows off*, an option not available for Japanese.

Figure 1b. Apple hits boy

Figure 1a. Hat blows off

Figure 1c. Girls racing

Figure 1: Examples of cartoon animacy vs. agency strips from Menn, Kamio, Hayashi, Fujita, Sasanuma, & Boles (1999).

Similarly, when the Undergoer was the protagonist/empathic focus (defocused Agent puts a number on a girl who is about to start a race), although 5 out of 7 Japanese speakers with aphasia had trouble with *she gets a number*, their errors did not include marking the girl as the Agent. And normal and aphasic speakers in both languages successfully used active-voice 'receive/accept' verbs for *she gets a prize*.

But there were no completed reversal errors, even when an inanimate object or force affected an animate Undergoer. The closest things to reversals in our data were utterances that began with the Undergoer and then fell apart; the most complete example was when a participant with anomic aphasia struggled valiantly to describe the final panel of Figure 1b, saying *He hits on the head – it – the apple.*

Figure 2: Snowball Series, varying animacy/empathic attraction of undergoer, from Menn, Reilly, Hayashi, Kamio, Fujita, & Sasanuma (1998)

So we could explain the discrepancy between isolated-sentence studies and narratives by saying that people with aphasia (at least those in the severity range capable of giving a minimal narrative) do know how the slots in various types of verb frames – including unaccusatives and other Undergoer-subject or Recipient-subject verbs – are supposed to map onto thematic roles in the active voice. But in both comprehension and in production they find it difficult to contend with verbs that are not in the active voice and with case roles that have to be explicitly marked (at least in English and Japanese). In the isolated active voice sentences of the more traditional studies, they could usually fall back on word order to interpret the active voice sentences they heard (none of which contained Undergoer-subject verbs); but on the passive voice sentences, that wouldn't work.

Now, was it animacy that pulled the speaker to mention a particular referent first, or causal power (in the English versions of 'Hat' story, the wind was chosen as the subject more often than the hat), or empathy, or all of these factors and perhaps others? And in what sense is an inanimate object like a hat an empathic focus? Surely it is the man's viewpoint that we share, not the hat's.

Or perhaps it was topicality, rather than this (somewhat stretched) factor of empathy that governed people's choices of which entity to mention first? (For other issues, see Menn et al. 1998.) Even at the design stage, we worried about this, so two more kinds of stimuli were created and presented in the same elicitation sessions; we hoped that the mix of materials would help to break up the monotony, reduce the unwanted priming, and give us a clearer picture of what was happening.

One of these additional kinds of stimulus sets gave closer control of the empathic-appeal-of-Undergoer variable (see Figure 2); in these stimuli (presented to participants as four separate pictures in quasi-random order with unrelated pictures in between), the Undergoer was the only thing that varied across the pictures of the set.

In the Snowball Series and in a parallel set involving a brick falling off a construction site, we attempted to influence the speaker's empathy with the Undergoers by making them more and more closely associated with a human, until in the final picture, the Undergoer was a person. We tried to keep the viewer's attention on the Undergoer by not showing an animate Agent. Our hypothesis, obviously, was that we would get more overt markings of empathy (both syntactic, i.e., various kinds of Undergoer fronting, and lexical, like saying *Ouch!* rather than *Bang!* to describe the impact of the snowball). This part of the study worked well: increasing the Undergoer's closeness-to-human did result in more expressions of empathy, for all groups of participants, although speakers with aphasia had to rely more on lexical marking than syntactic marking.

A further kind of stimulus set attempted to vary topicality. We had our artist create short cartoon strips in which the final picture of the strip could also stand alone to tell the whole story, and presented that picture both alone and in the context of the whole strip. In the 'context' condition, the earlier pictures served to introduce the Undergoer and establish him/her/it as the topic, as in Figure 3.

Our hypothesis was that in the context condition, the topicality of the Undergoer would be greater and that this would encourage more fronting of the Undergoer and other empathic markings than in the no-context condition. We defined the 'topic' of our cartoon narratives as the person whose history is followed; operationally, a character who was foregrounded when appearing in the illustrations, and who had at least two of the following three properties: being followed through time, appearing in all or almost all of the panels, or being reacted to by other characters. We designed the pictured events and the form of the examiner's question to maximize the yield of undergoer-focused responses for analysis, under the provisional assumption that both these variables would affect the form of the response of both normal and aphasic subjects. Undergoers were made as attractive as possible (with the exception of a teacher sneaking a drink) – children, puppies, innocent pedestrians. And they were all severely affected (or potentially affected) by the depicted event: hit on the head, shot, drowned, expelled, fired from a job.

Figure 3: Boy Saves Dog: Context condition. Story-elicitation picture presented either last panel only (no-context condition) or all four panels in sequence (context condition), from the unsuccessful topicality study, unpublished. Figures 2 and 3 drawn by Kuniko Tada.

But the context/no-context manipulation failed to work as predicted, although our design did produce plenty of lexical and syntactic empathic markings on the Undergoers. For English-speaking controls, there were *fewer* empathic markers – either lexical or syntactic (Undergoer-fronting) in describing the target picture when it appeared as the final panel of a strip, and for speakers with aphasia, there was no significant difference between the two conditions. The Japanese responses did appear to show the predicted context effect on the use of passive constructions for the aphasic as well as the normal speaker, but there were not enough data for statistical analysis. Perhaps the way in which the stories were constructed caused so many mentions of the Undergoer before the final panel that fronting him/her/it in the test sentence seemed unnecessary to the speakers. At any rate, someone will need to come up with better ways of testing the predicted effects of topicality on the choice of referent order.

Summarizing: No single factor controls the order of referring noun phrases in an utterance. Experimental work helps us to tease apart the interactions of cognitive factors that influence this order, but designing and interpreting experiments is complicated because the factors that are generally most interesting to functionalists are cognitive factors like empathy and the speaker's assessment of the knowledge of the listener. These are intermediate constructs, referring to internal states of the speaker, and cannot be manipulated directly. In addition, automatic processes like priming affect the accessibility of referring expressions and need to be controlled in order to study how speakers deploy language for communication.

However, speakers' internal states can be influenced by variables that the experimenter can control, like size, animacy, or order of presentation. We (provisionally) consider intermediate constructs valid to the extent that they are what is most useful in explaining the relationships between the variables we can control and what the participants in our studies say.

7.3 Pilot work on agreement: Functional orientation helps to improve the design of experiments.

So far, we've discussed why it is important for functional linguistics to test functional claims experimentally, focusing on word order. Now, we'd like to show how a functional linguistic approach can be beneficial for those doing experimental work in syntactic agreement, using a case study of subject-verb agreement in English as an example.

Psycholinguistic research investigating how speakers produce subject-verb agreement has typically investigated how speakers produce variation (or mismatch) in verb forms, as in the following examples.[4]
– *The committee*-sg *are*-pl voting tomorrow.
– *The label on the bottles*-sg *are*-pl peeling off.
– *Forty minutes*-pl *is*-sg too long to wait in the doctor's office.

From a functional perspective, the major problem with such studies is that they ignore the communicative context in which speakers typically produce subject-verb agreement. This problem is manifest in two ways: first, in the type of variation/errors that researchers have been investigating experimentally; and

---

4 The examples presented in this section are in English, but similar agreement variation has been examined in other languages (e.g., Hebrew: Deutsch & Dank, 2008; Russian: Lorimor, Bock, Zalkind, Sheyman & Beard, 2008; Dutch and French: Vigliocco, Hartsuiker, Jareman & Kolk, 1996; Spanish: Vigliocco, Butterworth & Garrett, 1996; Spanish (L2): Nicol & Greth, 2003; Italian: Vigliocco, Butterworth & Semenza, 1995)

second, in the procedures used during experimental investigation. Each of these will be discussed in turn, and current work that we are doing will highlight how a corpus-based functional approach can help experimenters escape these problems.

First, because subject-verb agreement is considered to be primarily a syntactic phenomenon, possible discourse factors affecting agreement errors have been ignored. To the best of our knowledge, very few psycholinguistic experiments have been based upon corpus studies of how speakers produce mismatch in spontaneous, communicative contexts (see Lorimor 2007); many studies are extensions of previous experimental results. The choice of factors to investigate in these experiments depends on the assumption that the types of errors that speakers produce in spontaneous discourse are similar to the errors produced in the lab. These are usually based on on-the-fly observations of naturally occurring errors, but they do not, for the most part, draw on the quantitative, distributional evidence that is now available from spoken language corpora.

Consider the following typical examples of subject noun phrases that are used to elicit agreement variation in production experiments (with examples of predicted elicited agreement errors in parentheses):

A1. The key to the cabinets... (*ARE on the table.*) (Bock & Miller 1991)

A2. The gang on the motorcycles... (*ARE wearing leather jackets.*) (Humphreys & Bock 2005)

A3. The picture on the postcards (*SHOW a cruise ship.*) (Eberhard 1999)

Example A1 shows how the number of the noun embedded in the subject noun phrase is the source of the speaker's error – the plural noun *cabinets* increases the likelihood of a speaker to produce a plural, rather than singular, form of the verb. A2 is an example of how the semantic or conceptual plurality of a collective subject head noun such as *gang* can lead the speaker to use a plural form of the verb. Similarly, A3 illustrates how the distributive (plural) conceptualization of the subject noun phrase can result in a plural form of the verb.

Examples A1–3 illustrate the tendency of psycholinguistic research in this area to focus only on the properties of the subject noun phrase. Experimenters generally assume that the type of agreement variation that speakers typically produce involves discrete features (syntactic or semantic number, or in some studies not discussed here, morphophonological form, e.g., Vigliocco, Butterworth & Semenza 1995; Franck, Vigliocco, Antón-Méndez, Collina, & Frauenfelder 2008) of the subject noun phrase alone, regardless of any other elements in the sentence and of the overall linguistic and situational context in which these features appear.[5] But is this type of agreement mismatch the most frequent type of mismatch error that speakers produce?

Recent corpus work (Duffield 2012) has demonstrated a new type of agreement mismatch in English that differs from previously examined examples in significant ways. Consider the following examples from the Switchboard corpus, a corpus of telephone conversations between strangers (Godfrey, Holliman, and McDaniel 1992):

B1. *The only thing*-sg we've taken back recently *are*-pl plants.

B2. *The other one*-sg is...*are*-pl the Saturns.

B3. *Repeating patterns*-pl *is*-sg what you have to check for when you buy your paper.

These sentences differ systematically from the types of sentences in the research discussed above. The prior work predicts that mismatch will occur when the semantic (conceptual) value of the subject noun phrase differs from its grammatical value – as in cases with "distributive" subjects (*The label on the bottles...*) and collective head nouns (*The gang on the motorcycles...*), and when there are plural nouns embedded in singular subject noun phrases. But agreement mismatch in the Switchboard corpus is strongly correlated with three new factors: the presence of semantically light nouns (such as *thing* or *one*), a predicate nominal that does not match in number with the subject, and a particular constructional context – the equative construction. To the best of our knowledge, nothing in previous psycholinguistic research predicts that agreement mismatch in equative constructions should readily occur in spoken language more often than in

---

5 Hartsuiker, Antón-Méndez, & van Zee (2001) have shown evidence that the grammatical form of pre-verbal objects in Dutch may also interfere with subject-verb agreement, but to the best of our knowledge, this effect has not been shown for objects that are produced after the verb, and it has not been shown to interact with the overall linguistic (constructional) or communicative context. Some more recent work in agreement lends itself to a more functional approach: Haskell & MacDonald (2003) propose a constraint-based account in which semantic and syntactic features of the subject noun phrase interact to affect the likelihood of a speaker producing agreement errors, which suggests that speakers may be more sensitive to overall linguistic context than purely syntactic accounts of agreement would claim. Haskell, Thornton & MacDonald (2010) provide evidence that speakers' production of agreement errors is influenced by statistical learning from past language experience, suggesting the possibility that speakers are not only sensitive to individual syntactic or semantic features that are activated on-line during production, but may also be sensitive to the entire context in which agreement patterns were previously produced. However, both of these studies focus on the properties of the subject NP, rather than the overall sentential or communicative context.

other sentence types, or that it should be more likely with a 'light' head noun and a plural predicate nominal. Furthermore, these correlations challenge current theories of agreement, and by extension, language production, because subject-verb agreement is not supposed to depend on the dynamic interaction of subject type, construction type, and material that comes after the verb. And what we are seeing is not only that plurality at the conceptual level can play a role in syntactic agreement, but that the weight of that conceptual plurality – whether it actually impacts agreement – depends upon other factors in the sentence.[6]

What does this have to say about the importance of combining a functional approach with experimental work on language processing? First, it demonstrates that what are commonly assumed to be syntactic processes can be sensitive to not only semantic information but also to contextual information – in this case, the context of the equative construction, which performs a particular communi-cative function: to equate two noun phrases (or, in certain cases, other constitu-ents; see Birner, Kaplan & Ward 2007). This doesn't necessarily mean that there is a functional *motivation* for such patterns; corpus investigation has so far failed to suggest a communicative reason why speakers would produce mismatches under these conditions. We suggest that the mismatch pattern arises from the way sentence production works, not from communicative design: In equating the subject and predicate noun phrases, the speaker may have greater access to the features of both noun phrases when computing the agreement features of the verb. In summary, the mismatch itself does not express a particular meaning; instead, processing factors may interact with the equative construction in a way that makes speakers more likely to produce agreement mismatch.

This study highlights the need to look to large samples of attested, natural language produced in communicative contexts as the data that form the bases for our experimental investigations of language processing. The examples of agreement mismatch in the equative construction were not singular examples of collected speech errors, nor were they based on the intuitions of the researcher. Rather, they came from a rigorous study of what speakers were doing in real com-municative situations. By failing to look at what speakers are actually doing in the real world, researchers will miss some key behaviors that provide insight into

---

6 Other variables may also influence how likely a speaker is to produce such patterns; language contact and/or dialectal variation could play a role. However, preliminary examination of the corpus data indicates that speakers who produced these tokens of mismatch come from several regions. Surveys from initial experimental investigation suggest that participants who produce such patterns exemplified in B1–3 do not share the same language background (either in terms of languages to which participants have been exposed, or in terms of length of exposure.) So while factors other than processing may be involved in a speaker's production of agreement mismatch, they do not appear to be the primary cause of such mismatches.

how speakers process language. In short, psycholinguistic investigation as well as linguistic analysis must be informed by observing how speakers actually use language in naturalistic contexts. Our own singular intuitions or grammaticality judgments should no longer be considered sufficient bases for our research, even though they remain necessary for formulating precise and testable hypotheses.

Another issue comes up in agreement production studies that do not consider language function: this is a matter of experimental design. Very few experiments have investigated speakers producing agreement within a communicative context (although several experiments do recognize the issue of whether or not speakers' behaviors are the result of experimental design: see Eberhard 1999 and Bock, Carreiras, & Meseguer 2012, Experiment 2). In most experiments investigating subject-verb agreement, speakers are presented with sentence preambles, such as, "The key to the cabinets..." They are then asked to repeat that preamble and then complete it so as to form a complete sentence. In some studies, the speakers are also presented with words that they should use to complete the sentences, including particular predicate adjectives or predicate nominals.

Pilot experiments on the agreement mismatch described by Duffield (2012), however, show something interesting. In the first pilot experiments, speakers were asked to perform the typical sentence completion task with preambles such as, "The thing on each boy's table," with a predicate nominal that mismatched the singular subject (e.g., *puzzles*). On the basis of the corpus work just described, speakers were predicted to be more likely to produce an agreement mismatch in the equative construction (e.g., *The thing on each workman's bench ARE hammers*) than when producing utterances that did not display the properties of the construction (e.g., *The hammer on each workman's bench IS hitting a nail.*) But when speakers were asked to do this type of task, they rarely produced the expected agreement mismatch.

However, once the task was changed to a more communicative situation, speakers' behaviors changed. In the more communicative version of the task, speakers were told that they were going to help the experimenter construct a story, and that to help them accomplish that task, they would first be given words that they should use in constructing the story. Then, they would hear the experimenter begin the story. At some point, the experimenter would stop mid-sentence (after presenting the preamble). They were then to complete the story (by completing the preamble) as quickly and as naturally as possible using the words that they had previously been given. (This is similar to the most recent paradigm employed by Bock, Carreiras & Meseguer 2012, Experiment 2, which only requires participants to complete, and not repeat, the preamble, but it takes the paradigm into an even more communicative context.) In this story completion condition, the number of mismatches produced by speakers increased. We might consider two hypotheses here: that there is a greater overall computational load in the story condition, or that when telling a story, ordinary speakers pay more attention to message content than to message form, increasing the 'leakage' from the conceptual level to the level of morphosyntactic formulation.

While this work is in preliminary stages, it highlights another important reason to combine experimental and functional approaches: functional ideas are essential in gradually bridging the gap between the laboratory and real-world language use, whether particular speaker behaviors are functionally motivated or are the result of processing demands. Several leading psycholinguistics research groups in addition to those cited in this paper clearly share this point of view. To adapt Allen's (2007: 254) comment on functional approaches, we might say that *the processing of* "linguistic structures can only be understood and explained with reference to the semantic and communicative functions of language."

8 Conclusion

Here are our principal experimental (psycho)linguistic take-home lessons for functionalists.

1. Not all valid explanations for why particular structures are used are functional. Some, of course, are historical, as DeLancey (1994) has been at pains to point out, but others come from priming, taking that term as shorthand for the way our brains repeat patterns of associations, irrespective of linguistic levels (and of cognitive divisions into language and non-language). We explored some aspects of structural and lexical-semantic priming as an introduction to the topic, but there is also phonological priming. Familiar phrases, such as proverbs and idioms, obtain their evident coherence from syntagmatic (sequential) priming (e.g. *A stitch in time saves nine*).[7] And, as one would predict from construction grammar, words can prime associated structures and vice versa; that is the process underlying the listener's expectation that particular verbs will most probably appear with their most frequent argument structures (Gahl, Menn, Ramsberger, Jurafsky, Elder, Rewega, & Holland 2003.

2. Experiments rarely work the first time (unless they are minor variations on a design that someone else has worked out); there are too many variables that

---

7 Syntagmatic priming (e.g. interference) arises when lexical access occurs in the context of other words that have been or are about to be produced. So, in 'A stitch in time', 'in' and 'time' are syntagmatic competitors when 'stitch' is accessed (Dell, Oppenheim, & Kittredge 2008).

one's theory fails to imagine. Experimental investigation of functional ideas requires careful design and re-design; but it is not impossible, and is still necessary.

3. Working back and forth among different levels of naturalness, from observation of relatively unconstrained language behavior to highly-controlled experiments, is the only way to build up a sufficiently rich, interpretable picture of how and why people choose the forms they use.

Obtaining experimental support for linguistic intuitions and corpus observations is a very slow and clumsy enterprise, requiring continual revision and refinement of the notions involved. But this is the typical course of scientific development, and it is how linguistics will become a real part of cognitive science.

Acknowledgements

Many thanks to Bernd Heine, Carmen Jany, and Victor Ferreira for their very helpful feedback on earlier versions of this paper.

References

Allen, Keith. 2007. *The Western Classical Tradition in Linguistics*. Equinox: London.
Arnold, J. W., T. Wasow, A. Losongco, and R. Grinstorm. 2000. Heaviness vs. newness: The effects of structural complexity and discourse status on constituent ordering. *Language*, 76, 28–55.
Baker, N. D., and P. M. Greenfield. 1988. The development of new and old information in young chidren's early language. *Language Sciences*, 10, 1, 3–34.
Bates, Elizabeth. 1976. *Language and Context: Studies in the Acquisition of Pragmatics*. New York: Academic Press.
Bates, Elizabeth, Suzanne Hamby, and Edgar Zurif. 1983. The effects of focal brain damage on pragmatic expression. *Canadian Journal of Psychology*, 37, 59–84.
Bates, Elizabeth, Angela Friederici, Beverly Wulfeck, and Juarez, L. A. 1988. On the preservation of word order in aphasia. *Brain and Language* 35, 323–364.
Bates, Elizabeth, Beverly Wulfeck, and Brian MacWhinney. 1991. Crosslinguistic research in aphasia: An overview. *Brain and Language*, 41, 123–148.
Belke, E., A. S. Meyer, and M. F. Damian. 2005. Refractory effects in picture naming as assessed in a semantic blocking paradigm. *Quarterly Journal of Experimental Psychology Section* A, 58(4).
Berman, Ruth A., and Dan I. Slobin. 1994. *Relating Events in Narrative: A Cross-Linguistic Developmental Study*. Erlbaum.

Bever, Thomas. 1970. The cognitive basis for linguistic structures. In: R. Hayes (ed.) *Cognition and Language Development*, 279–362. New York: Wiley & Sons.

Birner, Betty J., Jeffrey P. Kaplan and Gregory Ward. 2007. Functional compositionality and the interaction of discourse constraints. *Language* 83(2), 317–343.

Bock, J. Kathryn. 1977. The effect of a pragmatic presupposition on syntactic structure in question answering. *Journal of Verbal Learning and Verbal Behavior*, 16, 723–734.

Bock, J. Kathryn. 1982. Toward a cognitive psychology of syntax: Information processing contributions to sentence formulation. *Psychological Review* 89, 1–47.

Bock, J. Kathryn. 1986. Syntactic persistence in language production. *Cognitive Psychology* 18:355–387.

Bock, J. Kathryn. 1989. Closed-class immanence in sentence production. *Cognition* 31, 163–186.

Bock, K., Manuel Carreiras, and Enrique Meseguer. 2012. Number meaning and number grammar in English and Spanish. *Journal of Memory and Language* 66. 17–37.

Bock, K., and H. Loebell. 1990. Framing sentences. *Cognition, 35,* 1–39.

Bock, K., and C. A. Miller. 1991. Broken agreement. *Cognitive Psychology*, 23(1), 45–93.

Bock, Kathryn, Gary S. Dell, Franklin Chang, and Kristine H. Onishi. 2007. Persistent structural priming from language comprehension to language production. *Cognition* 104, 437–458.

Bock, J. K., and R. K. Warren. 1985. Conceptual accessibility and syntactic structure in sentence formulation. *Cognition* 21, 47–67.

Branigan, Holly P., Martin J. Pickering, and Alexandra Cleland. 2000. Syntactic co-ordination in dialogue. *Cognition* 25. B 13–25.

Caplan, D., and C. Futter. 1986. Assignment of thematic roles to nouns in sentence comprehension by an agrammatic patient. *Brain and Language*, 27, 117–134.

Chafe, Wallace (ed.). 1980. *The Pear Stories: Cognitive, Cultural, and Linguistic Aspects of Narrative Production*. Norwood, New Jersey: Ablex

Clark, H. H., and W. G. Chase. 1972. On the process of comparing sentences against pictures. *Cognitive Psychology* 3, 472–517.

Clark, Eve V., and Herbert H. Clark. 1978. Universals, relativity and language processing. In: J. Greenberg (Ed.), *Universals of Human Language Processing, Volume 1: Method and Theory*. Stanford: Stanford University Press.

Clark, H. H., and D. Wilkes-Gibbs. 1986. Referring as a collaborative process. *Cognition*, 22, 1–39.

Cooper, William, and John Robert Ross. 1975. World order. In: Robin E. Grossman, L. James San, and Timothy J. Vance (eds.), *Papers from the Parasession on Functionalism*, 63–111. Chicago Linguistic Society.

Daneš, Frantisek. 1970. One instance of the Prague school methodology: Functional analysis of utterance and text. In: Paul Garvin (ed.), *Method and Theory in Linguistics*. Mouton: Paris, The Hague.

DeLancey, Scott. 1994. Grammaticalization and linguistic theory. *Proceedings of the 1993 Mid-America Conference on Siouan/Caddoan Languages*, 1–22. Boulder CO: Department of Linguistics, University of Colorado.

Dell, G. S., Oppenheim, G. M., and Kittredge, A. K. 2008. Saying the right word at the right time: Syntagmatic and paradigmatic interference in sentence production. *Language and Cognitive Processes, 23,* 583–608.

Deutsch, A., and M. Dank. 2009. Conflicting cues and competition between notional and grammatical factors in producing agreement: Evidence from Hebrew. *Journal of Memory and Language* 60, 112–143.

Dickinson, Connie and Tom Givón. 2000. The effect of the interlocutor on episodic recall: An experimental study. In: Suzanne Kemmer and Michael Barlow (eds.), *Usage-Based Models of Language*, 151–196. Stanford CA: CSLI Publications.

Dimroth, Christine, and Bhuvana Narasimhan. 2009. Accessibility and topicality in children's use of word order. In: J. Chandlee, M. Franchini, S. Lord, and G. M. Rheiner (eds.), *Proceedings of the 33rd annual Boston University Conference on Language Development* (BUCLD), 133–138. Somerville: Cascadilla Press.

Dimroth, Christine, and Bhuvana Narasimhan. 2012. The development of linear ordering preferences in child language: The influence of accessibility and topicality. *Language Acquisition* 19, 312–323.

Duffield, Cecily Jill. 2012. Conceptual effects on agreement: A corpus study of mismatch in English copular constructions. Paper presented at the Annual Meeting of the Linguistic Society of America, Portland, OR. January 2012.

Eberhard, K. M. 1999. The Accessibility of Conceptual Number to the Processes of Subject–Verb Agreement in English. *Journal of Memory and Language*, 41(4), 560–578. doi: 10.1006/jmla.1999.2662.

Ertel, S. 1977. Where do the subjects of sentences come from? In: S. Rosenberg (ed.), *Sentence Production: Developments in Research and Theory*. Hillsdale, NJ: Erlbaum.

Ferreira, V. S. and C. E. Firato. 2002. Proactive interference effects on sentence production. *Psychonomic Bulletin and Review*, 9, 795–800.

Firbas, Jan. 1964. On defining the theme in functional sentence analysis. *Traveaux Linguistique de Prague* 1: 267–280.

Franck, J., G. Vigliocco, I. Antón-Méndez, S. Collina, and U. H. Frauenfelder. 2008. The interplay of syntax and form in sentence production: A cross-linguistic study of form effects on agreement. *Language and Cognitive Processes*, 23(3), 329–374.

Francis, Elaine and Laura Michaelis. 2012. Effects of weight and definiteness on speakers' choice of clausal ordering in English. Paper presented at the Annual Meeting of the Linguistics Society of America, Portland, OR. January 2012.

Gahl, Susanne, Lise Menn, Gail Ramsberger, Daniel S. Jurafsky, Elizabeth Elder, Molly Rewega, and Audrey L. Holland. 2003. Syntactic frame and verb bias in aphasia: Plausibility judgments of undergoer-subject sentences. *Brain and Cognition*, 53: 223–228.

Gennari, Silvia P. and Maryellen C. MacDonald. 2009. Linking production and comprehension processes: The case of relative clauses. *Cognition* 111. 1–23

Greenfield, Patricia and Joshua H. Smith. 1976. *The Structure of Communication in Early Language Development,* New York: Academic Press.

Godfrey, J. J., E. C. Holliman, and J. McDaniel. 1992. SWITCHBOARD: Telephone Speech Corpus for Research and Development. *Proceedings of ICASSP-92*, 517–520. San Francisco.

Grodzinsky, Yosef. 1984. The syntactic characterization of agrammatism. *Cognition,* 16, 99–120.

Gundel, Janet K. 1988. Universals of topic-comment structure. In: Michael Hammond, Edith A. Moravcsik, and Jessica Wirth (eds.), *Studies in Syntactic Typology*. John Benjamins, 209–239.

Hockett, Charles. 1958. *A Course in Modern Linguistics*. New York: Macmillan.

Hartsuiker, Robert J., Inés Antón-Méndez, & Marije van Zee. 2001. Object attraction in subject-verb agreement construction. *Journey of Memory and Language*, 45, 546–572.

Haskell, Todd R. & Maryellen C. MacDonald. 2003. Conflicting cues and competition in subject-verb agreement. *Journal of Memory and Language, 48,* 760–778.

Haskell, Todd R., Robert Thornton, and Maryellen C. MacDonald. 2003. Experience and grammatical agreement: Statistical learning shapes number agreement production. *Cognition, 114,* 151–164.

Hare, Mary L., and Adele E. Goldberg. 1999. Structural priming: Purely syntactic? In M. Hahn and S.C. Stones (Eds.), *Proceedings of the 21st Annual Meeting of the Cognitive Science Society,* 208–211. Mahwah, NJ: Erlbaum.

Harley, T. 2001. *The Psychology of Language: From Data to Theory.* 2nd edition. New York, NY: Psychology Press.

Hartsuiker, R. J., M. J. Pickering, and E. Veltkamp. 2004. Is syntax separate or shared between languages? Cross-linguistic syntactic priming in Spanish-English bilinguals. *Psychological Science, 15,* 409–414.

Humphreys, K. R., and K. Bock. 2005. Notional number agreement in English. *Psychonomic Bulletin and Review, 12*(4), 689–95.

Karmiloff-Smith, Annette. 1979. *A Functional Approach to Child Language: A Study of Determiners and Reference.* Cambridge, UK: Cambridge Univ. Press.

Kaschak, Michael, and Morton Ann Gernsbacher. forthc. *Changing language.* (this volume)

Kelly, Michael H., J. Kathryn Bock, and Frank C. Keil. 1986. Prototypicality in a linguistic context: effects of sentence structure. *Journal of Memory and Language* 25, 59–74.

Kuno, Susumu. 1987. *Functional Syntax: Anaphora, Discourse, and Empathy.* Chicago: Univ. of Chicago Press.

Ledoux, K., M. J. Traxler, and T. Y. Swaab. 2007. Syntactic priming in comprehension: Evidence from event-related potentials. *Psychological Science, 18,* 135–143.

Levelt, W.J.M., and S. Kelter. 1982. Surface form and memory in question answering. *Cognitive Psychology, 14,* 78–106.

Loebell, H. and K. Bock. 2003. Structural priming across languages. *Linguistics* 41, 791–824.

Lorimor, H. 2007. Conjunctions and grammatical agreement. (Unpublished doctoral dissertation). University of Illinois at Urbana-Champaign, Urbana, Illinois.

Lorimor, H., K. Bock, E. Zalkind, A. Sheyman, and R. Beard. 2008. Agreement and attraction in Russian. *Language and Cognitive Processes, 23*(6), 769–799. doi: 10.1080/01690960701774182.

MacWhinney, Brian. 1982. Basic syntactic processes. In Stan Kuczaj (ed.), *Language Development,* 73–136. Hillsdale, NY: Lawrence Erlbaum Associates

MacWhinney, Brian, and Elizabeth Bates. 1978. Sentential devices for conveying givenness and newness: A cross-cultural developmental study. *Journal of Verbal Learning and Verbal Behavior,* 17, 539 –558.

MacWhinney, B., and D. Price. 1980. The development of the comprehension of topic-comment marking. In: David Ingram, C. C. Peng, and Philip Dale (eds.), *Proceedings of the first international congress for the study of child language.* Lanham, MD: University Press of America.

McNamara, T., R. Ratcliff, and G. McKoon. 1984. The mental representation of knowledge acquired from maps. *Journal of Experimental Psychology: Learning, Memory and Cognition, 10,* 723–732.

Menn, Lise. 2000. Studying the pragmatic microstructure of aphasic and normal speech: An experimental approach. In: Lise Menn and Nan Bernstein Ratner (eds.), *Methods for Studying Language Production.* Hillsdale, NJ: Erlbaum. 377–401.

Menn, Lise, Michael Gottfried, Audrey L. Holland, and Merrill F. Garrett. 2005. Encoding location in aphasic and normal speech: The interaction of pragmatics with language output processing limitations. *Aphasiology* 19, 487–519.

Menn, Lise and Michael Gottfried. 2007. Aphasic errors in expressing location: Implications for production models. In: Carson T. Schütze and Victor S. Ferreira (eds.) *The State of the Art in Speech Error Research: Proceedings of the LSA Institute Workshop*, *MIT Working Papers in Linguistics* 53:305–351.

Menn, Lise, Akio Kamio, Makoto Hayashi, Ikuyo Fujita, Sumiko Sasanuma, and Larry Boles. 1999. The role of empathy in sentence production: A functional analysis of aphasic and normal elicited narratives in Japanese and English. In: A. Kamio and K. Takami (eds.), *Function and Structure*. Amsterdam: John Benjamins. 317–355.

Menn, Lise, and Loraine K. Obler. 1990. Chapter 20: Conclusion. In: Lise Menn and Loraine K. Obler (eds.) *Agrammatic Aphasia: A Cross-Language Narrative Sourcebook*. Amsterdam: Benjamins.

Menn, Lise, Kate F. Reilly, Makoto Hayashi, Akio Kamio, Ikuyo Fujita, and Sumiko Sasanuma. 1998. The interaction of preserved pragmatics and impaired syntax in Japanese and English aphasic speech. *Brain and Language,* 61: 183–225.

Menyuk, Paula. 1969. *Sentences children use*. Cambridge: MIT Press.

Mithun, Marianne. 1987. Is basic word order universal? In: Russell S. Tomlin (ed.), *Coherence and grounding in discourse*. Amsterdam: John Benjamins.

Narasimhan, Bhuvana and Christine Dimroth. 2008. Word order and information status in child language, *Cognition* 107. 317–29.

Narasimhan, Bhuvana and Christine Dimroth. (under revision) The influence of discourse context on children's ordering of 'new' and 'old' information.

Narasimhan, Bhuvana, Cecily Jill Duffield, C. Dimroth, and Albert Kim. 2010. Competing motivations in ordering 'old' and 'new' information: A psycholinguistic account. *Conference on Competing Motivations*, Max Planck Institute for Evolutionary Anthropology, Leipzig, Germany.

Nicol, J. and D. Greth. 2003. Subject-verb agreement in Spanish as a second language. *Experimental Psychology* 50, 196–203.

O'Grady, William. 1997. *Syntactic development*. Chicago: University of Chicago Press.

Pickering, Martin J. and Victor S. Ferreira. 2008. Structural priming: A critical review. *Psychological Bulletin* 134(3), 427–459

Pinker, S., and D. Birdsong. 1979. Speakers' sensitivity to rules of frozen word order. *Journal of Verbal Learning and Verbal Behavior* 18, 497–508.

Potter, M. C. and L. Lombardi. 1998. Syntactic priming in immediate recall of sentences. *Journal of Memory and Language*, *38*, 265–282.

Prat-Sala, M., R. Shillcock, and A. Sorace. 2000. Animacy effects on the production of object-dislocated descriptions by Catalan-speaking children. *Journal of Child Language* 27, 97–117.

Prince, Ellen F. 1981. Towards a taxonomy of given-new information. In P. Cole (Ed.), *Radical Pragmatics*. New York: Academic Press.

Ramsberger, Gail, and Barbara Rende. 2002. Measuring transactional success in the conversation of people with aphasia. *Aphasiology* 16:3, 337–353.

Saffran, Elinor, Myrna F. Schwartz, and Oscar S. M. Marin. 1980a. The word order problem in agrammatism. I. Comprehension. *Brain and Language* 10, 249–262.

Saffran, Elinor, Myrna F. Schwartz, and Oscar S. M. Marin. 1980b. The word order problem in agrammatism. II. Production. *Brain and Language* 10, 263 – 280.

Scheepers, C., and M. W. Crocker. 2004. Constituent order priming from listening to comprehension: A visual-world study. In M. Carreiras, & C. Clifton, Jr. (eds.), *The On-line Study of Sentence Comprehension: Eyetracking, ERPs, and Beyond* (pp. 167–185). New York: Psychology Press.

Schenkein, J. 1980. A taxonomy for repeating action sequences in natural conversation. In Brian Butterworth (ed.), *Language Production*, Vol. 1 (21–47). London: Academic Press.

Sgall, Petr, Eva Hajičová and Jarmila Panevová. 1986. *The Meaning of the Sentence in Its Semantic and Pragmatic Aspects*. Dordrecht: Reidel/Prague: Academia.

Slevc, L. R. 2007. Saying what's on your mind: Working memory effects on syntactic production. Unpublished dissertation, University of California, San Diego.

Sridhar, S. N. 1988. *Cognition and Sentence Production: A Cross-Linguistic Study*. New York: Springer-Verlag.

Sridhar, S. N. 1989. Cognitive Structures in Language Production: A Cross-Linguistic Study. In Brian MacWhinney and Elizabeth Bates (eds.) *The Cross-Linguistic Study of Sentence Processing*. Cambridge: Cambridge University Press.

Staub, Adrian. 2009. On the interpretation of the number attraction effect: Response time evidence. *Journal of Memory and Language* 60, 308–327.

Tanner, Darren. 2012. Structural effects in agreement processing: ERP and reaction time evidence for comprehension/production asymmetries. Paper presented at the Annual Meeting of the Linguistic Society of America. Portland, OR. January 2012.

Tanz, Christine. 1980. *Studies in the Acquisition of Deictic Terms*. Cambridge: Cambridge University Press.

Tomlin, Russell S. 1997. Mapping conceptual representations into linguistic representations: The role of attention in grammar. In: J. Nuyst and E. Pederson (eds.), *Language Conceptualization*, 162–189. Cambridge: Cambridge University Press.

Tomlin, Russell S. 1995. Focal attention, voice, and word order. In Pamela Downing and Michael Noonan (eds.) *Word Order in Discourse*. Philadelphia: John Benjamins. 517–554.

Vigliocco, G., R. J. Hartsuiker, G. Jarema, and H. H. J. Kolk. 1996. One or More Labels on the Bottles? Notional Concord in Dutch and French. *Language and Cognitive Processes*, 11(4)

Vigliocco, Gabriela, Brian Butterworth, and Merrill F. Garrett. 1996. Subject-verb agreement in Spanish and English: differences in the role of conceptual constraints. *Cognition*, 61(3), 261–98.

Vigliocco, Gabriela, Brian Butterworth, and Carlo Semenza. 1995. Constructing Subject-Verb Agreement in Speech: The Role of Semantic and Morphological Factors. *Journal of Memory and Language*, 34, 186–215.

von Stutterheim, C., and W. Klein. 2002. Quaestio and L-perspectivation. In C. F. Graumann and W. Kallmeyer (Eds.), *Perspective and perspectivation in discourse* (pp. 59–88). Amsterdam: Benjamins.

Wright, S. K., J. Hay, and T. Bent. 2005. Ladies first? Phonology, frequency, and the naming conspiracy. *Linguistics*, 43, 531–561.

Yule, George. 1997. *Referential Communication Tasks*. Mahwah, NY: Lawrence Erlbaum Associates.

Index

www.ingramcontent.com/pod-product-compliance
Lightning Source LLC
Chambersburg PA
CBHW070027100426
42740CB00013B/2620